LIMA

LIMA

A CULTURAL HISTORY

James Higgins

OXFORD
UNIVERSITY PRESS

2005

OXFORD
UNIVERSITY PRESS

Oxford   New York
Auckland   Bangkok   Buenos Aires   Cape Town   Chennai
Dar es Salaam   Delhi   Hong Kong   Istanbul   Karachi   Kolkata
Kuala Lumpur   Madrid   Melbourne   Mexico City   Mumbai   Nairobi
São Paulo   Shanghai   Taipei   Tokyo   Toronto

Published by Oxford University Press, Inc.
198 Madison Avenue, New York, New York 10016

www.oup.com

Oxford is a registered trademark of Oxford University Press

Co-published in Great Britain by Signal Books

Library of Congress Cataloging-in-Publication Data
Higgins, James, 1939–
Lima : a cultural history / James Higgins.
    p. cm. — (Cityscapes)
Includes bibliographical references and index.
ISBN 0-19-517891-2; ISBN 0-19-517890-4 (pbk.)
1. Lima (Peru)—Civilization. I. Title. III. Series.
F3601.2H54 2004
985'.25—dc22   2004058349

Drawings by Nicki Averill

9 8 7 6 5 4 3 2 1

Printed in the United States of America
on acid-free paper

In Memory of Tony
For all the books he was denied the time to write

Foreword

Lima is a mysterious city, the most mysterious of South American capitals.

Brasília, for example, comes up and hits you with its modernity, acquiring these days the first patina of age but still bearing the utopian hopes of its architects and planners. Every street in Buenos Aires cries out to you about its being Europe's orphan on the shores of the South Atlantic, its avenues imitating those of Paris, its great opera house those of Milan and Rome. Montevideo is the embodiment of a proud people conscious of having had a proud civic tradition till it was besmirched by a military coup in the 1970s but conscious, too, that Uruguay is stuck between the Brazilian giant to the north and the Argentine giant to the south. Asunción conducts itself in the knowledge that it is the chief town in the isolated and forgotten country of Paraguay which, to repeat the famous phrase, is an island surrounded by land. In French Guiana Cayenne carries the torch for modernity and the European space effort but senses, too, the ghosts of Captain Dreyfus and the *bagnards* from Paris and Montélimar and La Ferté-sous-Jouarre who lived and died in tropical exile. And so on round the continent.

Lima on the other hand doesn't say anything to you. It sits there inscrutable in its sandy desert, keeping itself to itself. Real rains never fall: the climate lours at you impassively, never drenching you yet never scorching you either. The waters of the Pacific, kept cold by the currents which obey some hidden law of the planet and well up from the Antarctic, do not favour skimpy bathing dresses. Thus they produce no perfectly tanned bodies. Indeed they discourage the sort of hedonistic exhibitionism and worship of the human form that make Rio de Janeiro and its beaches such as Copacabana and Ipanema what they are.

Lima's inhabitants are kind but discreet, polite yet impassive but above all in my experience enigmatic. There is, for instance, the enigma of the presidential escort. In front of the presidential palace the head of state's guards parade. If they are there to foil assassins why do they march up and down with the stately slowness of so many sleepwalkers?

Then there is the enigma of the Inca treasure. One day a friend of mine who represented a stoutly left-wing party in Congress suggested I met him for tea at this mother's house. I turned up at the appointed hour at a neat but otherwise unremarkable residence. After tea the three of us went downstairs where I saw several large rooms containing showcases carefully arranged with items dating back to the Inca empire. Had they been made of lead or ceramic their artistic and archaeological value would have been very great. But they were not made of lead or ceramic, they were fashioned in the finest gold and their value was enormous.

The splendour of the contents of that private house has never been matched by that of any other I have seen anywhere and is unlikely to be matched in the future. As I was shown them by their owner I began to understand a little of what the Spanish conquerors felt in the sixteenth century when the Incas had finished filling a room full of the gold the intruders had demanded as the ransom for the Inca emperor whom they were holding captive.

Then there is the potato question. Non-Peruvians can perhaps identify easily no more than two or three sort of potato, the vegetable which was sent out from Lima in the middle of the sixteenth century to Europe and immortality. But in Lima you can find hundreds of different potatoes, white ones, purple ones, red ones, green ones, small ones, big ones, delicate ones, flavoursome ones. The visitor will not find it hard to come across a market where a Lima stall-holder will impassively offer a greater selection of earth-apples than are to be found in any European supermarket.

In this book Professor James Higgins delights the reader with clues about how to pierce Lima's mysteries and riddles. He describes how the city came to its present eminence in the first years of the Spanish conquest. Its nearness to the sea and the connection to Seville meant that it was chosen by the Europeans as their base rather than the glorious old Inca capital of Cuzco. Cuzco, beautified by its palaces and by its massive stonework which continues to amaze the visitor with its marvellous accuracy, was fine for the purposes of administering a empire in the Andes. It was no good for keeping in touch with a foreign metropolis on another continent.

Like cities in other parts of colonial America Lima soon developed its own character, to which the author rapidly introduces us. Pious Lima, home of the Inquisition in South America, produced the continent's first saint. Santa Rosa was canonized in 1671, half a century after her death and Higgins deciphers the politics that lurks behind that weighty decision of the Vatican.

He also explains the conundrum which faces anyone who acquires the first smattering of Peruvian history, viz. why, at a time when the leaders of colonial society in the rest of Spanish America were fighting for their freedom from the rule of the Bourbons, did Peruvians do so little to liberate themselves and allow outsiders from the north and the south to break the relationship with the colonial power?

As a professor of literature Higgins comes into his own especially in his interpretation of the city as the home of some of the greatest writers Latin America has produced over the past century. Their story is bound up with the dynamics of a place which is constantly evolving. The flow of incomers from other parts of Peru never stops and Lima is thereby transformed from being little more than the seat of a European government into something which better reflects the indigenous roots of the country.

Lima's geographical position on the Pacific coast of South America always made it unfamiliar to Europeans and those from the East Coast of the United States. That fact, allied to the mysteries and enigmas the city wove about itself, made it difficult for the outsider to penetrate. In the pages which follow James Higgins brings Lima closer to non-Peruvians without at any time doing violence to the city's reserved character.

Hugh O'Shaughnessy

Preface and Acknowledgments

Peru has become increasingly popular as a travel destination. The main attraction is, of course, the ancient Inca capital of Cuzco and the nearby ruins of Machu Picchu, but other frequently visited locations are Lake Titicaca, the elegant colonial city of Arequipa, the Nazca lines, the impressive mountain scenery of the Huaraz region, and Iquitos and the Amazon region. Most people begin and end their journey in Lima, since it is Peru's gateway to the world and the hub of its domestic air and highway systems. Virtually every traveller to Peru, therefore, spends part of his or her stay in the capital.

Unfortunately, because their visit is part of a wider itinerary, many, if not most, visitors have time to see only a fraction of what Lima has to offer. I am fortunate in that for professional reasons I have been visiting the city regularly since the mid-1960s and have got to know it gradually over the best part of forty years. From the day I first stepped ashore at Callao after a three weeks' sea voyage from Liverpool, I have found it one of the most interesting cities I have ever known and with each new trip I keep discovering fresh dimensions. The aim of this book is to show that there is much more to Lima than can be glimpsed on a cursory visit and that a longer stay will be richly rewarded.

Lima was the viceregal capital of Spain's South American empire and the jewel in its crown is the old colonial centre, now a World Heritage Site. Yet the Historic Centre is not the only place where traces of its colonial past are to be found, since the olive grove in San Isidro, conserved colonial hacienda buildings in various parts of the city, and districts like Pueblo Libre, which originated as settlements where the indigenous population was congregated to facilitate evangelization and acculturation, all illustrate different aspects of colonial life.

Yet if the city tends to be identified with Spanish colonialism, there are other Limas. Evidence of its indigenous pre-history abounds, not just in museums, but in place names, in seaside districts like Barranco and Chorrillos which started life as Indian fishing villages, and in archaeological remains dotted around the city and the surrounding region, illustrating how pre-Hispanic man turned the coastal desert into a green oasis. Likewise, in the area ringing the old city centre and serving as a kind of border between it and the outward expansion of the twentieth century, the architecture and town planning point to the project of constructing a new city modelled on Paris, reflecting the aspiration of the elites of the post-Independence period to break with the Hispanic past and to pursue a European-style pattern of modernization. Finally there is the modern city, where the continuing socio-economic divisions of Peruvian society are mirrored in the contrast between leafy residential districts and the squalor of the ever-expanding shanty towns.

Lima is the gateway through which western culture was imposed on Peru, but it is and always has been the site of intercultural exchange. Though largely wiped out by European diseases, the pre-Hispanic peoples left a mark on the city that is seldom recognized. Today Afro-Peruvians constitute a tiny minority but in colonial times they made up the largest sector of the city's population and they, too, have had a lasting effect on its culture, exemplified by its major religious festival, the procession of El Señor de los Milagros. After Independence immigrants from Europe, mainly Italian but also German, French and British, and from Asia, Chinese and Japanese, exercised a significant influence on the local Hispanic culture. From 1940 onwards, as the coastal region began to undergo industrialization, Lima was flooded by an influx of migrants from the countryside. Today it is a city that is overcrowded and often squalid, but it is also a melting-pot where one only has to look at faces in the street to realize that after centuries of colonialism and post-colonial hierarchy a new rainbow society is emerging.

Lima is also a major cultural centre. Its museums house stunning collections of pre-Columbian textiles, pottery and gold work. It is renowned for its baroque architecture and art. It is a hive of literary activity and has been home to prominent writers such as Ricardo Palma, Julio Ramón Ribeyro, Mario Vargas Llosa, Alfredo Bryce Echenique and Antonio Cisneros. Its art schools have trained major painters, examples of whose work are to be seen in its art galleries. It also has a vibrant popular culture that includes distinctive brands of music such as the *canción criolla* and *chicha*. And since its cuisine enjoys a well deserved reputation for excellence, it can lay claim to being the gastronomic capital of South America.

Yet Lima is a city faced with tremendous problems as it struggles to cope with a population of nine million. It has run out of space to accommodate more migrants, it lacks the resources to provide basic services for its growing population, and its industrial growth is unable to match the demand for jobs. In effect, it is now reaping the consequences of the privileged position it enjoyed down the centuries as a colonial and neo-colonial enclave that flourished at the expense of the rest of the country. Lima has not always had a good press and, to counter the negative image which some people have of it, I have tried to highlight its positive features. However, I have also been at pains not to downplay the darker side of its history and I hope to have portrayed it with warts and all.

My method has been to tie a historical approach to descriptions of places of interest within relatively confined locations. In this I have been helped by the way in which Lima developed, since the colonial city occupied a small space in what is still referred to as the centre, the late-nineteenth and early-twentieth centuries saw the elites move out to new homes on the outskirts of the old city, and the rest of the twentieth century brought a massive expansion towards the sea till the whole of the Lima valley was urbanized. The city's history and evolving identity is explored through its architecture, literature, painting, music and popular culture. I have also made liberal use of the observations of local writers and foreign travellers.

I wish to express my thanks to John Crabtree for reading the manuscript and offering helpful suggestions. That apart, no one but myself has directly contributed to this book, so no one but myself can be blamed for its howlers. Even so, the book would never have been possible without the invaluable aid I have received over the years. I am indebted to the University of Liverpool, which financed visits to Lima to pursue research on Peruvian literature; to Augusto Arzubiaga, Peru's Consul General in Liverpool at a time when maritime trade still flourished, who not only paved the way for me in Lima but was a living example of the diplomat as man of culture; to the Pacific Steam Navigation Company, which on my first visit gave me a free passage on one of its ships and allowed me the experience of travelling to Lima the way it used to be done. I owe particular gratitude to Roque Carrión, my oldest Peruvian friend, who has taught me more about Lima than anyone else and made it fun. For all its size Lima is a small village and through Roque I got to know David

Sobrevilla, who among other things taught me all I know about Peruvian painting, and his anthropologist wife China. Through them in turn I became friends with Lima's last authentic old-style caballero, Lucho León, whose walking stick accompanied me on many a promenade and whose home was the scene of lively gatherings hosted by the long-suffering Vicha. Now an expatriate, Julio Ortega introduced me to up-and-coming poets of the 1960s like Antonio Cisneros and Marco Martos, who have remained great friends ever since. I have to profess a particular affection for all those associated with the Literature Department of the University of San Marcos, particularly Jorge Puccinelli and his wife Elsa Villanueva, the late lamented Wáshington Delgado, poet Carlos Germán Belli, and Carlos Zavaleta and his wife Tita, who not only showed me a magnificent view of the Pacific Ocean from their flat in Miraflores but represented Peru magnificently during his stint as Cultural Attaché in London. Others whose friendship and guidance have to be acknowledged are novelist Carlos Thorne, who served as a facilitator in his role as San Marcos administrator; literary critic Ricardo González Vigil and his wife María Antioneta, who have been consistently supportive and generous; and Jorge and Nelly Cornejo Polar, whom I first met in Arequipa in the 1960s and who since their move to Lima have been unfailingly hospitable. For showing me parts of the city few foreigners get the chance to know I thank Jesús Díaz, Cronwell Jara, the two Bethsabé Huamáns, mother and daughter, and Manuel Larrú, who gave me the privilege of visiting the pre-Hispanic settlement of El Paraíso. It was through all of these, and many others, that I got to know Lima and it was through their friendship that I came to love the city.

James Higgins

Contents

Part Five: The Expanding Metropolis 181

LIMA

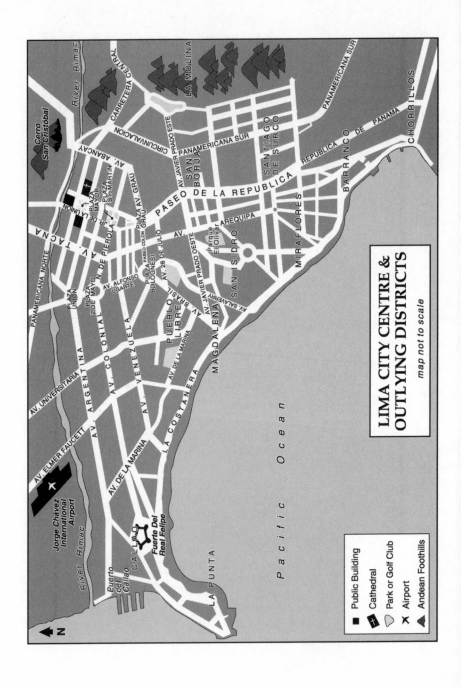

LIMA CITY CENTRE &
OUTLYING DISTRICTS

map not to scale

- ■ Public Building
- ✝ Cathedral
- Park or Golf Club
- ✕ Airport
- ▲ Andean Foothills

Part One
INTRODUCING LIMA: "THE STRANGEST, SADDEST CITY"

For many foreigner visitors Lima is merely a stopping-off point on their way to Cuzco, since a common perception is that the "real" Peru is the sierra, the Andean highland region, with its dramatic mountain landscapes, its colourfully dressed indigenous people and its majestic Inca archaeological sites like Machu Picchu. That perception, it must be said, has a certain validity, since Lima has traditionally been a western enclave from which the colonial elites and their Creole (American-born) descendants ruled a vast hinterland whose population was predominantly indigenous. The city has often been seen as something apart from the country. "In Lima I've learned nothing about Peru," wrote the German naturalist Alexander von Humboldt after a visit in 1802. "Lima is more remote from Peru than London." And in 1888 radical thinker and essayist Manuel González Prada asserted:

The real Peru isn't made up of the groups of Creoles and foreigners living on the strip of land situated between the Pacific and the Andes; the nation is made up of the masses of Indians living on the eastern slopes of the mountains.

Yet there are two senses in which Lima *is* Peru. Firstly, since the arrival of the Spaniards it has been the seat of power from which the country has been ruled. Secondly, Peru has ceased to be an Indian and rural society and has become a predominantly *mestizo* and urban nation. According to the 1876 census, Indians accounted for 57 per cent of the population, whereas in 1984 it was calculated that they made up about 35 per cent and since then the figure has fallen even further. In 1940 the urban population of 2.1 million was less than half the rural population of 4.8 million, but by 1991, 15.4 million Peruvians were concentrated in urban centres as against 6.5 million in the countryside. The main focus for mass migration from the countryside has been the capital, which is currently reckoned to have nine million inhabitants out of a total national population of 28.5 million. To quote a popular saying, the whole of Peru is now in Lima. The capital has become the space where a new rainbow nation is emerging, and the combination of its history as a centre of power and its current role as melting-pot makes Lima the most interesting and exciting city in Peru and, indeed, in all South America.

Setting and Climate

Lima is situated on the narrow strip of land running along the coast between the foothills of the Andes and the Pacific Ocean. The area occupied by today's city constitutes a micro-region extending between and beyond the rivers Chillón to the north and Lurín to the south, with the valley of the river Rímac at its centre. Its location places it in the tropics, but because of the cooling effect of the Humboldt Current that flows along the coast it enjoys a temperate climate. Temperatures rarely fall below 15°C (59°F) or rise above 27°C (81°F), the coldest period extending from the end of June to mid-September and the warmest from mid-January to mid-April. The transition between the seasons is gradual and almost imperceptible. Another effect of the Humboldt Current is that the moisture accumulating in the air above the sea is not sufficient to produce precipitation when borne towards the mountains by the incoming winds and, as a consequence, the nearest thing approaching rain is a very fine drizzle, known as *garúa*, which falls in the winter months. It is hardly surprising, then, that from colonial times onwards writers have enthused about the benevolence of Lima's climate. Typical are the words of the Franciscan Fray Buenaventura de Salinas y Córdova, written in 1630:

> *So habitable is this land that that there cannot be another in the world with a better climate, for it is neither too warm in summer nor too cold in winter; and the weather is so temperate that at no time in the year does the heat make one yearn for cool or the cold afflict men so much that it obliges them to heat themselves with fire.*

Yet, though it never actually rains, the air is always humid and some people find it enervating. In Antonio Cisneros' "Crónica de Lima" (Chronicle of Lima, 1968) the damp air is represented as corroding everything it comes into contact with and it becomes a metaphor for an insidious psychological climate that eats away at the will and initiative of the population, inducing an inertia against which it is impossible to immunize oneself. The image of a compass needle rusted by the damp suggests that the atmosphere of the city inevitably condemns all projects to lapse into aimless drifting:

> *This air—they'll tell you—*
> *has the property of turning any object red and eroded after the*
>   *[slightest contact]*
> *Thus,*
> *your desires, your undertakings will become a rusty needle*
> *before they've finished manifesting themselves.*
> *And that mutation—remember, Hermelinda—*
> *doesn't depend on anyone's will.*
> *The sea moves around in the channels of the air,*
> *the sea moves around,*
> *it is the air.*
>   *You can't see it.*

Though not cold by European or North American standards, winter can be depressing, for the city is shrouded by a damp blanket of low cloud trapped by the Andean foothills and skies are generally grey, with only intermittent sunshine breaking through the mist known as *neblina*. This phenomenon, too, has become a recurrent literary motif. In a poem written in the 1960s Carlos Germán Belli uses it as a metaphor for an oppressive socio-economic climate where the struggle to make a precarious living prevents him from pursuing higher things:

> *…I languished on the sublunar globe,*
> *captive in the stocks*
> *of the misty valley of my birth.*

As can be seen, Belli developed a distinctive poetic manner, replicating some of the traits of Spanish pastoral poetry of the sixteenth and seventeenth centuries in the context of twentieth-century urban Peru. Here, in an inter-textual allusion to neo-Platonism, the circumlocution "sublunar globe" evokes the distance separating the earth from the heavenly spheres, but that distance goes beyond the merely Platonic, for, since the valley of Lima is shrouded in mist, the heavens cannot even be glimpsed from afar. For his part, the narrator of Herman Melville's *Moby Dick* sees Lima's mist as one of a series of manifestations of an evil associated with whiteness: Lima is a city which "has taken the white veil," draping itself in an atmosphere of melancholy which makes it "the strangest, saddest city thou can'st see."

Another feature of the Lima environment is highlighted in Mario Vargas Llosa's novel *Conversación en La Catedral* (Conversation in The Cathedral, 1969), where the sight of "a run-down, shit-coloured adobe wall" leads the protagonist to reflect that shit is "the colour of Lima". The coastal region is mainly desert, and not only does much of the city's landscape consist of areas of sandy soil, but adobe, traditionally the basic building material and still used as a cheap alternative to brick and concrete, has the same drab colour. Yet the inhabitants of the region have always found ways of countering the drabness of their physical environment. In pre-Hispanic times the adobe walls of native shrines and administrative centres were painted in bright colours. Later, colonial settlers painted the walls of their houses in warm, light colours like blue, pink, yellow or ochre, and that practice has been followed in the renovation of buildings in the Historic Centre.

More positively, Lima traditionally enjoyed the reputation of being a garden city. The indigenous peoples brought the coastal desert under cultivation by channelling the waters of the river Rímac into irrigation canals, and when the Spaniards arrived they found a vast oasis of vegetation. In 1639 chronicler Bernabé Cobo waxed lyrical over the region's fertility: "Thanks to these irrigation channels which cross and fertilise the countryside, it is always green, pleasant and delightful, presenting to the gaze the freshness and bloom of spring."

Throughout the colonial period and the nineteenth century many houses had gardens and to the south there were areas of greenery within the city wall. In what is now the inner city gardens were still common in the early years of the twentieth century, as evidenced by Felipe Pinglo's "El huerto de mi amada" (My Beloved's Garden), a popular song from the 1920s:

If you pass by the verge/of my beloved's garden,
stretching your gaze/towards the back

you'll see a show of flowers/that adds tones of spring
to the pleasant peacefulness/created by the bushes.

Later, as the city began to develop and expand, the centre was entirely built over, but new housing developments in the outlying areas were designed to provide the middle and upper classes with gardens. One of the delights of Lima is to stroll through the streets of districts like San Isidro, Miraflores or Barranco and to admire the geraniums, roses and bougainvillaea in flower in gardens and on balconies.

A Brief History

Lima's history did not begin with the foundation of the colonial city in 1535, for the area had been settled for millennia. At the time of the Conquest the region was dotted with small rural communities organized as a confederation of petty fiefdoms, which around 1460 had been absorbed into the Inca empire. When the Spaniards arrived the local population offered no resistance but peacefully accepted the new order, just as they had earlier submitted to the rule of the Incas.

The foundation of Lima was the culmination of an enterprise that had begun more than a decade earlier. In the early 1520s Francisco Pizarro and his partner Diego de Almagro had obtained permission from the governor of Panama to undertake exploratory expeditions to the south. Eventually, after locating evidence of the existence of a high Indian civilization, Pizarro sailed to Spain to obtain royal support and financial backing for a campaign of conquest. Named governor of the new territory, he set out with an expeditionary force in 1531, leaving Almagro behind to follow with reinforcements. After establishing a base at Piura, he marched to Cajamarca in the northern highlands, where he captured the Inca Atahualpa and held him to ransom, only to have him executed when the ransom was paid. Meanwhile, Almagro and his reinforcements had arrived and the Spaniards then proceeded to capture the Inca capital Cuzco in 1533 and to subjugate the rest of the country. Lima was chosen as the site of the capital of the new territory primarily because the harbour at Callao provided access to the sea, facilitating communication with Panama and Spain.

Built on the south bank of the river Rímac, colonial Lima occupied only a tiny part of the area of the modern city. Originally it consisted of the so-called *damero de Pizarro* (Pizarro's draughtboard), a rectangle of 13 blocks by 9 laid out in a gridiron pattern. Later, as its population increased as a result of fresh immigration from Spain and the importation of black slaves as a work-force, it expanded piecemeal, northwards across the river and outwards on the southern side. By 1615 its population numbered 26,087 and by 1812 it had risen to 63,900, of whom 18,210 were Spaniards or Creoles, 10,643 Indians, 4,897 *mestizos*, 10,231 free coloureds, 17,881 black slaves and 2,056 other racial castes. The limits of the colonial city were marked by the defensive wall erected in the 1680s which formed a eight-mile semicircle around the river, corresponding more or less to the modern ring-road system constituted by Avenida Alfonso Ugarte, Paseo Colón and Avenida Grau, with the eastern part running through El Cercado district. The area between the city and the sea was agricultural land, originally shared out to the first settlers as *encomiendas*—grants entitling the holder to the use of the labour of the Indians living on the land but not to the land itself—which subsequently developed into small farms and haciendas. The Indians were concentrated in settlements, known as *reducciones*, such as Magdalena and Santiago de Surco. A road linked the city to the port of Callao, six miles to the west.

Power Struggles
In its early years the colony was destabilized by feuding among the conquistadors. As members of an expedition aimed at incorporating new territories into the Spanish empire, the conquerors of Peru were acting on behalf of the Crown, which lacked the resources to mount such expeditions itself. Yet rather than professional soldiers, they were partners in what was essentially a commercial enterprise from which all who participated were entitled to a share of the profits. The entrepreneurs behind the venture were Pizarro and Almagro, who between them organized and raised the finance to outfit the expedition, but relations between them soured as the latter became convinced that his business partner had double-crossed him, firstly by coming back from Spain with a royal contract that favoured him over Almagro, and secondly by allotting a greater share of the spoils of the enterprise to his own supporters. Following an unsuccessful expedition to the southern frontier of the former Inca empire, the disgruntled Almagro asserted his claim to be Governor of Cuzco by taking the city by force, but in a

battle at Las Salinas in 1538 he was defeated and captured and was subsequently executed. Nor did the strife end there, for the discontent of the Almagro faction erupted again in 1541 when they stormed Pizarro's residence, assassinated him and forced Lima city council to appoint his young *mestizo* son, also named Diego, as Governor. Order was eventually restored the following year when Cristóbal Vaca de Castro, sent from Spain as Governor to put an end the political chaos, marshalled the Pizarro loyalists to defeat young Almagro's forces and had him executed.

The following years were to see further upheaval. Though the Crown had to rely on the conquistadors to bring new territories into the Spanish empire, it distrusted the local dominance they came to acquire and was determined to impose its authority on its American colonies. To that end Blasco Núñez de la Vela was sent from Spain as the first Viceroy to implement the New Laws of 1542-3, which were designed partly to improve conditions for the Indians but mainly to curb the power of the *encomenderos* (grant-holders entrusted with responsibility for overseeing a tract of territory on behalf of the Crown, in exchange for which they were given rights to the personal services of the Indians belonging to that territory). That strategy backfired, as the new legislation threatened the interests of the most powerful men in Peru and a rebellion formed around Gonzalo Pizarro, who succeeded in defeating and killing the Viceroy in battle in 1546. Gonzalo had his own reasons for rebelling, since in his will his brother Francisco had named him his successor as Governor and he was resentful that the governorship had been taken away from his family, maintaining that those who had conquered the country with their sweat and blood deserved to rule it, an argument which was to be echoed again and again by later generations of colonials resentful of being ruled by Spanish bureaucrats. Yet it was not an argument that the Crown was prepared to countenance, as was demonstrated when a new royal emissary, Pedro de la Gasca, put down the rebellion and had Gonzalo executed in 1548. La Gasca's success was achieved at the cost of compromise; he was obliged to buy off Gonzalo's *encomendero* supporters by repealing the laws which threatened their interests. But this he was prepared to do in order to establish the authority of the Crown and by the end of the century a series of viceroys had effectively consolidated royal control over the colony.

With the creation of the Viceroyalty of Peru in 1542, Lima became the capital of a vast territory incorporating Panama and the whole of South America except the Venezuelan coastal region and Portuguese Brazil. It also became the hub of trade between the colony and the mother country, as Spain's commercial regulations granted it a monopoly by requiring that all shipping load and unload in Callao. Its major export was silver bullion, which was transported overland from Potosí in modern-day Bolivia and other mining centres and shipped to Spain via Panama. In return it imported textiles and other manufactured goods, which were then distributed to other parts of the viceroyalty. Despite these monopolistic advantages, Lima saw its privileged status diminish in the course of the eighteenth century when the Bourbon monarchs introduced a series of reforms designed to run Spain's overseas colonies more efficiently. With the creation of new viceroyalties centred on Bogotá in 1739 and Buenos Aires in 1776, it lost jurisdiction over the territories firstly of modern Colombia, Ecuador, Panama and then of Argentina, Uruguay, Paraguay and eastern Bolivia. It also lost its commercial monopoly as legislation was liberalized and other South American ports authorized to trade with Spain.

Painful Independence

Peru was the last of Spain's South American colonies to achieve independence. Partly this was because of the conservatism of the coastal elites, whose fear of being overwhelmed by the indigenous masses had been intensified by a series of uprisings in the Andes, culminating in the rebellion led by Túpac Amaru II in 1780. Mainly, though, it was because Peru was the main bastion of Spanish power in the continent. The two great leaders of Spanish America's struggle for independence, the Venezuelan Simón Bolívar and the Argentinian José de San Martín, both realized that their ultimate objective had to be to capture the Spaniards' Peruvian stronghold. Having liberated the territory occupied by the modern republics of Venezuela, Colombia and Ecuador, Bolívar closed in on Peru from the north, while San Martín did likewise from the south, having earlier led a patriot army across the Andes from the River Plate to liberate Chile.

It was San Martín who reached Peru first, landing his forces on the coast in 1820, and he was welcomed not only by the country's liberal Creoles but also by conservatives, who, alarmed at the rising tide of liberalism in Spain, had come to the reluctant conclusion that Peru would be better off on its own. The Spaniards, seeing themselves outnumbered on the coast, abandoned Lima and withdrew to the highlands. San Martín was able to enter the city in triumph without having to fight, and on 28 July 1821 he declared Peru's independence in front of a cheering crowd in the main square. At the request of the leading citizens, he assumed dictatorial power with the title of Protector, but in September 1822, disillusioned by the squabbling between competing factions, he resigned and left the country. Continued factional infighting impeded the prosecution of the war, and in 1823 Congress turned to Bolívar, inviting him to come to Peru and granting him dictatorial powers. Bolívar proceeded to mount a campaign against the Spaniards. Under his command a mixed Colombian and Peruvian army was victorious at Junín in August 1824 and in December of the same year his subordinate Antonio José de Sucre effectively put an end to Spain's power in Peru by inflicting a crushing defeat at Ayacucho. Even so, the Liberator's initial popularity among Peruvians soon gave way to resentment against his dictatorial manner, the influence of his entourage of Venezuelan and Colombian advisers and the continued presence of Colombian troops on their soil.

As a result, there was widespread relief when in 1826 he decided to return to Colombia. Now, with his departure and Congress' subsequent election of General José de La Mar as president, Peru was finally independent.

The capital of the new Republic was a city that had come down in the world. The territory under its jurisdiction had again been reduced by the independence of Chile and Bolivia. It also presided over a country beset by economic woes and political instability. The wars had devastated the economy and governments were forced to resort to borrowing, with the result that by the late 1820s the foreign debt was five times the government's annual revenue. To make matters worse, in the power vacuum created by the collapse of the colonial order ambitious military *caudillos* or regional warlords, thrown up by the wars, regularly mounted coups to seize power; between 1826 and 1895 no fewer than eighteen of them ruled the nation. Relative stability came with the emergence as president of General Ramón Castilla, who stamped his authority on the country and saw out two terms of office (1845-51 and 1855-62). During that period and the decade that followed Peru enjoyed an economic boom based on the export of guano—and later nitrates—as fertilizer, but, as a result of corruption, financial mismanagement and reckless overspending, the bonanza was squandered and by 1876 the country found itself bankrupt. Worse was to come, when in alliance with Bolivia Peru was drawn into a war with Chile in 1879—the War of the Pacific—and suffered a humiliating defeat. Lima itself was occupied and under the terms of the 1883 peace treaty Peru lost the nitrate-rich southern provinces of Tarapacá, Tacna and Arica, though Tacna was eventually restored to it in 1929.

Modernization and Change
With independence Spain's monopoly of trade came to an end and foreign merchant houses, mainly British, established themselves in the country as Peru was incorporated into the international economic system as exporter of primary products and importer of manufactured goods. During the guano era Peru's economy was dependent on a single product, but as the country recovered after the War of the Pacific a new economy was created based on a varied range of agricultural and mineral exports. There was also a progressive growth of foreign investment, mainly from the United States and Britain, albeit at the cost

of a loss of national control over the mining and oil sectors. From 1895 onwards the country enjoyed a quarter of a century of political stability and economic prosperity. The nineteenth century had seen the steady growth of Lima's population, which by 1890 had risen to 114,788, mainly as a result of immigration, mostly internal but also from Europe and Asia. After 1895 that growth accelerated, and by 1920 the city's population numbered 223,807.

This period was dominated by the Partido Civil, Peru's first modern political party, which had emerged in the late 1860s as a focus for all those opposed to military rule but which came to represent the interests of the coastal elites. The era came to be known as the Aristocratic Republic, for the *civilista* oligarchy were an unrepresentative elite and under the limited democracy of the period governments were voted in by a small minority of literate male electors who constituted only about four per cent of the total population. Nonetheless, the *civilistas* were far from being traditional in their thinking, since they embraced liberal ideas and pursued a project of modernization aimed at turning Peru into an ordered, prosperous and cultivated nation on the European model.

Modernization had, in fact, been the great aspiration of the nation's elites ever since independence but it was not until the guano bonanza that resources became available to invest in developments like the railroad-building programme initiated by President José Balta (1868-72). One of the priorities, of course, was to modernize the capital, which had remained virtually unchanged since colonial times and whose fabric had badly deteriorated as a result of war damage and economic decline. As a site for the Great Exhibition held in 1872 a park—the Parque de la Exposición—was landscaped outside the city wall, and in the following decades it was to be the capital's most popular recreation spot. In 1870 the wall itself was demolished to enable the city to grow and develop. Unfortunately, the planned development was hindered first by economic crisis and then by the War of the Pacific, and was not until the period between 1895 and 1930 that most of it actually took place.

Though projects tended to be carried out in a piecemeal fashion, behind them lay the grand design of creating a city of wide avenues flowing into squares on the model of the nineteenth-century Paris designed by Baron Haussmann. One element in the design was a ring road along the route of the old city wall, made up of Avenida Alfonso Ugarte, Paseo Colón and Avenida Grau. A second was an avenue intersecting the city west to east—Avenida Nicolás de Piérola (more commonly known as La Colmena)—and running through a modern square, the Plaza San Martín. The construction of these avenues was accompanied by the erection of modern houses and apartment blocks, again with a strong French influence. From the 1920s onwards the area around the Plaza San Martín and La Colmena constituted the new city centre and remained so until the 1960s.

A third element in the design was a series of avenues such as Avenida Brasil and Avenida Arequipa, which radiated from the ring road, linking the city to outlying districts. The most important of these districts were the port of Callao, the long-established village of Pueblo Libre (formerly Magdalena) and the seaside villages of Miraflores, Barranco and Chorrillos, which from late colonial times had been holiday resorts for the city's elites and gradually evolved into residential areas. Expanding Lima came to have the shape of a triangle, with the city centre as its apex and a base formed by the line of settlements on the coast stretching between Callao and Chorrillos. Improved communications led to the further growth of those settlements as more and more people opted to live in the suburbs and travel into the centre to work, first by tram and later by bus or car. At the same time, agricultural land adjoining the new avenues was sold off to permit further urban development, and new districts like Magdalena del Mar and San Isidro came into existence. This development reflected a steady growth in the city's population, which by 1940 had risen to half a million.

The single greatest driving force behind this modernization was President Augusto B. Leguía (1919-30). Capitalizing on the discontent of the emergent middle classes, Leguía effectively put an end to *civilismo* as a political force and under his rule there was a significant increase in the number of middle-class professionals, small businessmen and public employees. This period also saw the foundation of Peru's first mass political party, the reformist Alianza Popular Revolucionaria Americana (APRA). Following the overthrow of Leguía, political life was dominated by the struggle between APRA and the oligarchy, which regained its control over the country through alliances with conservative military figures. For much of the next twenty-five years

APRA was outlawed and persecuted, and in its spells of legality the military sent out clear signals that it would never be allowed to take power. Eventually its leaders resorted to the tactic of entering into alliances with its former political enemies as a means of exercising influence and as a result the party lost its credentials as the champion of radical change.

By the 1960s pressure for such change had become so great that in 1968 a new breed of army officers, headed by General Juan Velasco Alvarado, intervened to forestall the threat of revolution by mounting their own brand of revolution from above. A sweeping agrarian reform expropriated large estates and turned them into peasant co-operatives, and the petrol, mining and fishing industries were nationalized. In many respect Velasco's revolution proved a failure, but it drastically changed Peru forever, finally breaking the centuries-old power of the oligarchy and raising the expectations and self-esteem of the country's lower classes.

From the mid-1970s Peru went through a prolonged economic crisis, which intensified in the late 1980s, when at one stage inflation reached a staggering 7000 per cent annually. The crisis was also political. In 1980 the Maoist movement Shining Path, seeking to capitalize on the widespread discontent caused by state's failure to meet the expectations created during the Velasco era, unleashed an insurgency campaign that developed into a bloody civil war. Over the next fourteen years the insurgency claimed close on 70,000 lives and caused economic damage estimated at $20 billion. In the 1990s, during the long presidency of Alberto Fujimori (1990-2001), Shining Path was finally defeated and peace restored, albeit at the cost of widespread human rights abuses and the imprisonment of hundreds of innocent people. Fujimori also succeeded in stabilizing and reactivating the economy by restructuring on the neo-liberal model. State enterprises were privatized, financial and labour markets were deregulated and Peru was incorporated into the new global system. Inflation, too, was gradually brought under control after an initial phase of rising prices. But such policies caused great hardship for ordinary Peruvians, and poverty levels soared as workers were laid off.

Meanwhile, other major developments had been taking place since the 1940s. Thanks mainly to improvements in basic health care, Peru underwent a demographic explosion that tripled its population in the space of fifty years: from 6.5 million in 1940, 13.5 million in 1972, to 22.6 million in 1993. Depressed conditions in the countryside and other factors led to a massive movement of population from rural areas to the cities and, as Lima was swamped by an influx of migrants, the number of its inhabitants rose from half a million in 1940 to two million in 1961 and, if one includes Callao, its population today almost certainly exceeds nine million. Immigration changed the city's ethnic composition, since the majority of its inhabitants were now of Andean origin. It also led to the proletarianization of the city centre, where once-elegant housing was turned into slum dwellings and the streets were taken over by market stalls and itinerant traders. Even so, the city lacked the infrastructure to accommodate the influx and shanty towns proliferated in its peripheral areas. In the meantime, businesses and residents had been moving out to relocate in more salubrious districts like San Isidro and Miraflores. Not only did both areas grow in population, but the former became the new financial and business centre and the latter the main shopping and recreation area. Subsequently, the eastern edge of the valley was also urbanized as affluent new suburbs—La Molina, San Borja, Monterrico, Camacho, Las Casuarinas, etc.—were created with their own infrastructure of shopping and leisure facilities. The result was that, whereas until 1920 only 15 per cent of the Lima area had been urbanized, by the end of the century a progressive process of urban development had completely built over the green land contained with the Lima-Callao-Chorrillos triangle and squatter settlements had spilled over its sides in so-called "cones" to the north, south and east of the city.

Local Sources and Foreign Travellers
Among the many local writers whose work conveys an image of the Peruvian capital, a few are particularly useful as a source of information. In the colonial period the Franciscan Buenaventura de Salinas y Córdova sang the praises of his native city in *Memorial de las historias del Nuevo Mundo Pirú* (Memorial of the Histories of the New World: Peru, 1630). Jesuit chronicler Bernabé Cobo wrote an early history, *Fundación de Lima* (The Foundation of Lima, 1639). From 1640 until his death in 1686 the Spanish-born soldier Josephe de Mugaburu kept a diary, which was continued until 1697 by his son Francisco, though in much lesser detail. Later, Manuel Atanasio Fuentes produced a guide

to the nineteenth-century city: *Lima, apuntes históricos, descriptivos, estadísticos y de costumbres* (Lima, Notes Historical, Descriptive and Statistical and on its Customs, 1867). Starting with a first series in 1872, Ricardo Palma published over five hundred *Tradiciones peruanas* (Peruvian Traditions), a collection of chatty anecdotes recounting episodes from the nation's history, most of them set in colonial Lima. Evocations of the modern city are to be found in the fiction of writers such as Julio Ramón Ribeyro, Mario Vargas Llosa and Alfredo Bryce Echenique.

During the sixteenth and seventeenth centuries Spain's American empire was officially closed to foreigners. But following the accession of the Bourbons to the Spanish throne in the early eighteenth century, France as Spain's ally was granted permission to operate merchant fleets along the Pacific coast. One of the earliest descriptions of Lima as seen through foreign eyes is to be found in French naval officer Amadée F. Frézier's *A Voyage to the South Sea, and Along the Coast of Chili and Peru*, the English version of which appeared in London in 1717. But the major travel book of the colonial era was the work of Jorge Juan and Antonio de Ulloa, two Spanish naval officers who were detailed to accompany a French scientific expedition which carried out field-work in the region between 1735 and 1744. Their account of the expedition, *A Voyage to South America*, which was first published in Spanish in 1748 and was in fact almost entirely the work of Ulloa, contains a substantial section on Lima.

In the nineteenth century some famous figures visited the city and made reference to it in their writing. German naturalist Alexander von Humboldt stayed there for two months in 1802. English scientist Charles Darwin called at Callao in 1835 during his voyage on HMS *Beagle*. North American novelist Herman Melville got to know the area during his seafaring days in the 1840s. Much more informative, however, are the accounts of lesser-known travellers who spent more time in the city and had the opportunity to observe it more closely. Scotsman Basil Hall, officer in command of the British navy's Pacific squadron in the years 1820-22, evokes the atmosphere in the city at the time of the struggle for independence in *Extracts from a Journal written on the coast of Chili, Peru, and Mexico* (1824). Robert Proctor spent ten months in the country in the 1820s as an agent for British investors and describes his impressions in *Narrative of a Journey across the Cordillera of the Andes and of a residence in Lima and other parts of Peru* (1825). Lima features prominently in William B. Stevenson's *A historical and descriptive narrative of twenty years' residence in South America* (1825), an account of adventures that saw him involved in contraband trade, imprisoned as a suspected spy and working in the service of the patriot forces. Frenchwoman Flora Tristan, whose father was Peruvian, travelled to Peru in 1833 in an unsuccessful attempt to claim an inheritance and records her experiences in *Peregrinations of a Pariah*, first published in French in 1838. Her compatriot, naval officer Max Radiguet, had ample opportunity to become acquainted with the Peruvian capital in the 1840s, since his ship remained anchored at Callao for more than three years awaiting orders from France, and the observations contained in his memoirs (1856) are particularly sensitive and perceptive. Swiss naturalist Johann Jakob von Tschudi carried out field-work in Peru and his impressions of Lima and the coastal region are included in his *Travels in Peru, during the years 1838-1842* (1847), an abridged English version of the German original. German Ernst W. Middendorf made three extensive visits to Peru, working first as a doctor and later devoting himself to linguistic and anthropological research, and in 1893-94 he produced a monumental three-volume description of the country.

There is also a corpus of visual material to help us re-create an image of nineteenth-century Lima. Local water-colourist Pancho Fierro (1807-79) produced some 1,200 paintings portraying a gallery of social types and documenting scenes that were part of daily street life. Léonce Angrand, French vice-consul between 1836 and 1839, depicted local characters and customs in paintings and sketches, as did German artist Johan Moritz Rugendas in the period 1838-44. French immigrant Eugenio (Eugène) Courret became Lima's most prestigious photographer in the latter half of the nineteenth century and his work constitutes a photographic history of the period.

Part Two
THE PRE-HISPANIC PAST

The Pre-history of Lima
The Spaniards' decision to site their capital on the coast radically re-oriented the course of Peruvian history, as the country's traditional core is the sierra, the Andean highlands, whose valleys and plateaux supported the bulk of the population until modern times. In the pre-Hispanic era a number of major civilizations had flourished in the coastal region—Paracas (1100 BC-300 BC) and Nazca (200 BC-500 AD) in the south; Moche (500 BC-500 AD) and Chimú (1100 AD-1470 AD) in the north; and Chancay (1100 AD-1450 AD) in the centre—but the most dynamic and expansive of Peru's indigenous cultures had their roots in the Andean highlands, culminating in the Incas (1440 AD-1532 AD), who in the century before the arrival of the Spaniards expanded outwards from their heartland around Cuzco to create the mighty empire of Tahuantinsuyo, which embraced not only present-day Peru but also Bolivia, Ecuador and parts of Colombia, Chile and Argentina. The pre-Hispanic era is conventionally divided into periods, known as "horizons", when the expansive highland cultures extended their hegemony throughout the country—thus, Early Horizon: Chavín (1200 BC-200 AD), Middle Horizon: Tiahuanaco/Huari (700 AD-1100 AD) and Late Horizon: Inca (1440 AD-1532 AD)—and "intermediate periods", in which the country fragmented into small fiefdoms and local cultures blossomed. From now on, however, it was from the coast that hegemony was to be exercised over the rest of the country.

Lima is very much a western city. Founded as an enclave of European colonialism, it followed a western model of development as it grew and was modernized in the course of the twentieth century and, though the indigenous origins of many of its inhabitants are evident in their facial features and copper-coloured skin, the majority of those who are not recent migrants wear western clothes and live an essentially western lifestyle. Yet, ironically, Lima is the best place to acquire an overview and understanding of Peru's indigenous past, since because of the centralization of wealth, power and institutions in the capital it is here that the country's best museums are concentrated. The Museo Nacional de Antropología, Arqueología e Historia (Plaza Bolívar, Pueblo Libre) and the Museo de la Nación (Av. Javier Prado Este 2465, San Borja) have collections covering all the various periods. The former's main attractions include Chavín stone carvings, Paracas textiles and Nazca pottery, while the latter houses the famous Señor de Sipán display until such time as an on-site museum is constructed. Also worth a visit is the Museo Arqueológico Rafael Larco Herrera (Av. Bolívar 1515, Pueblo Libre), which is particularly strong on the cultures of the northern coast. The Museo Oro del Perú (Av. Alonso de Molina 1100, Monterrico) has a stunning, if rather congested, collection of pre-Hispanic artefacts crafted in gold and silver.

The area occupied by the present-day city also has its own indigenous past, whose remains greatly impressed Charles Darwin in 1835:

I had an opportunity of seeing the ruins of one of the ancient Indian villages, with its mound like a natural hill in the centre. The remains of houses, enclosures, irrigating streams and burial mounds, scattered over this plain, cannot fail to give one a high idea of the condition and number of the ancient population. When their earthenware, woolen clothes, utensils of elegant forms cut out of the hardest rocks, tools of copper, ornaments of precious stones, palaces and hydraulic works are considered, it is impossible not to respect the considerable advance made by them in the arts of civilisation. The burial mounds, called Huacas, are really stupendous.

Traces of that past still survive in a variety of forms: local place names like Lima, Lurigancho and Surco are deformations of native words; the seaside suburbs of Barranco and Chorrillos were Indian fishing communities; the city and its environs are dotted with *huacas* (temples and/or administrative centres) like the Huaca Pucllana (popularly known as the Huaca Juliana) in Miraflores (General Borgoño, cuadra 8).

When the Spaniards arrived they encountered a native population of some 200,000 people—150,000 of them concentrated in the Chillón-Rímac area—organized as a confederation of petty fiefdoms that had been absorbed into the Inca empire around 1460. In the Inca imperial scheme the region was of relatively minor importance, but its people had a history which went far beyond that of their new masters. The last of a series of cultures that flourished in the pre-Hispanic period, the Incas did not come onto the scene until around 1440 AD, barely a century before the arrival of the Spaniards. In contrast, the earliest civilization in Peru—Caral-Supe in the valley of the River Supe some 110 miles to the north of Lima—dates from 3000-2500 BC, and El Paraíso, the earliest settlement in the Lima region, is only slightly younger, dating as it does from around 2000 BC. The history of the Lima area stretches back, in short, to the very origins of civilization in Peru.

Today's visitor to Lima is confronted by a massive metropolis where virtually every available scrap of land has been built over. But when the Spaniards arrived they were delighted to find a green and pleasant valley where, according to one document, the fruit trees were so high and so extensive that they rode two leagues sheltered from the sun. Yet, like the rest of the coastal region, the Lima area was arid desert when men first settled there. The history of the pre-Hispanic period is essentially the story of the long process whereby man learned to dominate nature and turned that desert into a green oasis.

Despite the desert conditions prevailing in the coastal region, two factors enabled the area's earliest inhabitants to live off the land. The first was the proximity of the sea, which provided them with a diet of fish and shellfish. The second was the local micro-climate, which drapes the area in a damp blanket of low cloud from May to October. The moisture trapped by the hills fed vegetation on their slopes, allowing the population to supplement their diet by hunting and gathering. Later they developed a primitive agriculture in low-lying areas irrigated by the rivers and freshwater springs and lagoons. The earliest settlement in the region, the archaeological complex known as El Paraíso (c. 2000 BC), provides an excellent illustration of this early phase of human development. Unfortunately, it is not easy to get to and it is not officially open to the public, but with a little initiative it is possible to find and gain access. Located a mile and a quarter from the sea on the northern bank of the river Chillón, it stands on sandy wasteland, recalling the practice of restricting building to unproductive areas. A track leads to the sea, whose produce is believed to have supported a population of 1,500-3,000 inhabitants, and others to the surrounding hills, where they hunted animals and gathered berries and roots. A green area near the river and another around a lagoon correspond to the zones where the first cultivation of crops took place. The main building—which does not look very impressive, since it is in poor condition—is a terraced pyramid built with stone obtained from the surrounding hills. It is not clear whether this was a temple or an administrative centre, but what is certain is that the inhabitants of El Paraíso, having resolved the basic problem of subsistence, had evolved some form of government to direct their communal affairs.

A major leap forward occurred during the Early Horizon (1200 BC-200 AD) in the wake of the emergence of Peru's first major culture, Chavín, in the Ancash region in the central sierra. In the absence of the abundance provided by the sea, the people of the sierra were driven by the need to find alternative means of feeding themselves. With the advantage of regular rainfall, they learned to domesticate animals and plants, and a population surplus led to migration towards the coast, where the in-comers settled and farmed irrigated areas around rivers and lagoons. Later, the Early Intermediate Period (200 AD-700 AD) saw the flourishing of a local culture known as Maranga. Having assimilated the agricultural technology of the Chavín, the Maranga successfully exploited the area comprising Bellavista, La Perla, Callao and La Punta, where annual flooding caused by the overflow of the Rímac laid down rich deposits of sediment and humus. The Maranga also learned to imitate nature, constructing artificial canals upriver to irrigate the adjacent desert lands. The first drew water from the Rímac at the level of the Palacio de Gobierno and carried it to the outskirts of Callao, with side channels feeding neighbouring districts. The second, known as the Canal Huatica—part of which still exists and is used to water the city's main parks—started upriver from the Historic Centre and provided irrigation for much of the eastern part of the valley.

This irrigation system was not only an impressive feat of engineering but involved a sophisticated social organization, since it required a team of specialists to run and maintain the system and an official to oversee the fair distribution of the water to the consumers. During the Middle Horizon (700 AD-1100 AD) the Huari (or Wari), who from their heartland in the Ayacucho area came to dominate the central Andes and coast, further extended the system by constructing the still surviving Surco canal—which came to be known as the river Surco, an indication of the volume of water it carried—running some twelve miles from Vitarte to Chorrillos. The system left in place by the Huari was still operating when the Spaniards arrived. Taulichusco, the chieftain of the Lima area, who is commemorated by a monument in the Paseo de los Escribanos in the Historic Centre, controlled and administered the distribution of irrigation waters throughout the valley from his residence on the site of today's Palacio de Gobierno. It was precisely to control that vital resource that Pizarro opted to build the Governor's Residence on the same spot.

Pachacámac

The Lima area abounds in archaeological remains of its pre-Hispanic past, though sadly many of them are in a sorry state of repair. Local children used them as playgrounds and, if we are to believe Julio Ramón Ribeyro's story "Sobre los modos de ganar la guerra" (On the Ways of Winning War, 1969), the military instructor at a Miraflores school was in the habit of taking his pupils to the Huaca Juliana to play war games. Indeed, it is only in recent decades that serious attempts have been made to conserve these sites as part of the national patrimony.

Dating from the Chavín era is the Huaca Garagay, located in the El Pacífico district of San Martín de Porras. A ceremonial centre, it consists of three pyramids laid out in the "U" shape favoured by the Chavín. Painted on one of the walls of the main pyramid is the head of an anthropomorphic deity symbolizing the duality of life, with a huge mouth and jaguar's teeth evoking the powerful and unpredictable forces that ruled the natural world and a nose in the form of a snake (a primeval fertility symbol) representing him as the giver of life. The Maranga left behind a complex of *huacas* that were subsequently adapted and added to by later peoples, the main ones being the Huaca Maranga and the Huaca Tres Palos, both located in the Parque de las Leyendas (Av. de la Marina, cuadra 24), the Huaca Huallamarca (or Pan de Azúcar) in San Isidro (Nicolás de Ribera 201) and the Huaca Juliana in Miraflores. Consisting of pyramids built with adobe bricks and accessed by a zigzagging ramp, these seem to have served as administrative centres for the different irrigation zones. The museum at the Huaca Huallamarca contains examples of funeral bundles and the mummy of a local princess.

Near Huachipa, eight miles along the Central Highway, lie the ruins of Cajamarquilla, a major commercial, administrative and military conurbation founded by the Huari and thought to have supported a population of some 15,000. The city appears have been abandoned after the decline of Huari power, and the site has suffered badly from flash-floods, which destroyed large parts of the city. The palace of Puruchuco, located at 7.5 kilometres on the Central Highway, was built by the Incas as an administrative centre on a site dating back much earlier. On display in the museum is the figure of the so-called "Señor de Puruchuco", a local pre-Inca chief or an imperial functionary, whose regalia includes a silver death mask, a coat of mail of silver plate and a feathered head-dress.

But the major pre-Hispanic site in the Lima area is Pachacámac, a vast religious complex standing on a rocky outcrop overlooking the sea at kilometre 31 on the Panamerican Highway South. The oldest existing building dates back to the Maranga, but it flourished particularly during the Huari period. The shrine was dedicated to Pachacámac, the "creator of the world", a carved wooden image of whom is on display in the museum. The most important place of pilgrimage in the coastal region, it drew worshippers from all over Peru. Although sadly deteriorated, the Temple of Pachacámac, built of adobe, still survives and in front of it stands a raised rectangular space where pilgrims would leave their offerings. So popular was the cult of Pachacámac that, following their conquest of the area, the Incas deemed it prudent not to tamper with it. Instead they allowed it to coexist alongside their own religious practices. On a rocky hill overlooking the Temple of Pachacámac they constructed a Temple of the Sun, built of stone and adobe blocks, and in another part of the site they built a House of the Elect, a kind of convent for young maidens dedicated to the service of the deity. Inevitably, with the passing of time, the new cult came to displace the old.

The Art of Chancay
In the period 1000 AD-1450 AD, following the decline of the Huari, a major local culture developed in the valley of Chancay, sixty miles to the north of Lima, and extended its influence as far south as Pachacámac. That influence seems to have been cultural and commercial rather than political in that the ceramics and textiles

manufactured by the Chancay acquired great prestige, and they flooded the region with their products. Examples of their art are to be found in all the capital's main museums, but the fullest and most varied collection of Chancay textiles is that of the Museo Amano (Retiro 160, Miraflores).

The Chancay produced two distinctive forms of ceramic. *Cuchimilcos* are figurines representing standing figures, usually female, with tiny arms raised upwards like wings. They wear a head-dress and ear-rings and their faces are painted, details which make each piece unique. The figures are naked but their sexual attributes are depicted with great delicacy. It is believed that they represent a lunar deity or a fertility goddess. *Chinos* are "fun objects", pitchers humorously shaped in the form of a man. The vessel has a wide neck modelled as a human head with a variety of facial expressions.

Yet the Chancay are renowned, above all, for their textiles, their weavers having developed a sophisticated expertise in virtually every technique of weaving and decoration then known. Their main activity, of course, was the production of woven cloth for articles ranging from everyday clothing to ceremonial robes for religious and political elites, burial mantles and wall-hangings for temples and palaces. At the same time, their output included cloth *cuchimilcos*, little dolls to which magical properties are thought to have been attributed, and decorative three-dimensional objects, such as houses, trees and models of women weaving, made out of cotton, wool and vegetable. They also developed fine open-work gauzes with knotted-in patterns, which were used mainly as scarves, and created painted cotton fabrics whose apparently naive and childlike style is reminiscent of the work of modern painters like Miró and Klee.

Since the ancient Peruvians never developed a system of writing, the images and signs woven into cloths or embroidered and painted on fabrics served as a pictorial language to communicate their beliefs about their world. That language has a naturalistic base but it privileges stylization, reducing natural forms to their essential characteristics, so that what is represented is a generic archetype. Their world-view was essentially magical-religious in that they saw the natural world as being animated by spirits on whose benevolence the fertility of the land and the health of the community depended. The motifs that feature in Chancay textiles are essentially local variants of the iconography common to all pre-Hispanic cultures. A frontal staff-bearing figure represents power, sometimes human, sometimes supernatural. Trophy heads—the severed heads of slain enemies—reflect the belief that blood fertilized the earth, that the gods required human sacrifice as the price of their beneficence. The two-headed snake symbolizes the supernatural force that maintains the harmony of the cosmos by uniting the opposed but complementary elements making it up. Special honour is accorded to fishes and sea-birds which, as food and the source of fertilizer for the fields, were the bases of life in the coastal region. What this pictorial language conveys, in other words, is a sacred view of the world. At the same time, though, it is clear that Chancay's textile artists took pleasure in design for its own sake, as illustrated by the frequent use of the so-called interlocking pattern, where a series of geometrically stylized animal figures interlock so skilfully that the same pattern appears in another colour when the fabric is looked at upside down.

Part Three

CITY OF THE KINGS

The Monument to Pizarro

For close on seventy years an equestrian statue of Lima's founder Francisco Pizarro stood in the Plaza Mayor. Leader of the expeditionary force which conquered the Inca empire and governor of Spain's new South American colony, Pizarro has always been a controversial figure and over the years his monument likewise has been a source of controversy. The work of the American sculptor Ramsey MacDonald, it was donated to the city by the artist's widow and unveiled in 1935, on the occasion of the fourth centenary of Lima's foundation. Initially it was situated in front of the cathedral, but in 1950 it was moved to a site in the north-west corner of the square. While some saw it as only fitting that the city should commemorate its founder, others denounced the statue's presence in the main square as a celebration of colonialism and an offence to Peru's subaltern peoples. Eventually, in 2003, the municipal authorities bowed to pressure and had the statue removed, replacing it with a fountain and renaming the square Plaza Perú. Even so, this is not to say that Pizarro has been relegated to oblivion, for the monument is scheduled to be relocated to a new site that is being developed behind the church of San Francisco.

It is significant that the statue should date from 1935, and not just because it was Lima's fourth centenary. It never occurred to the elites of the nineteenth and early twentieth centuries to erect a monument to Pizarro, for their great aspiration was to shake off the colonial legacy and to modernize the country on the model of advanced European nations like Britain and France. Yet by the 1930s, Peru's political rulers were on the defensive as their grasp on power was threatened by the emergence of new social forces and left-wing political movements At the same time, their European model of the nation was challenged by the *indigenistas* (indigenists), who proposed the construction of a new national identity rooted in the autochthonous tradition.

To contain these new social forces the oligarchy resorted to repression and, above all, to the persecution of APRA, the political formation which constituted the vanguard of those forces. Conservative intellectuals also waged an ideological campaign to combat the arguments of the *indigenistas* and to defend the status quo. Likening the conquest of Peru to the Romans' colonization of the Iberian Peninsula, José de la Riva-Agüero argued that, though Peru had inevitably evolved into a *mestizo* nation, its essence was Hispanic since Inca civilization had been primitive by comparison with Europe and it was the Spaniards who had implanted the superior civilization that was to shape the character of the country. The defence of the Hispanic model and of the social order which it legitimized also involved the rehabilitation of Pizarro as a national icon, and Riva-Agüero waxed eloquent in praise of his hero:

> *The Marquis Don Francisco Pizarro, uneducated but wise, illiterate but sagacious, brought to this land, with the heroic thrust of arms, all the rich and splendid civilization of Castile, the indisputable heir of the Roman; and it is not the first time in history [...] that war has fathered a superior order of things.*

The monument, too, was part of the conservatives' ideological campaign, for though the municipal authorities did not actually commission it, but received it as a gift, they allocated it pride of place in the Plaza Mayor as a visual emblem of the concept of the nation and the social order which the elites were resolved to uphold.

The monument, in fact, was never simply a commemoration of Pizarro but was an assertion of the values underpinning the old oligarchic order. Moreover, despite the attempts of conservative intellectuals like Riva-Agüero to cast Pizarro as the founder of a civilization, the image that comes across is very much that of a conqueror, since the statue depicts him astride a war-horse, wearing full armour and brandishing a sword. Given the social changes that have taken place in Peru in recent decades, it is proper that it should be moved to a more discreet site, since for Peruvians of Andean origin, who now constitute the majority of Lima's population, its central location was an obtrusive reminder of their ancestors' defeat and subjugation at the hands of foreign invaders. Yet it is equally proper that the statue should be displayed, for not to do so would be to deny the past, since for better or worse Peru has been incorporated into the orbit of western civilization and Pizarro was the person who initiated that process.

The Historic Centre

On 18 January 1535, on the site of Lima's Plaza Mayor, Pizarro ceremonially founded the city which was to be its capital. By the end of the century the city had come to be known as Lima, a corruption of the native name of the river on whose bank it was sited, but its official title was "City of the Kings". The name is less pretentious than it at first sounds, as it commemorates the fact that the holy day closest to its foundation was the feast of the Epiphany, the "Day of the Kings" in Spanish. Subsequently, though, it was to carry connotations not originally intended, reinforced by the fact that two years later the city was granted a coat of arms bearing the emblems of the Emperor Charles V and his mother Juana together with the stars of the three Magi. For in 1542 Lima was named capital of the Viceroyalty of Peru, a vast empire incorporating Panama and the whole of South America except the Venezuelan coastal region and Portuguese Brazil. The name "City of the Kings" thus became synonymous with the status and prestige which Lima enjoyed as the centre of Spanish imperialism in South America.

For Pizarro and his companions the principal advantage of Lima as a site for their capital was that it gave access to the sea and communication with the mother country. The City of the Kings was to be an outpost of European colonialism, the base from which Spain exercised control over the conquered territories and their native inhabitants, and in the post-colonial period it was from here that the Creole elites, descendants of the Spanish settlers, ruled over a nation where, until the 1930s, the population was predominantly indigenous. It was also to be the hub of colonial economic exchange, since it was through its port at Callao that Peru's mineral wealth was exported to Spain and manufactured goods from the metropolis were imported, and that pattern continued after independence as the new nation state was incorporated into the world economy as an exporter of primary products and importer of manufactures from the industrial nations. Lima was also to be the main gateway linking Peru to the outside world and from here western culture was disseminated and imposed on the rest of the country, from the writing and Catholicism introduced by the Spaniards to the computers and capitalist neo-liberalism of the late twentieth century. Following the founding of Lima, Peru was to be increasingly drawn into the orbit of western civilization.

Lima's Historic Centre essentially comprises the area lying between the Plaza San Martín and the Plaza Mayor and bounded by Avenidas Tacna and Abancay, though in practice the colonial city extended further in all directions. If the core of the colonial city still survives, relatively few of its buildings are actually colonial. The catastrophic earthquake of 1746 left much of the city in ruins and another severe earthquake in 1940 also caused extensive damage. Most building dates, in fact, from the late nineteenth and early twentieth centuries, when the Republican elites were intent on constructing a modern capital on the model of Paris. Much more insensitive to the city's cultural heritage was the urban development of the late 1930s and early 1940s, when many old buildings of recognized architectural merit were pulled down or partially demolished in order to widen Avenidas Tacna and Abancay, the two main thoroughfares running through the city between north and south. The modernization of that period is held to have wreaked more damage than earthquakes and in Julio Ramón Ribeyro's short story "Dirección equivocada" (Wrong Address, 1957), set in those years, the protagonist sadly notes that the city is being stripped of its distinctive character:

As he was waiting for the bus that would take him to Lince, he whiled away the time watching the demolition of Lima's old houses.

A day didn't go past without them pulling down a colonial mansion, a carved wooden balcony or at the least one of those quiet republican villas, where in days gone by more than one revolution was hatched. All around haughty, impersonal buildings were rising up, exactly the same as those that could been seen in a hundred of the world's cities. Lima, the adorable Lima of adobe and wood, was turning into a kind of concrete barracks.

Moreover, from the late 1950s and 1960s onwards the area succumbed to inner-city decay as residents and businesses relocated to other districts, and in the 1980s Andean migrants took over its streets and turned them into a gigantic open-air market. Today the centre of Lima remains rather dingy, but since the 1990s things have looked up, thanks to the efforts of the municipal authorities—in particular, Mayor Alberto Andrade—to recuperate the city's cultural heritage and to promote tourism. Street traders were moved to sites away from the main tourist areas; citizens were encouraged to take a pride in their city; buildings were cleaned and renovated; tourist services were laid on. In 1988 the Historic Centre was designated a UNESCO World Heritage site.

Pizarro's Draughtboard

In line with a practice characteristic of Spain's colonization of the Americas, Lima was built on the site of an existing indigenous settlement. There were practical reasons for that policy, of course, since the existence of such settlements was proof that the location was suitable for human habitation and enabled the Spaniards to take advantage of an already established infrastructure. At the same time, though, it was an assertion of dominance and a declaration of the Spaniards' intent to impose their culture on the subjugated Indians. In the case of Lima, Pizarro appropriated the seat of the local chieftain, Taulichusco, for his own residence as governor; a church that was later to become the cathedral was built on top of an Indian temple; and the conquistadors were allotted plots of land to build European-style houses and granted *encomiendas* in the countryside to enable them to live in a style befitting a colonial elite.

Though most of its colonial buildings have gone, the Historic Centre still retains the original gridiron pattern known as Pizarro's draughtboard. Lima's design followed a blueprint, because in their instructions from Spain the leaders of military expeditions in the New World were required to create "ordered" towns laid out through careful measurement according to a gridiron or draughtboard plan, that is, in symmetrical fashion with a series of straight streets emanating from the central square. The plan that Pizarro had drawn up was in the shape of a quadrilateral draughtboard with a longitude of 13 blocks and a latitude of 9, each block consisting of a square whose sides were 400 feet in length and with 40-foot-wide streets between them. This layout departed from the blueprint in one major respect, for since the Spaniards chose to base their city on the existing native settlement, which was located on the bank of the Rímac, the main square was on the edge of the draughtboard rather than in the centre. Nonetheless, Lima's straight streets and regular, symmetrical design were held to embody an ideal of what a civilized community should look like and were celebrated as such in 1630 by Fray Buenaventura de Salinas y Córdova:

> It has a singular beauty in the layout and proportion of the squares and the streets, all of them the same [...] The form and layout is squared off with such order and harmony that all the streets are alike [...] They are all extremely beautiful because of their uniformity, wideness and straightness.

Later, the city was to grow up more organically and haphazardly as it expanded. And in spite of its symmetry colonial Lima could be confusing for outsiders, as every block in the same street was identified by a different name. Thus, the main street—what was to become the Jirón de la Unión—was made up of ten blocks, each with its own name: Palacio, Portal de Escribanos, Mercaderes, Espaderos, La Merced, Baquíjano, Boza, San Juan de Dios, Belén and Juan Simón. In 1861 the authorities, committed to modernizing the city and deeming such a custom to be backward, introduced the system which now operates. Streets running from north to south were named after provinces, while those from east to west were given the names of departments. The main street running from north to south, now called Jirón de la Unión, symbolically unites the various departments, with the numbering of the streets on either side starting from there. It appears, however, that for many years afterwards the locals continued using the old names.

The draughtboard plan was born of a Mediterranean tradition that conceived the city as the locus of civilization, a community of citizens living together in accordance with the principles of law and justice. Within that tradition cities were architecturally designed as a visual expression of the civilization they represented, and in that sense Lima's layout self-consciously sets itself up as European in order to body forth a European value-system in an alien environment. It was also, of course, part of an imperial project. During the re-conquest of Spain from the Moors, Christian monarchs had formally taken possession of new territories by founding towns, and that policy was carried over to the New World, where, in contrast to British North America, Spanish colonization was urban-based. Those towns were the base from which the surrounding countryside was to be colonized, governed, Christianized and absorbed into Spanish civilization. Ultimately, that policy derived from the practice of the Romans, who had regularly established towns as a means of imposing their laws, institutions, customs and religion upon newly conquered lands. Likewise, in the New World, the city was the means whereby Spanish civilization would replace native barbarism. Architecturally, it was intended to impress on the natives the superiority of the culture of their conquerors.

The Plaza Mayor

For the best part of two hundred years Lima's Plaza Mayor was known as the Plaza de Armas, for in the nineteenth century the square was re-christened to mark the break with Spain, its new name deriving from the fact that troops paraded there during the struggle for independence. It was only in the 1990s that the municipal authorities decided to revert to the original name.

Despite the many changes it has undergone over the years, the square's layout still corresponds to the original conception. It was designed to be the core of the city, the site of institutions representing the major components of the social order. On the north side, backing on to the river, stands the Palacio de Gobierno, the presidential residence, formerly the site of the house of Governor Francisco Pizarro and, later, of the Palace of the Viceroys. On the east side the imposing cathedral is flanked by the Archbishop's Palace, while the Palacio

Municipal (town hall) is located on the west. In the centre of the square, on the spot occupied today by a fountain erected in 1651, there originally stood a pillar of justice known as the *picota*.

Given that Lima started out as a frontier settlement, the transformation of the grand design into reality was a slow process. Though in the act of foundation Pizarro ceremonially laid the first stone of the building that was eventually to become the cathedral, Lima did not have a church in the early years, and Sunday mass was a makeshift affair celebrated on a portable altar in the square. In 1540 a church was opened on the site, but it was a very basic building with adobe walls, mangrove beams and a roof of woven reeds, and in 1543 Governor Vaca de Castro condemned it as unworthy of a viceregal capital. Work began on a more fitting building in 1550, but it was not until 1625, some 89 years after the first stone was laid, that the cathedral was actually completed and consecrated, largely because of setbacks caused by earthquakes. Modelled on Seville's cathedral, it emblematized the Church's role as the spiritual and cultural focus of the community. Its sheer size, its two bell-towers, its imposing three-arched entrance and the opulence of its interior all conveyed to settlers and natives alike a sense of the power and might of the Church and of the Christian God whom it represented on earth.

Although the cathedral has retained its basic structure, it has undergone a series of modifications over the centuries. Its present style is basically late eighteenth-century, since its towers had to be rebuilt after the 1746 earthquake and its baroque interior was dismantled and replaced by adornment in the more austere neoclassical style fashionable in the period. It was further modified at the end of the nineteenth century and again after the 1940 earthquake.

Adjoining the cathedral is the Archbishop's Palace. The modern edifice, inaugurated in 1924, was the first example of what was to become the favoured style for public buildings: the neocolonial, which sought to create a national style of architecture by adapting forms from the past to modern tastes and materials. Its doorways, carved wooden balconies and grilled windows replicate characteristic aspects of Limeñan architecture from the eighteenth century. Despite the fact that in 1546 Lima was elevated to the status of metropolitan archdiocese, with a jurisdiction covering most of South America, its colonial predecessor seems to have been a very modest structure and Robert Proctor, who saw it in the 1820s, described it as being "unworthy" of the imposing cathedral. Its most illustrious occupant was Santo Toribio Alfonso de Mogrovejo (1538-1606), who played a leading role in the establishment of Catholicism in Peru.

In contrast with Mexico, where military conquest was followed up by a concerted evangelization campaign, the conversion of the natives does not seem to have constituted a priority for the majority of Peru's clergy, who preferred the comfort of urban parishes or monasteries to the rigours of missionary work in the interior. In 1581 Mogrovejo arrived from Spain as newly appointed archbishop and energetically set about the task of reforming the Peruvian Church. The following year an archdiocesan council required all priests to undertake a specified period of missionary work and to have knowledge of the natives' language. To facilitate the evangelization process the council ordered the compilation of a catechism with versions in Spanish, Quechua and Aymara. The archbishop himself set his fellow churchmen an example by learning Quechua and by embarking on long and arduous pastoral visits throughout his archdiocese, during which he confirmed tens of thousands of new Catholics. Santo Toribio, in short, championed a Church committed to the mission of converting native Americans to Catholicism and to serving the people as a whole rather than just the

Spanish elites. His remains are interred in the cathedral, where a chapel is dedicated to him. He was canonized in 1726.

Across the square the Archibishop's Palace is complemented by the Palacio Municipal, another neocolonial building with carved wooden balconies and arched portals. Completed in 1944, it replaced earlier structures that were destroyed by earthquake and fire. Inside, it has a particularly fine stairway and houses an important collection of paintings from the Republican period. On display in its library are the original Declaration of Independence and the Charter of Foundation signed by Pizarro.

A variant of the neocolonial style was employed in the reconstruction of the Palacio de Gobierno, designed by the Polish architect Ricardo Malachowski and completed in 1938. To enhance its stateliness, it was also set back from the street and enclosed with iron railings. The colonial palace, which had been a humble structure unbefitting its status, had faced directly on to the square, and traders' booths, shaded with awnings, were lined along its front. French mariner Gabriel Lafond, who saw it in the 1820s, was one of several travellers shocked by the meanness of the building: "It has an insignificant appearance and it is almost completely hidden by a mass of shabby wooden shops that lean against its façade." In 1857 Manuel Atanasio Fuentes complained that the seat of government conveyed a poor image of the nation: "The Palace is one of our worst buildings; judging by it one would be right in thinking us one of the poorest nations in the world." The modern Palacio was designed precisely with the aim of changing that image.

Located on the same site, the Governor's Residence was the scene of what was effectively Peru's first *coup d'état* when in 1541 it was stormed by the Almagro faction, who assassinated Pizarro and imposed young Diego Almagro as governor, thereby setting a precedent for the palace take-overs that were later to be an all too common feature of Republican times. The instability caused by continual conspiracies, coups and rebellions in the decades following independence is illustrated by an incident which occurred in 1835 when, while the country's feuding *caudillos* were waging war in the interior and the majority of the local garrison were out on patrol, the black bandit León Escobar led his gang into the city, occupied the Palacio de Gobierno and extorted a levy from the municipal authorities as the price for withdrawing. The incident is described by Ricardo Palma in "Un negro en el sillón presidencial" (A Black in the Presidential Chair), where he claims that he was informed at first-hand by one the councillors who negotiated with Escobar that the black bandit "had behaved in as cultivated a manner as white-skinned presidents, if not more so."

Among the forty-two viceroys who occupied the colonial palace, some in particular stand out. Francisco de Toledo (1569-81) brought stability and organization to the colony. After carrying out a five-year inspection tour, Toledo drew up regulations for the efficient administration of the viceroyalty and the structures he set up remained in place for the rest of the colonial period. He also consolidated royal control by checking the power of the *encomendero* class and by eliminating the final vestiges of Inca resistance through the capture and execution of the last Inca, Túpac Amaru.

José Manso de Velasco has gone down in history as Lima's second founder, winning universal admiration for the energy with which he supervised the reconstruction of the city in the wake of the disastrous earthquake of 1746. In recognition of his services he was ennobled with the title Conde de Superunda (over the wave), which alludes to the tidal wave that destroyed Callao and honours him as the man who prevailed over the disaster. He is commemorated by a portrait in the cathedral sacristy that shows him, dressed in the elegant French style of the period, overseeing the rebuilding of the damaged church.

The achievements of Manuel de Amat (1761-76) have been overshadowed by the fame of his mistress, Micaela Villegas, who is the subject of Jacques Offenbach's fictional light opera, *La Périchole* (1868) and features in Thornton Wilder's novel *The Bridge of San Luis Rey* (1927). The long-lasting affair between the sexagenarian Viceroy and the twenty-year-old actress scandalized Lima society and kept it entertained with gossip. Micaela acquired her nickname when Amat, during a quarrel, shouted the insult "¡Perra chola!" (half-breed bitch!), mispronouncing the words because of his Catalan accent, and thereafter she was known as La Perricholi. In local folk-history she has come to personify a distinctive Creole behaviour-type, though there are differing views as to what that type is. For some she embodies the astuteness that enables Creoles to get ahead despite social obstacles, while for others *perricholismo* is synonymous with fawning deference and opportunism. Yet in the history of Lima, Amat was an extremely significant figure, for he not only continued the Conde de Superunda's reconstruction of the city but oversaw a change of architectural style and urban design marked by a strong French influence and based on the thinking of the Enlightenment.

The Plaza Mayor was also the economic heart of colonial Lima. The arcade in front of the Palacio Municipal was known as the Portal de los Escribanos, because it was there that the city's notaries conducted their business. The arcade on the south side was called the Portal de Botoneros, since it was originally occupied by traders specializing in buttons and braid, though merchandise on sale later became more varied, with small traders working from stalls under the arcade in front of the big shops in the buildings behind. Also full of shops was the narrow lane dividing this side of the square, now Pasaje Olaya but formerly called Callejón de Petateros because cigarette vendors were located there. Merchants also had shops in adjacent streets, the most up-market being Mercaderes (Jirón de la Unión, cuadra 3).

Also to be found in the square was the market, described in 1639 by chronicler Bernabé Cobo:

> *The commerce and bustle of people which is always to be seen in this square is very great [...] all kind of fruit and foodstuffs are sold by black and Indian women, so many in number that it is like an ants' nest [...] the things to be found in this market are all that a well provisioned republic can desire for its sustenance and comfort. There are likewise many Indian pedlars' stalls where they sell a thousand knick-knacks.*

In contrast, V. M. Golovnin, a Russian mariner who visited Lima in 1818, was appalled by the squalor and the disregard of hygiene and felt that the market lowered the tone of the city centre:

> We came to a large square which was very dirty and full of foodstuffs. Everything is sold there: meat, vegetables and fruit. It is a market, but who could imagine that such a filthy place was the city's main square!

Nonetheless, the presence in the main square of a market where people of all races and conditions intermingled points to one of the idiosyncrasies of colonial Lima; if on the one hand this was an extremely hierarchical society where everyone had their place, it was also a society where all classes shared the same public space.

Place of Pageantry

The Plaza Mayor was also the city's ceremonial centre, the place where religious and state processions were held, where entertainments such as bullfights took place, and where arriving dignitaries were received. Pageantry was a distinctive feature of colonial Lima. Every major event in the life of the colony—the arrival of a new viceroy or archbishop, news of a Spanish military victory or of a royal birth or marriage, a religious feast—was the occasion for elaborate and ostentatious celebration involving processions, cavalcades, allegorical floats, bell-ringing, firework displays, theatrical performances and bullfights. An indication of the scale of such jamborees is that the celebration of the birth of Prince Baltasar Carlos, son of Philip IV, lasted almost four months, from 3 November 1630 until 22 February 1631. Municipal elections were postponed to avoid disrupting the festivities and even a strong earth tremor interrupted them only briefly.

Such festivities served to relieve the tedium of life in an isolated colonial city. At the same time, though, ceremonial functioned as a ritual reaffirmation of the colonial order in that it was a public display both of imperial power and of the colonists' allegiance to Spain and what it stood for. A new viceroy, for example, was received with all the solemnity due to the king's deputy. He was preceded by an emissary bearing letters informing his predecessor and local officials of his arrival, which was then publicly announced by the town crier. On the day of his public entry into the city the streets were cleaned and hung with tapestries and magnificent triumphal arches were erected at regular intervals. On the edge of the city—at a street called Arco (Jirón Callao, cuadra 6)—he was conducted to a throne on a raised platform in front of a triumphal arch and from there he reviewed a parade of militia, university professors, magistrates, bureaucrats and the various corporations. Then, after taking his oath of office, he joined the procession mounted on a horse whose bridle was held by two councilmen acting as equerries and under a canopy borne by four aldermen. He was escorted through the arch into the city and as he passed through the streets flowers and sometimes silver coins would be thrown at his horse's feet from the balconies above. In the Plaza Mayor he alighted in front of the cathedral, where he was received by the archbishop and the chapter with a *Te Deum* and given the Church's blessing. From the cathedral he then made his way to the Viceregal Palace, where he was greeted with artillery salutes, while in the square outside his arrival was celebrated with music, bonfires and fireworks.

Lima's festivals were marked by their lavishness. For the entry of a viceroy it was standard practice for the area around the triumphal arch in Calle Mercaderes to be paved with silver bars, but in 1682, on the occasion of the entry of the Duque de la Palata, the city's merchants excelled themselves by paving the whole street as well as the nearby Calle de la Merced. In 1674 the Count of Castellar's entourage included twenty-four pages and twenty-four mulatto lackeys; for his family there were three mule-drawn carriages with six coachmen, all wearing identical livery of red, silver and blue; behind came twenty-four mules, laden with silver baskets; each mule had silk ropes and halters and was covered with a silk cloth bearing the viceroy's coat of arms, which also figured on three silver plates, one on the forehead and two hanging from the ears. Royal officials and members of the nobility demonstrated their largesse by hurling coins into the crowd; they and the guilds provided free entertainment by financing bullfights and firework displays; and in 1659 the wine merchants and grocers set up a fountain of wine, which flowed all day.

Official processions replicated the social hierarchy as the various sectors of the elite paraded in their respective place: the militia companies; the viceroy's mounted guards and halberdiers in blue and red uniforms; the municipal kettledrummers and buglers in crimson cloaks trimmed with silver fringes; the religious orders, recognizable by the different colours of their habits; the city's students, wearing blue, green, red or brown tunics and breeches; the university professoriat in academic dress; the magistrates and ministers of the Audiencia—an institution which combined the functions of high court and council of state—mounted on horses with black saddle-covers; the municipal magistrates and aldermen, dressed in scarlet; the corps of nobles; the gentlemen-at-arms; and the ladies of the aristocracy in their ceremonial carriages. On such occasions the role of the lower orders was to re-enact their subordination as spectators of their social superiors or, in the case of blacks, to parade as liveried pages escorting their masters and enhancing their status.

Festivals, on the other hand, allowed all sectors to participate, including Indians and blacks, suggesting that though these were regarded as inferiors they were nonetheless recognized as part of colonial society. It would seem, too, that both groups had accommodated themselves to the colonial order and, like other sectors, they made public demonstration of their allegiance to the Crown. In 1659, as part of the celebration of a birth in the royal family, Indians staged an allegorical pageant in which the Inca captured a castle after defeating two kings in combat and then offered the keys of the castle to the Spanish prince. Likewise, in 1631, as part of the celebration of the birth of Prince Baltasar Carlos, a mulatto brotherhood staged a re-enactment of the Trojan War in which the great figures of Greek history—Helen, Ulysses, Priam, Hector, Agamemnon, Menalaos, Achilles—bore insignia proclaiming their homage to the Spanish prince.

While festivals reaffirmed the colonial order, they also bolstered it by defusing social tensions. Such events provided diversion to relieve the hardness and monotony of the lives of the poor majority. They also accorded them a measure of social recognition, for blacks and Indians were allowed to be part of the celebrations and to perform their traditional dances and music and, though their status was clearly subordinate, they were able to enjoy a momentary sense of importance as they and their culture became the centre of attention. The festivities were also organized so as to permit a controlled letting-off of steam on the part of the subjugated. It was members of those sectors who played the main part in mummery, dressing up as dragons, gigantic ugly women or dwarves with enormous heads. One of the most famous of such mummeries was the Dance of the Devils, in which blacks dressed up as demons and went around attacking the crowd and shouting defiance of the authorities. Masquerades sometimes took the form of making fun of their betters, as blacks dressed up in the clothing of the men and women of the colonial aristocracy and exaggeratedly mimicked their mannerisms.

The Cerro San Cristóbal

From the Plaza Mayor, tourist buses do a trip across the river to the top of the Cerro San Cristóbal. One of the Andean foothills forming a semicircle around the capital, the Cerro affords a panoramic view of the city as far as the sea. As English foreign correspondent James Morris vividly pointed out in *Cities* (1963), that view reveals Lima's ugly side as well as its splendours:

> The best vantage point in the capital is the hill of San Cristobal, which rises steep and pyramidical within sight of the Presidential Palace, covered with ash-like dust and crowned with a cross of pilgrimage... From here you may survey the whole panorama of the City of the Kings, from the drab wilderness of its attendant deserts to the ineffable blue sheen of the Pacific. The pale prosperous suburbs lie in a splurge of gardens. The brave new office blocks tower above the business streets. Lima of the Viceroys lies there intricate and higgledy-piggledy, a meshwork of greys, browns and duns. It is a splendid prospect, a famous one, with the Andes behind you and the ocean horizon in front.
>
> Look below your feet, though, over the crest of the hill, and there lies misery: for straggling up towards the summit, clinging to San Cristobal like some nightmare belvedere, squats a slum so bestial, so filthy, so congested, so empty of light, fun, colour, health or comfort, so littered with excrement and garbage, so swarming with barefoot children, so reeking with pitiful squalor that just the breath of it, borne on the fresh sea wind, makes you retch into your handkerchief. From these unspeakable hovels and rubbish-piles a stench of degradation rises: it veils the City of the Kings in a kind of haze...

For all around her lie these dreadful slums, the notorious barri-
adas of Peru, in which 250,000 people live like gutter-creatures in
the dirt, and they give to Lima the reproach of a guilty conscience.

The cross on the Cerro's summit also serves as a reminder of Lima's vulnerability in the early years when it was still a small frontier settlement. In 1536 Manco Inca rose up in rebellion in the highlands and an army of some 50,000 men under general Titu Yupanqui was despatched against Lima. Massing their forces on the hill, the Incas launched a series of attacks on the city, which seemed in such imminent danger of being overrun that panic spread among the residents, some of whom pressed Pizarro to abandon the settlement and to flee on the ships anchored at Callao. Eventually the Spaniards succeeded in driving off the Inca army after two weeks of siege and, as was their wont, they attributed their delivery to divine intervention. While the two armies were facing each other across the river, they had called on St. Christopher to protect them and, according to legend, each time the Indians tried to cross the current grew fiercer and engulfed them, while the Spaniards were able to ford the river safely to attack the enemy forces. In thanksgiving they named the hill after him and on its summit they erected a cross to watch protectively over the city.

Even after it had established itself Lima remained vulnerable, since, given the relative smallness of the settler community, it would have been overrun if the subject peoples had joined in common cause against their European masters. In the event, that did not happen, as blacks and Indians were divided by mutual antipathy and distrust and the blacks as a group were too heterogeneous and dispersed to organize collectively on a large scale. Nonetheless, the settlers were haunted by fear of Indian insurrection. Josephe de Mugaburu recorded in his diary that in December 1666 the authorities uncovered an Indian plot to seize the city and massacre the Spanish population. Eight Indians were hanged for their part in the conspiracy and, as a warning to others with seditious notions, their heads were cut off and placed on spikes on the bridge over the Rímac and their bodies quartered and displayed in the streets.

Yet for most of the colonial period it was blacks who constituted the largest sector of Lima's population, and another of the colonists' nightmares was the prospect of a slave uprising. A source of great unease was the existence of communities of *cimarrones* (runaway slaves) in the vicinity of the city. As early as 1544 runaway blacks were reported to be assaulting and killing men and raiding farms on the outskirts, and the following year a force of 120 men was sent against some 200 *cimarrones* who had entrenched themselves in a well-organized settlement in a reedy marsh at Huara, a few miles north along the coast. The runaways had accumulated large quantities of Spanish weapons and armour and, according to reports, they had allies among the city's slave population and were planning to overthrow the Spanish settlers and assume rule over the Indians. The community was wiped out, but only after a bloody battle that left eleven Spaniards dead and many more wounded. Throughout the colonial period other such communities grew up sporadically in the hills surrounding the valley of Lima. The story of the most important, located in Huachipa around 1713, is recounted in Gregorio Martínez's novel *Crónica de músicos y diablos* (Chronicle of Musicians and Devils, 1991). Huachipa had an organized economy and defensive system and terrorized the region by waylaying travellers and raiding the neighbouring haciendas for provisions till it, too, was eventually suppressed after long and fierce resistance.

Nonetheless, the nightmare refused to go away, and in the years leading up to independence old fears were rekindled by events in Haiti, where in 1804 a slave revolt had established a black republic. Basil Hall was in Lima in 1821 when the royalists withdrew to a more defensible base in the Andes, abandoning the capital to the approaching patriots. Panic spread throughout the capital, he records, and many people took refuge in the fort at Callao or in the monasteries. The main cause of the panic, he explains, was the fear that blacks would rise up against their masters:

> *I landed and proceeded along the Callao road. It was with no small difficulty that I could make head against the crowd of fugitives coming in the opposite direction: groups of people on foot, in carts, on horseback, hurried past; men, women and children, with horses and mules and numbers of slaves laden with baggage and other valuables, travelled indiscriminately along and all was outcry and confusion. In the city itself the consternation was excessive; the men were pacing about in the fearful doubt what was to be done; the women were flying in all directions towards the convents; and the narrow*

streets were literally choked up with loaded wagons and mules and mounted horsemen. [...] An indistinct dread of some terrible catastrophe was the principal cause of this universal panic; but there was a definite source of alarm besides, which contributed considerably to the extraordinary event which I have been describing. This was a belief, industriously propagated, and caught up with all the diseased eagerness of fear, that the slave population of the city meant to take advantage of the absence of the troops to rise up in a body and massacre the whites.

Peru's vulnerability to attacks by foreign enemies was likewise exposed by the activities of English and Dutch corsairs. As early as the late 1550s the English adventurer Francis Drake was terrorizing the Peruvian coast; in the 1570s his compatriot John Oxenham did likewise; and at various times towns like Guayaquil, Paita, Huacho and Pisco were sacked. As is indicated by its title, Juan de Miramontes y Zuázola's epic poem *Armas antárticas* (Antartic Arms), written between 1608 and 1615, celebrates Spanish feats of arms in the southern hemisphere, but it is significant that though the opening cantos narrate the events of the Conquest and the civil wars that followed, the main body of the book is concerned with the defence of Peru against the likes of Drake and Oxenham, campaigns in which Miramontes personally participated. For the citizens of Lima the danger was brought closer to home in 1615 when a Dutch expedition led by Joris van Speilbergen defeated the Spanish Pacific fleet off Cañete and approached Callao, seemingly intent on forcing a landing and attacking the capital itself. Again in 1624 the Dutch corsair Jacques l'Hermite very nearly succeeded in landing at the head of eleven ships and 1,600 men. In both cases the danger was eventually averted, but such incidents spread panic throughout the city. What frightened authorities and settlers, above all, was a nightmare scenario in which Indians and blacks would rise up in support of a foreign invasion and their fears appear to have had some foundation, for it seems that l'Hermite had been counting on such support and that it might well have been forthcoming.

Such experiences made Limeñans uncomfortably aware of how ill-prepared they were to resist attack. And as Spain became embroiled in European wars, it was less and less able to deploy troops to defend its American empire and came to rely on local militias. A steadily increasing proportion of local revenues was diverted towards defence but, even so, the settlers, fearing that pirate raids were merely the first phase of a foreign campaign to seize possession of the colony, were unhappy about the lack of protection which Spain afforded them. In 1630 Fray Buenaventura de Salinas y Córdova complained that though Peru was subsidizing Spain with its mineral wealth, the Crown seemed unwilling to provide resources to improve its defences, leaving it to fend for itself as best it could:

> *Is it not too much that, after Peru has given its Kings its blood and its substance, melted down into so many millions, they disregard and forget it when enemies harass and attack it; and that, with so many of them invading its straits, Spain never comes to its aid and ties the viceroy's hands to keep him from spending money in its defence?*

In 1684-7, in response to such fears, Viceroy the Duque de la Palata constructed an immense defensive wall around the city. Built of adobe, the wall measured 15 to 20 feet high, was of a similar thickness and had 34 ramparts. It formed an eight-mile semicircle around the river, corresponding more or less to the ring-road system constituted by Avenida Alfonso Ugarte, Paseo Colón and Avenida Grau. The eastern part ran through El Cercado district, where a section still survives in the vicinity of the square. It had nine gates, the most important at the end of the road from Callao, which was located at today's Plaza Dos de Mayo. As a defensive structure the wall was never actually put to the test, but it is generally reckoned that it would have been totally ineffective against a determined attack. It would seem that it was primarily intended as a psychological deterrent and, above all, to provide the populace with a reassuring sense of security. The wall was eventually demolished in 1870 to allow the city to expand. The part of the city lying within the former wall's boundaries is sometimes referred to as El Cercado de Lima, which is not to be confused with the district known as El Cercado.

In the late 1980s and early 1990s Limeñans' old fears of being overrun by barbarian hordes seemed close to becoming a reality. In 1980 the Maoist movement Sendero Luminoso (Shining Path) unleashed an insurgency campaign in Ayacucho that over the following years developed into a bloody civil war. Most of the killing took place in rural areas, where peasants found themselves victimized by insurgents and army alike, but it was Shining Path's declared strategy to encircle the cities from the countryside, and the capital itself was subjected to terrorist attacks. Ancestral anxieties were fuelled by the widespread perception that Shining Path was an essentially Andean movement and by the support it enjoyed in the shanty towns. Such fears were heightened by its favourite tactic of plunging the capital into darkness by sabotaging electricity installations and then lighting up the surrounding hills with torches to signal the shining future that the revolution would bring. On one occasion the Cerro San Cristóbal was lit up by lanterns in the shape of a giant hammer and sickle. In fact, the brunt of the terror was borne by the inhabitants of the *pueblos jóvenes*, where the group waged war on community leaders and grassroots organizations, and it was they, too, who put up the most heroic resistance, exemplified by María Elena Moyano, the deputy mayor of Villa El Salvador, who was murdered in February 1992 for daring to speak out against the movement. Yet no one could feel safe. In July of the same year a week-long wave of bombings, assassinations and random killings attacked civilians and private property in nearly all of Lima's neighbourhoods. One of the most horrifying incidents occurred in the heart of Miraflores, where a powerful car bomb completely destroyed an apartment block in Calle Tarata, killing twenty people and wounding 132 others. The capture of Shining Path's leader Abimael Guzmán a couple of months later proved to be the beginning of the end, and by the mid-1990s the nightmare was finally over.

El Cercado

To the east of the Historic Centre, in the district of Barrios Altos, lies the neighbourhood of El Cercado, which in colonial times was a kind of Indian ghetto on the outskirts of the city and separated from it by fields. To facilitate the process of conversion and acculturation, the Spanish authorities, most notably during the administration of the fifth viceroy Francisco de Toledo (1569-81), pursued a policy, already practised in Spain's other American possessions, of bringing the natives together in settlements, known as *reducciones*, where they could be more easily controlled and indoctrinated. The *reducciones* served the interests of the Crown and the settlers, since by congregating the Indians in stable communities they made it easier to collect taxes and facilitated access to a sedentary labour force, but they were designed primarily to integrate the natives into the colonial order. Santiago del Cercado was established as a settlement for Indians belonging to neighbouring *encomiendas*. Other *reducciones* were established in rural areas to the south of the city: Santa María Magdalena and Santiago de Surco, which subsequently became the villages of Magdalena and Surco, which in their turn were later absorbed into the city as districts.

The task of evangelizing the natives of El Cercado was entrusted to the Jesuits. Religious indoctrination went hand in hand with a policy of acculturating the Indians to the Spanish way of life. One of the premises underlying the *reducciones* was that the natives would acquire civilized habits through exposure to an urban lifestyle and accordingly such settlements were built on the model of Spanish colonial cities, with streets laid out in a draughtboard pattern around a central square where the church and municipal council were sited. El Cercado has a typical colonial church around which the settlement was built, but it is unusual in that its square has the shape of a rhombus. Together with the priest a secular administrator was responsible for supervising the settlement, but it had its town council to govern local affairs, a means by which it was hoped that the Indians would learn to exercise their rights and responsibilities as subjects of the Crown.

Because of its proximity to the viceregal capital El Cercado had certain special features that distinguished it from other *reducciones*. Firstly, it was surrounded by high walls—hence its name (The Enclosure)—and each evening its gates were closed at curfew. The official reason for these measures was to protect the Indians from molestation by Spaniards, blacks or *mestizos*. It is likely that another unspoken reason was a lurking fear of Indian uprisings, but that is not incompatible with the official explanation. In fact, the Crown and the settlers viewed the Indians differently. Considering the natives to be racial inferiors who were there to be exploited, the settlers subjected them to frequent abuse, and in this they were emulated by blacks and *mestizos*. The Crown, on the other hand, regarded the natives as free men with the same rights as other subjects and, though its good intentions were often sacrificed to expediency, it did endeavour to protect the Indians against the depredations of the settler community.

El Cercado was also the site of the Colegio del Príncipe, a school for the sons of Indian chiefs founded in the 1610s. The Spanish colonial authorities adopted a double strategy with regard to the traditional Andean elites. On the one hand, they sought to consolidate Spanish power by diminishing their influence; on the other, they co-opted them as mediators between the colonial order and the indigenous masses. The latter strategy, favoured by the Jesuits, aimed to exploit the prestige still enjoyed by the indigenous elites as a means of propagating the Christian faith and allegiance to the Crown among the native population. To that end, the sons of chiefs received an education designed to acculturate them and to send them back to their communities as a bridge between the Spanish and indigenous worlds.

Another institution based in El Cercado, the Casa de Santa Cruz, was linked to the campaign to extirpate idolatry. Despite mass conversions of the natives, the destruction of Inca temples and the building of churches up and down the country, the Spaniards' apparently successful imposition of the Catholic faith was revealed to be illusory by the widespread persistence of indigenous religious practices in rural areas. In 1609 the ecclesiastical authorities became alarmed when Francisco de Avila, the parish priest of Huarochirí, reported to his superiors that his parishioners continued to practise their ancient rites in secret. The authorities' response was to initiate a series of persecutory campaigns of extirpation, organized and co-ordinated by the Archbishop of Lima and involving judicial trials for the offence of idolatry. The Casa de Santa Cruz was established as a correction centre where shamans found guilty of heathen practices were secluded and subjected to a process of ideological brainwashing.

Whether or not the Colegio del Príncipe and the Casa de Santa Cruz achieved their objectives, El Cercado seems to have been effective as an agent of acculturation. In 1639 Bernabé Cobo claimed that its inhabitants had become thoroughly hispanicized, to the extent that they had acquired black slaves as an emblem of social status:

> At present it has around two hundred houses and eight hundred souls and these Indians are so well instructed in civilized manners and Christianity that they stand out among the others of this kingdom; they are so hispanicized that all of them, men and women, understand and speak our language and in the care of their persons and the tidiness of their houses they are just like Spaniards, and as proof of

that it suffices to say that among them they have more than eighty black slaves.

It appears, too, that the Jesuits trained a highly accomplished parish choir and orchestra, which were frequently asked to perform at functions in the city. At the same time, though, the Indians of El Cercado clearly retained a strong sense of pride in their own cultural heritage. In public festivities they performed indigenous music and dances as well as masquerades commemorating their Inca ancestors.

Colonial Houses

Relatively few of Lima's original colonial houses remain standing, and it is in the nature of things that it is upper-class residences rather than humble lower-class housing which have survived. Of these only two—the Casa Aliaga (Jirón de la Unión 224) and the Casa Esquivel y Jarava, popularly known as the Casa de Pilatos (Ancash 390)—go back to the sixteenth century. The others—the Casa del Oidor (corner of Carabaya and Junín), the Palacio de Torre Tagle, now the Ministry of Foreign Affairs (Ucayali 363), the Casa Goyeneche (Ucayali 358), the Casa de las Trece Monedas (Ancash 536), the Casa Riva-Agüero, now a research institute of the Catholic University (Camaná 459), the Casa Negreiros (Azángaro 536), the Palacio de Osambela (Conde de Superunda 298), the Casa Larriva, now the Asociación Cultural Entre Nous (Ica 426)—date from the seventeenth and eighteenth centuries. Most have undergone modifications over the centuries and have found a new role as headquarters of institutions of one kind or another. Nonetheless, between them they enable us to reconstruct an image of the homes of the colonial elites.

Since settlers sought to re-create the environment of their homeland, colonial houses were typically modelled on those of Seville, with interior patios and tiled internal walls. In keeping with the cultural assumptions they had brought with them from Europe, the Spaniards believed that buildings should be constructed in "noble" materials such as stone and brick and regarded as primitive the mud, canes, reeds or wood used by the natives. In practice, though, they were obliged to make concessions to local conditions. Firstly, they had to adjust to shortages of the materials that they were accustomed to use for building. Stone was very expensive, since it had to be brought from a distance, and if in the neighbourhood there were groves of trees which they could exploit as a source of timber, overuse of that resource rapidly led to deforestation. Secondly, the danger of earthquakes militated against the construction of high buildings and roofing with heavy materials, as was discovered during the protracted building of the cathedral, which proved vulnerable to earthquakes and had to be reconstructed several times. As a result, the type of colonial house that evolved was an adaptation of a Mediterranean, more specifically Andalusian, model to the local environment, and as such it could be said to exemplify the emergence of a Creole culture. (The term "Creole", first used to designate native-born settlers as distinguished from those born in Spain, subsequently came to describe customs that were distinctively local.) In other words, it was the beginnings of a European culture adapted to and influenced by the conditions prevailing in the Peruvian coastal region.

As a precaution against earthquakes houses tended to be of only one or two storeys and, since it never rains in the Lima area, rooftops were not sloped but had flat surfaces, sometimes laid out as terraces (*azoteas*). External walls were constructed of adobe brick on the ground floor and *quincha* (panels of canes coated with mud) on the first floor; internal partitions were also made of *quincha*; *esteras* (panels of woven reeds) were used for the roofs; timber-work was held in place by leather thongs which, moistened in advance, contracted as they dried and formed a ligament that was both solid and elastic.

The settlers also found ways of compensating for the poverty of the materials they were forced to use. Façades were painted in warm, light colours (blue, pink, yellow, ochre) by distempering directly on to the rough surface. Ornamentation was obtained by using coatings of stucco—a mixture of slaked lime, marble dust and chalk worked into shapes and left to harden—as a substitute for marble.

The mansions of the elites were spacious, and, in addition to the family and an extended family of dependants, accommodated a household of servants and slaves. Traditionally they were divided into three zones. Inside the doorway, which was always open during the day, an entry hall gave access to an inner patio, separated from the street by wrought-iron gates. This first zone was the area of contact between the household and the outside world. The doorway was wide to allow passage to the inner patio for carriages, visitors on horseback and tradesmen making deliveries carried by mule. Distributed around the entry hall and the inner patio were various rooms, either used to conduct business or rented out as apartments. Rooms facing on to the street were often rented out as shops, the window having been converted into a door for that purpose. The central zone consisted of one or two drawing-rooms where guests were received and was the part that was most elegantly furnished and decorated. At the back of the house a second patio was the centre of the family's private space. Here the bedrooms and dining-room were located, and further back were the kitchen area, the stables and the quarters of servants and slaves. Many houses also had a garden.

Prominence was given to doorways as a statement of the status of the owner. The entrance was flanked by two broad pillars, embellished with mouldings and reliefs and surmounted by a decorated entablature, and the family coat of arms was displayed on the lintel. The Casa de Pilatos is unique in that its doorway is constructed entirely of dressed stone; in the case of the Palacio de Torre Tagle and the Casa Goyeneche the lower part of the doorway is in stone and the upper part in stucco; more common was the use of brick plastered over with stucco, as exemplified by the Casa de las Trece Monedas and the Casa Riva-Agüero. The doors themselves were of solid wood decorated with studs and ornamental knockers of iron and bronze. A particularly fine example is the Palacio de Torre Tagle.

Another status symbol were the richly decorated wrought-iron gates shutting off the inner patio. These gates were an assertion of the social and economic position of the family, and house-owners competed with one another to show off the most beautiful and finely wrought ironwork. Huge, low outer windows were likewise protected by elegant wrought-iron grilles. Inside, the patios were decorated with ornamental glazed tiles, at first imported from Spain but later manufactured locally. The Casa de Pilatos and the Casa Riva-Agüero are good places to see examples of both tiles and wrought ironwork.

Perhaps the most distinctive feature of Lima's colonial houses were the enclosed wooden balconies with lattice-work windows which projected from the upper storey and ran along the façade. Such balconies derived from Moorish Spain and allowed the occupants of the house to take the air and observe the street without being seen, but they also served a practical purpose in that they kept out the dust in a city where the climate was dry and the streets unpaved. Many examples can be seen in the Historic Centre, but the finest are generally held to be those of the Palacio de Torre Tagle. The enclosed balcony continued to be popular in the early decades of the Republican period, but in the late nineteenth century modernizing authorities, concerned for the health and safety of the population, prohibited it in the construction of new buildings on the grounds that it prevented the circulation of air and constituted a fire hazard.

Encomenderos, Bureaucrats and Merchants

Apart from their architectural interest, some of the houses cited are significant because they encapsulate aspects of colonial history. One such is the Casa Aliaga, which was built by Jerónimo de Aliaga, a member of the expedition that captured the Inca Atahualpa at Cajamarca. Identified as they were with Spanish Peru's epic foundational events, veterans of the Cajamarca and Cuzco campaigns enjoyed great status and prestige in early colonial society; they dominated city councils and, as holders of *encomiendas* granted to them as a reward for their services, they constituted a socio-economic elite. Aliaga himself held important municipal offices and was one of the colony's great *encomenderos*. Like many of his comrades, he opted to return to Spain in 1550, but he left his sons behind to inherit the *encomienda* and to maintain the position he had won, and to this day the house remains in the possession of his heirs.

An *encomienda* was not a grant of land, but charged its holder with responsibility for an area of territory and entitled him to the service of the Indians living on it. In the course of time, however, many *encomenderos* succeeded in acquiring title to the land and turned their *encomiendas* into large estates. The prosperity of the *encomenderos* derived from their control of Indian labour. Though the primary obligation of the *encomienda* Indians was to provide for the upkeep of the *encomendero* and his household, *encomenderos* used them for a range of economic enterprises such as producing food and textiles for the urban market and also put them to work in the construction of houses for sale or rent and hired out their services to others on short-term contracts. With the income generated they invested in mining and in the ventures of merchants and artisans, so that in time the *encomienda* itself often ceased to be their main source of revenue.

Encomenderos did not actually live on their *encomienda* but employed stewards to oversee it for them. They were theoretically required to reside in the city to fulfil a public role as pillars of the community, but that obligation sat easily with the ambition for a lordly lifestyle that most Spaniards shared. A typical *encomendero's* urban mansion such as that of the Aliagas was a large establishment with a retinue of Spanish and Indian servants and black slaves, and a table where many guests were maintained. Virtually all the early colony's social and economic activity effectively revolved around the *encomenderos*, as a huge number of relatives, friends and retainers were dependent on them for a living and their ostentatious spending was the main source of income for artisans and merchants.

Little is known about the house standing in the north-east corner of the Plaza Mayor, except that it dates from the late seventeenth century. It came to be known as the Casa del Oidor because it was speculated that here magistrates attached to the Audiencia heard complaints from the public. The highest court in the colony, the Audiencia also had legislative and executive functions and acted as a kind of advisory council to the viceroy and its meetings were held across the street in the Viceregal Palace. As royal authority was consolidated after the upheavals of the early decades, a key group in Peruvian society were to be men like the anonymous magistrate after whom the house is named, a class of professional bureaucrats who effectively ran the colony for the Crown. These were the men who interpreted and implemented royal policy, provided general administration, meted out justice, collected and disbursed taxes, performed ceremonial roles and dealt with local problems. They also ensured stability and continuity, for whereas viceroys came and went after a limited period of tenure, they mostly held lifetime appointments and thus constituted a permanent civil service.

The Peninsular authorities viewed Creoles with distrust and regularly sought to renovate the colonial administration with Europeans whose loyalty could be counted on. Yet though Creoles repeatedly complained that they were excluded from senior public posts, they actually constituted a relatively substantial proportion of the colonial bureaucracy. Indeed, in the course of the seventeenth century, as the Crown resorted to the sale of public offices as a means of resolving its increasing financial difficulties, control of the local administration virtually passed into the hands of the Creole elite. Yet, as part of the reform of Spain's American empire carried out by Bourbon regime in the latter decades of the eighteenth century, measures were taken to block the appointment of Creoles, with the result that by 1803 the Audiencia had only two Creole members. This exclusionary policy produced discontent that contributed to the eventual growth of a desire for independence among certain sectors of the Creole population.

Lima's colonial houses also include a number of opulent mansions erected by rich merchants who made their fortune in the import-export trade: the Palacio de Torre Tagle, built in the 1730s by José Bernardo de Tagle y Bracho; the Casa Riva-Agüero, built around 1760 by Domingo Ramírez de Arellano; and the Palacio de Osambela, built in 1808 by Martín de Osambela. A feature of the latter is a *mirador* from which the merchant could watch out for the arrival of his ships at Callao, a reminder that Lima was the hub of a colonial system of economic exchange.

Colonial Peru's major export was silver bullion, which was transported overland from Potosí and other mines in the viceroyalty to Lima and from there shipped to Spain via Panama, and in return it imported textiles and other manufactured goods. But Spain's trade regulations, which required all shipping to load and unload in Seville and, at the South American end, in Callao, effectively ensured that commerce between the two countries was monopolized by Seville's merchant guild and its associates in the viceregal capital. Working in partnership with their colleagues in Seville, Lima's wholesale merchants, who after 1613 likewise operated as a monopolistic guild, controlled the import-export market and were able to amass huge profits by forcing down the price of silver and forcing up the price of imports. One effect of such price-fixing was to restrict the growth of the colonial economy, as investment in mining decreased as a consequence. In the course of the seventeenth century the system underwent a long period of crisis as transatlantic trade declined as a result of a slump in mining production, Spain's growing inability to supply the colonial market, a growing contraband trade and the colony's increasing capacity to produce many items previously imported. Of our three merchants mentioned above Osambela belonged to a later era when trade had been revitalized by the late-eighteenth-century reforms introduced by the Bourbons. They gave incentives to revive mining, which was now centred on Cerro de Pasco; the quality of Peninsular manufactures improved; freight charges fell as Atlantic crossings became quicker with the abandonment of the cumbersome fleet system previously employed to protect shipping from attack; and the old monopolies gave way to a liberalization authorizing other ports to trade with Spain and foreigners. Lima's merchants seem to have adjusted to the loss of their monopoly and, as demonstrated by the mansion that Osambela built for himself, they prospered under the new system as they had under the old.

A City of Churches

Colonial Lima was a city of churches. In the eighteenth century it had a cathedral, 6 parish churches, 15 nunneries and 19 monasteries serving a population of about 50,000. Apart from the cathedral, the most impressive are Santo Domingo (corner of Conde de Superunda and Camaná), San Agustín (Ica 251), San Pedro (corner of Azángaro and Ucayali) and La Merced (Jirón de la Unión 621). But the magnificence of Lima's ecclesiastical architecture is exemplified, above all, by the church and monastery of San Francisco (corner of Ancash and Lampa), a vast complex which was once even vaster, part of the property having been sacrificed to the widening of Avenida Abancay in the 1940s. In its heyday San Francisco housed more than 200 monks together with a huge staff of servants and slaves and was a city within the city. Its main cloister gives access to the communal rooms—chapter hall, library, refectory—and to the church and sacristy. Laid out in the form of a Latin cross, with a dome over the intersection and a twin-towered façade, the church was the spiritual centre of the monastic community. It also served as its link with the city, since the public could enter it from the street. In front of it is an open square that was used for open-air services. Worked in stone, the main doorway incorporates all the main architectonic elements of seventeenth-century altars, so that it itself becomes a kind of reredos projecting the sacred space of the temple out towards the street.

Foreign travellers such as the Spaniards Jorge Juan and Antonio de Ulloa, who visited the viceroyalty in the 1740s, marvelled at the opulence of Lima's churches:

> The altars, from their very bases to the borders of the paintings, are covered with massive silver, wrought into various kinds of ornaments. The walls [...] are hung with velvet, or tapestry of equal value,

adorned with gold and silver fringes [...] The lower part of the church [...] is equally dazzling with glittering objects, presenting themselves on all sides: among which are candlesticks of massive silver, six or seven feet high, placed in two rows along the nave [...] the gold of the sacred vessels, the chalices, the ostensoriums is covered with diamonds, pearls and precious stones [...] In short, whatever is employed in ornamenting the churches is always the richest of the kind possible to be procured.

Such opulence is perhaps not so surprising, since Lima was a wealthy city. It was home to affluent *hacendados* and merchants and, as one of the poles of the silver trade, it reaped vast profits and revenues from the shipping of bullion to Spain. The Church benefited from that wealth in that it was the recipient of generous endowments and bequests. It also generated its own wealth. The religious orders acquired urban property and agricultural lands, either donated or purchased with donated money, and through efficient management of their estates turned them in to prosperous businesses. The Jesuits became the most powerful landowner in the coastal region, two of their estates being located in the

Lima area: the Hacienda San Juan Grande in Surco and the Hacienda Villa in Chorrillos.

Part of the Church's income was channelled into the upkeep of its communities and the funding of its educational and charitable activities. The religious orders, the Jesuits in particular, founded schools to educate the sons of the Spanish and Creole elites, and they also ran hospitals, hospices and orphanages. At the same time, a substantial proportion of the Church's wealth was devoted to the embellishment of its temples and monasteries, particularly the interiors. Such embellishment was intended to glorify God, but it was also a triumphal affirmation of the colonial order in that it projected the majesty of the faith underpinning that order. It also conferred prestige both on the religious establishments and their members and on the patrons and the community whose generosity made the system possible.

It is an indication of the purchasing power of the Lima Church that hanging on the walls of the capital's religious establishments are paintings commissioned from the studios of major Spanish artists, some of them by the master himself. The monastery of San Francisco has a collection of 15 pictures depicting the apostles from the studio of Francisco de Zurbarán, while from the same studio a series featuring archangels is housed in the convent of La Concepción (Abancay 325). The church of San Pedro has a series on the life of St. Ignatius of Loyola by Juan de Valdés Leal. Church patronage also encouraged Italian and Spanish artists like Mateo Pérez de Alesio, Angelino Medoro and Leonardo Jaramilla to move to Lima and set up studios there and led, too, to the emergence of local painters trained by the former. The major work by local artists is a series of paintings on the life of St. Francis of Assisi in the main cloister of the monastery of San Francisco, a group effort completed in 1673 and involving Francisco de Escobar, Pedro Fernández de Noriega, Diego de Aguilera and Andrés de Liévana, the last of whom was a black slave hired out for the project by his master Francisco de Liévana. In contrast with the Cuzco school of painting, where the indigenous cultural heritage left its imprint on ecclesiastical art, the work of the Lima school is very much within the western tradition since its artists were Spaniards and Creoles. Even so, the work of the former was enthusiastically received in the viceregal capital, as can be gauged from the collection in the monastery of Los Descalzos (Alameda de los Descalzos 164, Rímac).

The Spanish cultural heritage also manifests itself in the use of ornamental glazed tiles to decorate the walls of monastery cloisters. Initially these were imported from Seville but they later came to be manufactured locally. Dating from the early seventeenth century, the tiles adorning the lower walls and pillars of the monastery of San Francisco include a series depicting Franciscan missionaries martyred in Japan. Other examples can be seen in the monastery of Santo Domingo.

A distinctive feature of Lima church interiors is the range of ornate wood carvings and sculptures of their reredos, pulpits and choir-stalls. Monumental pieces filling the whole wall space behind the altar, reredos usually contain a mixture of paintings and carved statues in their niches and panels and they are often gilded. Some were commissioned from Spain, such as the reredos of the chapel of St. John the Baptist in the cathedral, which is the work of the famous Sevillian artist Juan Martínez Montañés. Other Spanish artists like Pedro de Noguera, attracted by the wealth of the viceroyalty, settled in Lima and set up workshops, where local craftsmen were to learn their skills. The characteristic style of seventeenth-century reredos was baroque, but many have been lost, when, as a consequence of a later reaction against baroque exuberance and extravagance, they were dismantled and replaced by more austere neoclassical pieces produced by Matías Maestro, the most influential artist of the late eighteenth century. Such was the case of the high altars of the cathedral, San Francisco and San Pedro. Fortunately, some fine examples have survived, notably the high altar of the church of Jesús, María y José (Camaná 765) and the side chapels of San Pedro, particularly those dedicated to San Francisco Javier and San Francisco de Borja. In the second half of the eighteenth century, during the reconstruction that followed the disastrous earthquake of 1746 and reflecting the influence of the new Bourbon dynasty, French rococo came to replace the baroque as the dominant style, as exemplified by the reredos of the chapel of the Virgin of Lourdes in the church of La Merced.

Wood carving was not restricted to reredos. Choir-stalls were decorated with carvings and panels featuring statues of saints or angels. The cathedral choir-stalls are a masterpiece and reckoned to be the finest in the Americas, but other splendid examples are to be found in the churches of Santo Domingo, San Francisco and La Merced. The high level of artistry achieved by colonial carvers and sculptors of wood is further illustrated by the pulpit of the church of San Pedro and the monastery of San Francisco's carved ceilings in the Mudejar style.

Given that Lima's prosperity was based mainly on the output of the silver mines of Potosí, it is hardly surprising that silverwork should have figured in the adornment of its churches in the shape of tabernacles, crosses and the various accessories of divine worship. Today's church interiors are considerably less opulent, since much of their silver was requisitioned at the time of the struggle for independence to finance the war effort. Nonetheless, evidence of their former opulence is still to be seen. The decoration of the front part of the high altar of the church of La Merced, for example, consists of a huge elliptical silver medallion depicting the order's protectress, the Virgin of Mercy. The convent of Nuestra Señora del Prado (Junín 1411) houses one of the masterpieces of Limeñan baroque silverware, a piece in which Christ's sacrifice is symbolically represented by the figure of a pelican opening its breast to feed its chicks. Many other examples of religious art in silver and gold are on display in the museum in the monastery of San Francisco.

Limeñan Piety

Colonial Lima produced five saints and numerous other men and women who were venerated for their saintliness. It had an exceptionally high number of churches and monasteries for a city of its size and population and, according to a census carried out in 1613, more than one in ten of its inhabitants had committed their lives to the service of God. And the opulence of its religious establishments constituted visible proof of the community's support of the Catholic faith. Yet, while a minority of the city's inhabitants distinguished themselves by their piety, it would be a mistake to conclude that Lima was a particularly pious society. As in all societies where there is an established church, religious faith was a given that had been handed down and which no one would have thought to question, but for most people it was a no more than a matter of habit and convention. And that was true of the clergy as much as the laity. Indeed, the sheer number of Lima's churches is an indictment of the Peruvian Church's failure to fulfil its mission. Since it was the evangelization of the natives which officially justified the Spaniards' presence in Peru, it was in country areas where priests and churches were most needed, but most priests were reluctant to endure the hardships of life in the countryside, preferring instead the comfort and status of work in the city. Essentially the religious life was a career which brought them an adequate income, earned them respect in the community and integrated them into the social fabric of the city. Donning the cloth did not prevent them from leading fairly worldly lives. The secular clergy mingled with their fellow citizens at social events such as the theatre or bullfights and, though the regulars were more constrained by the rules of their order, they too led a way of life that was only semi-monastic since their various activities frequently took them outside the walls of the monastery.

The same was true of female religious. Some women opted for the religious life out of a sense of vocation, but for many it had other attractions: it offered independence from male domination; for the impoverished daughters of good families convents provided a refuge; and, more generally, having a nun in the family was seen as conferring social prestige. In the smaller convents the rules were strictly enforced, but in larger ones such as La Concepción and Santa Clara (Jauja 449) the atmosphere was relaxed and worldly. Nuns often had their own private cell, with a servant or slave to prepare their meals, and far from being isolated from the outside world, they were allowed regular visits from family and friends, whom they entertained with music and refreshments. Flora Tristan visited one such convent in the 1830s and was shocked by what she saw:

> *Inside that convent there is no sense of religious feeling. Convent rule is nowhere to be seen. It is a house where everything goes on that goes on in any other house. There are twenty-nine nuns; each of them has her own lodging, in which she is cooked for, works, teaches children, chats, sings, in short, does as she fancies. We even saw some who were not wearing their order's habit. They have pupils who come and go; the convent door is always open. It is a way of life whose purpose is beyond comprehension; one would be tempted to believe that these women have taken refuge in this cloister to be more independent than they would have been in the outside world.*

The Cloisters as Battleground: Creoles Versus Peninsulars

Lima's monasteries were pillars of the colonial order, but they were also an arena where the tensions between Spaniards and colonials were acted out. This was particularly the case on the occasion of the three-yearly election of the provincial of the various religious orders. Initially it had been Spanish priests who occupied positions of responsibility, since Creole churchmen constituted a small minority and were young and inexperienced. In time, however, the Spaniards were to be displaced. Spain found it increasingly difficult to recruit priests to serve its vast overseas empire and to replace locally-based Spanish monks as they grew old and died out. At the same time, as the number of Creole friars increased, so too did their voting power in the communities and chapters. By the end of the sixteenth century some orders, such as the Dominicans, had already come under Creole control. Reluctant to accept that development, Spanish clerics pressed for the introduction of the *alternativa*, a system whereby rival groups alternated in power every three years and which was commonly used in Europe to avoid conflicts. The Creoles, for their part, strongly resisted it, claiming that, while it was justified in cases where rival groups were more or less numerically balanced, the Spaniards were invoking it merely to cling to power.

Far from being in-house disputes, these power struggles affected the entire city. Though Lima was a wealthy city, life was precarious for those who were not landowners, merchants or bureaucrats, and the religious life came to be viewed as a career opportunity: at the very least it provided material security; it offered the sons of humble families a means to better themselves; and it enabled the scions of noble families to find a position appropriate to their social status. Given that in 1613 more than one-tenth of the population had entered the religious life, virtually every family in Lima almost certainly had a relative in one or other of the monasteries and therefore had a stake in the outcome of these elections. Moreover, since the position of provincial was unique in that appointment to it was decided by election—major posts in the administration and in the secular clergy went to government appointees—electoral campaigns were the only forum where competition between Spaniards and Creoles was fought out in public. Most of the colonists supported the Creoles, of course. Spanish priests, on the other hand, enjoyed official backing, since Peninsular political and ecclesiastical authority took the view that colonials were less able and qualified. The king, the Council of the Indies and the ambassador to the Holy See repeatedly and insistently put pressure on the pope and on the generals of the orders to have the *alternativa* introduced, and likewise viceroys intervened to ensure that the decisions made in Rome were implemented. Hence, the controversy over the *alternativa* often turned into a confrontation between the colonial authorities and the local Creole population.

In some cases, such disputes led to violence. In 1680 the Creole faction of the Franciscans, believing that Commissar General Fray Terán had been sent to impose the *alternativa*, subjected him to harassment and intimidation and, fearing for his safety, he took refuge in another monastery. Apparently unaware of this, a group of hot-headed young monks set fire to his cell and, armed with sticks and stones, waited for him to emerge, and an unfortunate priest who had been using the cell in his place was badly beaten. The viceroy sent in troops and arrested nine of the ringleaders, but their colleagues attacked the soldiers with stones and in the scuffle a friar was shot dead. The monks then paraded the corpse through the streets, protesting against what they claimed was repression. To restore order the viceroy was eventually obliged to issue an edict forbidding public gatherings.

Emergence of a Creole Consciousness
These disputes within the walls of monasteries like San Francisco were merely the most visible and dramatic expression of an evolving Creole consciousness. As churchmen and educators, most of Peru's writers were members of the colonial establishment and it would never have occurred to them to challenge the imperial ideology within whose parameters they operated, but that did not prevent them from striving to assert their status and identity as colonials within the imperial order. Such was the purpose of the Franciscan Buenaventura de Salinas y Córdova's *Memorial de las historias del Nuevo Mundo Pirú* (Memorial of the Histories of the New World: Peru, 1630), where he informs the king about his overseas territory, diagnoses failings of colonial practice and offers advice for the better government of the colony.

"Are those born in Peru perhaps made of different stuff and blood from the people of Spain?" Salinas asks rhetorically, voicing the grievance that colonials were looked down upon as inferiors by Europeans. Such complaints were more than mere paranoia, as from the outset Creoles were the target of European prejudices. The term "Creole" itself carried pejorative connotations on the lips of the

European. Originally used to designate a black slave born in the Americas, it came to be applied to the descendants of Spaniards, thereby associating them with the subject peoples and implying that they were degenerate offspring of Europe. In keeping with beliefs of the period, the geographic and climactic conditions in the Americas were held to be unfavourable to human development, as a consequence of which its inhabitants underwent a process of physical and intellectual degeneration. According to this environmental determinism, the indigenous Indians were natural inferiors, but the degeneration process also affected the descendants of Spaniards settled in the New World. Furthermore, Creoles were regarded as having been contaminated by contact with the inferior races with whom they mingled, either as a result of sexual intercourse or because they had been suckled by black or Indian wet-nurses.

Creoles also saw themselves as victims of a policy of discrimination which privileged Spaniards over colonials. As the descendants of those who had conquered and settled the colony, the Creoles felt that it should have been their birthright to govern their country and enjoy the privileges and profits of political dominion. Looking to public office as their chief hope for security and status, they repeatedly complained that viceroys favoured their own extensive entourage of relatives and clients and gave preference to Spaniards over Creoles. Salinas laments that "the best magistratures, the governorships, the revenues and *encomiendas*, rightfully due to the sons and descendants of those who conquered this land and who now defend it with their lives, are now enjoyed by outsiders." In-comers from Spain were a bigger threat than Dutch pirates, he claims, for whereas the latter merely came to plunder, the former rob the Creoles of their honour by denigrating their capabilities and of their inheritance by monopolizing positions of prestige within the country.

Like other self-justifying agendas, Creole discourse tended to be selective with the truth, glossing over facts that conflicted with their image of themselves. While Creoles resented the affluence and status acquired by immigrants from Spain who enriched themselves through commerce, they themselves failed to take advantage of the opportunities afforded by the expansion of the export economy based on silver-mining and transatlantic trade. Salinas himself unwittingly offers an insight into the Creole mentality when he asserts that those born in Peru grow up "with such elevated spirits that there are none who are inclined to learn the mechanical arts and crafts that their fathers brought from Spain; and so one will not find Creole cobblers, barbers, smiths or taverners." It would appear, therefore, that the Creoles' obsession with gaining access to public office stems from the fact that, as heirs of the conquistadors, they viewed themselves as a noble elite entitled to positions of prestige and were reluctant to sully their hands by entering trade.

Seeking to refute prevailing prejudices and to demonstrate that Creoles are every bit as gifted and capable as Europeans, Salinas addresses the issue of environmental determinism by emphasizing the benignity of Lima's climate and the beauty of its surroundings, claiming that few cities can match it as a site for human habitation. He then exploits the determinist argument for his own ends by suggesting that if climate shapes personality, a benevolent environment such as Lima's could not fail to produce human beings possessed of the highest abilities and virtues. "The temperament of the people is peaceful and gentle," he claims, "and those who are born here are extremely acute, sharp, subtle and profound in every branch of learning." And he goes on: "What causes most wonder is to see how early the use of reason dawns in children and that in general they all emerge with such elevated spirits that there are none who are inclined to learn the mechanical arts and crafts that their fathers brought from Spain [...], for the constellation and climate of Peru elevate and ennoble them in spirit and thought." Salinas thus effectively turns the tables on the Creoles' detractors by implying that the Peruvian environment has an improving rather than a degenerative effect and produces a breed of men superior to their Peninsular forbears.

Like most Creole writing, Salinas' *Memorial* focuses almost exclusively on Lima. Though it contains a general description of Peru, the only other area of the country to merit substantial discussion is Potosí, whose silver mines sustained the urban splendour of which he boasts. His is the perspective of a settler elite who, ensconced in their coastal enclave, regarded the interior as a source of wealth to be exploited. In privileging Lima over the rest of the country, he exalts the most European part of the colony, therefore effectively defining himself and his class as American Spaniards. In that respect it is significant that he asserts Lima's claims to be regarded as a major centre of civilization by measuring it against the most prestigious cities of the Old World. Lima, he enthuses, is

> *a holy Rome in its temples, ornaments and religious cult; a proud Genoa in the style and brio of those who are born in it; a beautiful Florence for its benign climate; a populous Milan because of the crowd of people who flock there from all quarters; a wealthy Venice because of the riches it produces for Spain and prodigally distributes to all, remaining as wealthy as ever; a copious Bologna because of the abundance of foodstuff; a Salamanca because of its thriving university and colleges.*

As we have seen, such eulogies of the Creole homeland were intended to put colonials on a par with Peninsular Spaniards by demonstrating that Creoles were their equals in merits and achievements. At the same time, though, they constituted a psychological appropriation of the colonial territory, enabling Creoles to define themselves as "hijos de la tierra" (sons of the country) as opposed to Spanish officials who had come on a limited term of service or opportunist immigrants who planned to return home to the Peninsula after making their fortune. The Creoles' sense of themselves accordingly came to be less a question of ethnicity than of having roots in the colony and, though made up mainly of the descendants of Spaniards born in America, the Creole sector was not limited to that group since it also included acculturated *mestizos* and mulattoes as well as Spaniards who had established themselves in the country.

So we find Salinas deploying a line of argument that enables him to claim for his class the rights due to the descendants of the conquerors while distancing them from the ills stemming from the Conquest. It is the Creoles who are Peru's natural leaders, he implies, since they are committed to its long-term development in contrast to transient Spaniards, who are interested only in milking the country. The greatest threat to Peru's future, he claims, are not foreign invaders but Spanish immigrants who come to the colony not to settle but to enrich themselves and return to Spain in style. Unlike the settlers, such people cannot be relied on to fight to defend the country in times of danger. They also dominate commerce, "sucking the land like parasites, extracting the blood from the Indians like leeches" and bleeding the country of its wealth. And in their greed to enrich themselves Spanish merchants, government officials and *encomenderos* are destroying the country's greatest asset by exploiting and oppressing the Indian work-force to the point of exterminating it. "If the farmer is concerned only with picking the fruit rather than caring for the trees," he observes, "it is inevitable that the orchard will soon become a wasteland." The solution, he advises the king, is to limit immigration to those committed to establishing themselves in the colony with their families and to building their future there, since they would have a personal stake in the long-term well-being of the country. Peru would thus become a country of colonists under the Crown, with the old-established Creoles constituting its dominant elite.

The Museum of the Inquisition

One of colonial Lima's great spectacles was specifically designed to uphold the colonial order by making a public example of those found guilty of offences against the Catholic faith. This was the *auto de fe*, where those condemned by the Inquisition were formally sentenced and handed over to the civil authorities for punishment. Anyone convicted of serious offences such as heresy or witchcraft was condemned to death either by hanging or, if refusing to recant, by burning; lesser offences were punished with fines, flogging, confiscation of property, exile or service on the galleys; those who expressed remorse for their sins and asked to be reconciled to the Church were absolved and given penance but carried the social stigma with them for the rest of their lives. In the course of its existence (1570-1820) the Lima Inquisition held forty-odd *autos de fe*, but they dwindled in number from the mid-seventeenth century onwards.

Held on a raised platform in the Plaza Mayor, *autos de fe* involved elaborate ceremony. On the morning scheduled for the event—usually a holiday to ensure a large public—all the city's civil and ecclesiastical authorities would congregate at the headquarters of the Inquisition, together with companies of troops and militia, to escort the Inquisitors and the convicted to the square. At the head of the procession four priests carried a cross covered with a black cloth indicating the presence of excommunicates and the clergy intoned the *miserere*. The convicted wore a tall conical hat, on which were painted devils and flames, and a *sanbenito* (penitential cloak), which was later placed in the cathedral or parish church as a reminder of their shame; around their neck they had a rope and they carried a candle. When the procession reached the Plaza Mayor, the viceroy, the Audiencia and the public would swear to defend the faith and, after a sermon, the convicted would be called to hear their sentence and be taken away for punishment.

In the Plaza Bolívar a museum stands on the site of the Inquisition's headquarters. The exterior is somewhat misleading, as the neoclassical columns of the entrance date from the nineteenth century when the building functioned as the Senate Chamber. Inside, however, are the hall where trials were held, cells where prisoners were kept, and the chamber where they were tortured. The Inquisition initiated proceedings on the basis of information received and in the initial stages the accused was not informed of the charges against him nor allowed to confront witnesses. Instead, he was given a warning that was effectively an invitation to confess his offence. If he failed to do so, he was subjected to torture. It was only at a later stage that he was made aware of the charges and given the opportunity to defend himself. Such a system, of course, laid innocent people open to malicious accusations.

The Inquisition was introduced to Peru to maintain the purity of the Catholic faith against the spread of heretical Protestant beliefs brought to the Americas by foreign interlopers. In practice, though, a large proportion of the cases it tried related to matters of morality or ecclesiastical discipline. The single offence most frequently punished was bigamy, committed by men who remarried in Peru when they already had a wife in Spain or in some other part of the Americas, and twenty per cent of those it sentenced were churchman, usually for sexual offences. It also persecuted blasphemy and superstitious practices such as witchcraft, most of the latter involving blacks, mulattoes or *mestizos*, particularly women, though Indians, it should be emphasized, did not come within the Inquisition's jurisdiction. In fact, though numerically relatively small (21.2 per cent of all cases), it was offences of a heretical nature, the bulk of them involving foreigners, which aroused the strongest feelings among the public. Protestants deemed to be heretics were usually the crews of captured pirate ships or foreign artisans resident in the city, but these were outnumbered by New Christians (converted Jews) found guilty of persisting in the faith of their ancestors, and no fewer than 36 Jews, mostly Portuguese in origin, were sentenced to death.

On the whole the colonists supported the Inquisition, considering it to be a body that protected their values and way of life, since they regarded themselves as Spaniards and shared the cultural values of the mother country. Any challenge to Catholic orthodoxy was perceived by them as a threat to their world, as their sense of identity was grounded in their allegiance to Catholicism. This sentiment is illustrated in diarist Josephe de Mugaburu's description of César de Bandier (a.k.a. Nicolás Legras), a French-born physician and priest sentenced to life imprisonment in Spain for heresy at an *auto de fe* held in October 1667:

> *This so-and-so denied the immortality of the soul, and his errors were worse than Luther, Arius, Mohammed, or any of the sectarians. He was of such a type that he went up to paintings of the crucified and dying Jesus Christ and one of the Virgin of Solitude, and he said to the holy Virgin, "Why is that lying woman crying for a son who has deceived the world?" There were so many insults and blasphemies and dishonest words that he said to the holy Virgin, that I do not write them for the great horror and scandal they cause to Christian hearers. They were so bad that in relating his wickedness and evil deeds all those who heard became enraged, and if the gentlemen of the Inquisition had not ordered that no more be read, they would have killed him right in the chapel of the Holy Office.*

Such was the public indignation Bandier aroused, Mugaburu tells us, that the Inquisition had to keep him away from the cathedral, where an angry mob was waiting to lynch him:

> *The following day, Sunday, the 9th of October, more than two thousand souls awaited for him to be brought out to the Cathedral to hear Mass, determined, young and old, to stone him to death. But the gentlemen of the Inquisition, knowing that there was such a tumult, ordered that neither he nor the other two go out to hear Mass.*

The Santuario de Santa Rosa
The church (built in 1728) and sanctuary of Santa Rosa (Tacna 100) stand on the site of the family home of Latin America's first saint, Santa Rosa de Lima (1586-1617), who was canonized in 1671. The daughter

of a middle-class Creole family, Rosa made the life choice followed by a significant minority of women in the Hispanic world. Rejecting marriage as an option, she espoused Christ as her husband and she built a hermitage in her home where she devoted herself to prayer, mortification of the flesh and mystic contemplation. She also established an infirmary for destitute children and old people. She eventually left the family home to join the Dominican order but, like many pious women of the period who wished to pursue a religious life without taking the irrevocable vows demanded by convent life, she did so according to the rules of the Third Order, which required her to wear a habit and to lead a secluded life but allowed her to live in the home of a wealthy patron rather than in a convent.

During her lifetime she acquired a reputation for saintliness and numerous miracles were attributed to her. In the church there is an image of the Infant Jesus, which is popularly known as the "Little Doctor" because he reportedly cured the sick at Rosa's request. The garden in the sanctuary features the tiny hermitage of adobe where she allowed herself two hours of sleep a night on a bed of two tree trunks with stones as pillows. It also includes a well where she is said to have thrown the key to the girdle of thorns which she wore round her waist. The convent and church of Santa Rosa de las Monjas (Miró Quesada 605), built on the site of the home of the patron where she spent the last five years of her life, contains relics and portraits.

Santa Rosa was one of five saints produced by colonial Lima. The others include the aforementioned Santo Toribio Alfonso de Mogrovejo (1538-1606), San Juan Masías (1585-1645) and San Francisco Solano (1549-1610), but the most famous is San Martín de Porras—sometimes written "Porres"—(1579-1639). The son of a Spaniard and a free black woman, he became a lay brother in the Dominican order. Known as the "Saint of the Broom" because of his willingness to undertake the most menial tasks, he was noted for his love of animals and his concern for the needy. As a nurse in the monastery infirmary he became famous for healing the sick, and as the "brother of the poor" he wheedled funds and favours from the wealthy and the powerful to support his charities, among them the rescue and education of abandoned orphans. He was reputed to have miraculous powers that gave him the ability to be in different places at the same time or to make a dog, a cat and a mouse eat from the same plate.

Santa Rosa was canonized a little over fifty years after her death, whereas Santo Toribio had to wait until 1726 and San Martín until 1962 before they were elevated to sainthood. This prompts two related questions. Why was it she rather than one of the other equally worthy candidates who became America's first saint? And why was her canonization process so remarkably speedy? It is easy to understand why San Martín was never a serious competitor. Among the colony's lower classes he was beloved and revered and he enjoyed the patronizing affection of the elites, who saw in his humility a model of how coloured people should behave, but in the climate of the times it was unthinkable that American Catholicism could be equated with a mulatto, and official recognition of him only came in the twentieth century when the Church began to rethink its attitude towards the black populations of Africa and the New World. Santo Toribio would appear to have had a stronger case, since his apostolic endeavours had consolidated the Catholic religion in Peru and he was much beloved by the indigenous masses to whom he had brought the word of God, but his reforming zeal had not endeared him to his fellow churchmen and as a Spaniard he had the disadvantage of being associated with the metropolis. Rosa, conversely, as the daughter of a respectable and well-connected Creole family, had the ideal profile.

Rosa's canonization is connected to an emerging sense of Creole identity. Regarding themselves as American Spaniards, the settler community nursed the grievance that colonials were treated as inferiors and hankered after official recognition of their equal status. The elevation of one of their own to sainthood was one form of such recognition. Lima's Creole leaders mounted a particularly well orchestrated campaign and the Crown and the Papacy responded positively, realizing the political advantages of giving the American colonists a saint of their own, since it would strengthen allegiance to the Catholic religion. Accordingly, not only was she canonized, but she was also declared patron saint of the Americas and the Philippines. As such she was adopted as an emblem of Latin American identity and became the object of particular devotion, not only among colonials but also among the empire's subaltern population.

Rosa was also named patron saint of Lima and, despite her continental appeal, for Limeñans she was very much a local saint, an icon of her city and her class. This was illustrated by a poem penned by

Luis Antonio de Oviedo y Herrera, the Conde de la Granja. The central episode of his life of the saint—*Vida de Santa Rosa* (1711)—evokes the Creoles' worst nightmare, the fear of an alliance between Indians and European heretics to overrun Catholic Peru. A conspiracy between the Inca leadership and the Protestant powers is thwarted when Rosa's intercession drives a fleet of Dutch privateers from the coast of Callao. Rosa is celebrated as the patron watching protectively over the Peru founded by the Christian warrior Francisco Pizarro.

After independence Santa Rosa was to be a recurring figure in Lima's imaginary as an emblem of Peruvian identity. On display in the Palacio Municipal is a famous painting by Francisco Laso (1823-69) where she is portrayed in a state of mystic ecstasy. Ricardo Palma was later to adopt a distinctly less solemn approach to the saint in "Los gobiernos del Perú" (Peru's Governments). The narrative recounts a popular anecdote concerning Santa Rosa, who one day intercedes with God to bestow a number of blessings on her country: a benign climate, rich resources, beautiful and virtuous women and intelligent men. God indulges her but begins to weary of her endless demands and by the time she gets round to her final request He has lost patience with her and in typically Limeñan language tells her to leave Him in peace:

"Lord! Lord!"
"Eh? What? You still want more?"
"Yes, Lord. Give my country good government."
At that point the good Lord, peeved, turned his back on her, saying:
"Rosita! Rosita! Why don't you go and make fritters?"

If only Rosa had made her requests in reverse order, comments Palma, Peru might have been a happier country. In this story Palma establishes a sense of shared community with his readership, both of them forming part of a society whose misfortune it is to have to put up with misgovernment as a fact of life. Instead of venerating Santa Rosa as an icon, he humanizes her, depicting her as a typical example of Limeñan womanhood, as "one of us", and by so doing he turns her into an emblem both of that shared community and of the flaws inherent in it.

Somewhat more irreverent is Creole popular culture's tongue-in-cheek treatment of the saint. A well-known refrain consists of a mock appeal to her followed by a line describing some activity of which she would have disapproved, a good example being the drinking song "Salud contigo" (Good Health):

Saint Rose of Lima, Saint Rose of Lima, how can you permit
that here in Lima people drink so much liquor?

The refrain works, in effect, by invoking Santa Rosa as the accepted symbol of cultural identity only to assert a counter-culture more life-affirming than the rigid self-discipline which she embraced.

The Church of Las Nazarenas and El Señor de los Milagros

Opened in 1730, the church of Las Nazarenas (corner of Huancavelica and Tacna) has a long prehistory. The inhabitants of the Lima region live under the permanent threat of earthquakes and since its foundation the city has periodically suffered varying degrees of damage caused by tremors. The greatest catastrophe was the earthquake of 28 October 1746. The quake lasted for four minutes and was so strong that it brought most of the city's buildings tumbling to the ground. Some 6,000 people—ten per cent of the population—were killed and the disaster was made worse by a huge tidal wave which swamped Callao, claiming 5,000 victims. Even then the city's misfortunes did not end, for in the following days the area was hit by freak weather in the form of strong winds and heavy downpours, and 2,000 of the homeless population died of diseases.

Earthquakes had been a fact of life in pre-Hispanic times as well, of course. Among his other attributes the pre-Columbian deity Pachacámac was believed to be the Lord of Tremors, whose anger made the earth tremble, and his cult was born in part of a primitive wish to placate his wrath. Despite their supposed cultural superiority, it would appear that the colonial settlers responded to earthquakes and other natural disasters in the same elemental fashion as their indigenous predecessors, seeing the hand of God behind them. Earthquakes were commonly interpreted as a manifestation of the wrath of God for the sins of men, as is clear from diarist Josephe de Mugaburu's account of reaction to the earthquake of 1687:

More than a month earlier someone had been going about saying
that through a revelation he knew about this earthquake. God look

on us with eyes of mercy that such a thing was not listened to. It was clear from the way it shook that it was a slap from the hand of God. At that hour all the churches were opened, there were confessions and many priests preached through the streets advocating penance.

On the evening of Wednesday the 2nd the very Reverend Father Luis Galindo de San Ramón preached in the cathedral. Never had such a crowd of people been seen as that day in the cathedral, filling the whole church and even the steps; and there were also people in the halls. He preached that God was very angry about our faults, and that which has him most annoyed is the nefarious sin which is practiced between members of the same sex, women with women, and men with men. May God liberate us from such faults; with good reason is His Divine Majesty angry, and may He give us His grace so that we will offend Him no more.

As we shall see, the church of Las Nazarenas owes its existence to the same primeval fear of earthquakes that gave rise to the cult of Pachacámac.

The church's history is also linked to that of Lima's black slave population. In colonial times it was the custom for different social groups such as the various trade guilds to band together in *cofradías* (brotherhoods) under the protection of a patron saint. Such associations participated collectively in the celebration of religious festivals and they met regularly for devotions, discussion of brotherhood business and socializing. The city's blacks were likewise organized into a number of brotherhoods overseen by the clergy and loosely corresponding to place of origin, these associations being seen as a means of facilitating the process of acculturation, though in practice they also fulfilled an opposite role by becoming havens for African culture. One black brotherhood held its meetings in a house on the site now occupied by the church and on one of its walls was an image of the crucified Christ painted by one of its members.

It is here that the two strands of the story come together. Amidst the devastation caused by the earthquake of 1655, the wall bearing the image of Christ somehow remained intact, an event deemed to be miraculous. Some time later a local resident began to venerate the image and to take care of the site, and it developed into a shrine where blacks and mulattoes of the area met to worship. The cult was a classic example of religious syncretism, since in addition to offering candles, flowers, incense, prayers and hymns, the worshippers often performed semi-pagan rituals and dances of African origin. Such practices aroused the disapproval of the ecclesiastical authorities, who condemned them as indecent and pagan, and in 1671 the archbishop ordered that the image be painted over. To forestall resistance, troops accompanied the work party but, according to folklore, every attempt to obliterate the image was miraculously thwarted, for the workmen entrusted with the task either fell into a faint or suffered paralysis of the arm. Whatever actually happened, it is clear that the authorities' efforts to put an end to the cult ran up against strong popular opposition and that in the end they were obliged to back down and give it official recognition.

Originally called the Cristo de Pachacamilla after the neighbourhood where the brotherhood's meeting-house was located, the image came to be known as El Señor de los Milagros (Our Lord of the Miracles). The cult always remained primarily associated with the Afro-Peruvian population, who saw comforting evidence that the Christian god was watching over them in the miracles associated with the image and in the fact that Christ took on a dark complexion as the image was blackened by the smoke of candles placed before it. Gradually, however, the cult came to acquire greater respectability as it won devotees among the Creole middle classes, and the church of Las Nazarenas was built to house the miraculous image. The growth of the cult was further boosted by subsequent earthquakes. During the tremors of 1687 a copy of the image was taken out in procession and later, following the quake of 1746, it became the practice every 28 October to parade it to invoke protection against earthquakes.

Over the years the cult of El Señor de los Milagros became increasingly popular, even attracting devotees from among the Creole upper classes, and today it is the biggest religious cult in the country. In the process it has undergone changes and has become institutionalized as it has been assimilated into national culture. What has come to be one of its most distinctive features—the purple habit worn by devotees as a symbol of penitence—is an innovation introduced in 1760 by Antonia Lucía del Espíritu Santo, founder of an association of pious Creole women linked to the church of Las Nazarenas. The state and the Church hierarchy have associated themselves with it, the former to turn its popularity to political advantage, the latter to exercise ecclesiastical control. The Brotherhood of El Señor de los Milagros, originally a spontaneous black organization, has become formally structured and elections and appointments are vetted by the archbishop. Even so, the annual procession of El Señor de los Milagros has retained its popular character and blacks and mulattoes still play the central role of shouldering the heavy litters.

October has come to be known as the month of El Señor de los Milagros, since there are actually several processions taking place over several days; it is also known as the "purple month" after the colour of the habits worn by the devotees. The procession begins and ends with a service in the church of Las Nazarenas. From there a copy of the original image is paraded through the streets in a shrine of solid gold placed on a silver litter weighing almost a ton, and the devotees form an immense sea of purple as the procession wends its way through the narrow streets of the Historic Centre. Hundreds of thousands turn out to watch and many more identify themselves with the event by displaying reproductions of the holy image in houses, cars and buses. Various customs have also grown up around the procession. A food traditionally associated with it is one of Lima's favourite sweets, a type of nougat known as "turrón de doña Pepa". Though this is in fact a traditional recipe, legend has it that, after El Señor de los Milagros cured her of paralysis, a mulatto woman, Josefa (Pepa) Marmaguillo, invented the sweet and distributed it among the poor at the church of Las Nazarenas. Ever since, street vendors having been plying the sweet to the public throughout the month of October.

The housing of the image of El Señor de los Milagros in the church of Las Nazarenas can be seen as symbolic of the way in which black culture has been appropriated and domesticated by Creole society. At the same time, though, the massive popularity of the cult reflects the influence that Afro-Peruvians have had on the shaping of Creole culture. The procession has become one of the great emblems of Peruvian identity and as such it figures as a recurrent theme in modern painting in the work of artists such as Camilo Blas, Enrique Camino Brent, Víctor Humareda, Teodoro Núñez Ureta, José Sabogal and Jorge Vinatea Reinoso.

Afro-Peruvians

Walking through the streets of modern Lima it is hard to imagine that in colonial times Afro-Peruvians constituted the single largest sector of the population. According to the 1940 census—the last to include racial categories—only 0.48 per cent of the national population was black. Yet in 1790, 45 per cent of the capital's inhabitants were either black or of African descent.

Because of the decline of the coastal region's indigenous population, mainly as a result of European diseases, black slaves were imported as a labour force. Some worked on rural farms and haciendas. Others were resident in the city, where they were mainly household servants or hired out as temporary workers on an individual basis. From the earliest days of the colony there had also been a small minority of free blacks and in the course of the colonial period their numbers swelled, as did the number of black *mestizos*. Some slaves were manumitted by their masters—sometimes as a reward for faithful service, sometimes as an unwanted liability—or bought their liberty with their earnings from outside employment or with money provided by family, friends or patrons. The number of free black *mestizos* also increased through reproduction, particularly since the numerous offspring fathered by African males with Indian women—known as *zambos*—were automatically free, and since Spanish males often freed the mulatto children they had fathered by slave women. By the end of the eighteenth century free Afro-Peruvians slightly outnumbered the slave population. Slaves lived in the homes of their masters or in neighbouring *callejones*—communal housing in the form of an enclosed alleyway with individual one-room apartments leading off it—but certain neighbourhoods on the margin of the city centre, such as San Lázaro across the river and the area behind the cathedral, became home to large concentrations of blacks.

Initially slaves seem to have retained a sense of their African heritage and tried to keep it alive. Black brotherhoods painted the walls of their meeting-houses with scenes evoking their African past and at their Sunday meetings, after discussing brotherhood business, they sang and danced into the evening to the music of African instruments. At public festivals they paraded as "nations" (ethnic groups) wearing African dress, playing African music and performing African war-dances. But local conditions militated against the preservation of

African cultural identity. Slaves came to Peru from heterogeneous tribal origins. In contrast with other parts of the Americas, where huge plantations congregated massive numbers of slaves, Peruvian coastal haciendas tended to be small, with no more than forty slaves each, and urban slaves were dispersed throughout the city and isolated from one another. Moreover, though the majority of slaves came directly from Africa, many were imported from other parts of America and already spoke Spanish and were familiar with Spanish customs, while the nature of the work carried out by urban slaves brought them into daily contact with the settler community and required them to adopt Spanish ways. Though some broke free from their servitude to form runaway communities or bandit gangs, the majority resigned themselves to the fact that there was no viable future for them outside the colonial order and aspired to improve their condition within it by becoming acculturated. The eagerness with which they adopted the ways of their white superiors is suggested by discriminatory legislation intended to keep them in their place, such as a viceregal edict of 1667 which decreed that "no mulatto woman, negress or *zamba*, freed or slave, without exception, wear a dress of silk, nor trimming of gold or silver, nor black trim of silk or linen."

Most free blacks and black *mestizos* remained at the bottom of the socio-economic scale. Some managed to establish themselves in the artisan trades and other areas of economic activity that lacked prestige among whites, and by the eighteenth century some were even able to bypass discriminatory legislation and gain access to university, practise professions like law and medicine and hold public posts. The gallery of eminent professional men painted by nineteenth-century water-colourist Pancho Fierro, for example, includes pictures of two mulatto doctors, one of whom, José Manuel Valdés, became the country's Chief Medical Officer in 1836.

But these were very much the minority and, like all Afro-Peruvians, they had to contend with colour prejudice, as illustrated by Juan del Valle Caviedes' "Vejamen que le dio el autor al zambo Pedro de Utrilla" (Mock eulogy given by the author to the *zambo* Pedro de Utrilla), a seventeenth-century poem satirizing the surgeon named in the title as an example of the ignorance and ineptitude of the medical profession. Caviedes, to be sure, was not attacking Utrilla just because he was a surgeon. Utrilla was also a mulatto, one of a substantial number of individuals of mixed race who had practical experience of treating disease but little in the way of official credentials and who, because of the shortage of qualified doctors and because whites tended to shun the medical profession as lacking prestige, were able to make successful careers for themselves and thereby improve their social position. Yet by so doing, they came to be perceived as an economic threat by the more vulnerable sectors of the white settler population, whose response was to exploit the race card in an attempt to defend their own position. Such is the case with Caviedes' satire, which makes repeated allusions to Utrilla's colour to belittle his intellectual and professional competence by stereotyping him as a member of an inferior racial group. The text draws attention to Utrilla's lack of medical training by ironically conferring spurious titles on him and then attaches modifiers that emphasize his colour and associate blackness with ignorance and incompetence:

> *Licentiate Black Pudding*
> *and Bachelor Chimney; [...]*
> *doctor of the Dark Room*
> *of the Congo king of Guinea.*

The mock titles "Licentiate Black Pudding" and "Bachelor Chimney" allude to his colour but also imply that his only training has been in butchery and that his expertise is limited to generating dross. Then, having established an equivalence between ineptitude and colour, Caviedes goes on to suggest that the only fitting place for Utrilla to practise his supposedly primitive brand of medicine is the land of his ancestors, as doctor to some African chief.

The decline in the numbers of Lima's black community was inevitable, given the lack of fresh blood to renew it after the slave trade came to an end in 1817—slavery was eventually abolished in 1854—and its decline relative to the rest of the population was to become progressive as the birth rate among other sectors increased. Another factor in that decline seems to have been blacks' response to the discrimination which disadvantaged them. This theme is explored in Julio Ramón Ribeyro's "Alienación" (Alienation, 1975), a story set in the 1950s. The protagonist, Roberto López, is the son of the local black washerwoman, and his marginal position in the social hierarchy is indicated by the fact that he is relegated to watching from the side-lines while a group of middle-class boys play football. He shares their infatuation with Queca, the local beauty, but when he eventually finds an opportunity to gain her attention by retrieving her ball for her, her reaction of disgust and her contemptuous racist snubbing of him inflict a humiliation that scars him for life:

> Queca [...] seemed to be adjusting her focus, observing something that only now was she really seeing for the first time: a short, dark, thick-lipped being with kinky hair, something very ordinary that she probably saw daily, just as one sees park benches or pine trees. Abruptly, she turned away, terrified.
>
> Roberto never forgot Queca's words as she fled: "I don't play with zambos."

Roberto's response is to seek to erase the stigma of blackness by turning himself into a white. In fact, he goes even further, when, perceiving that the local Creoles play second fiddle to the North Americans, he decides to go the whole hog and transform himself into a gringo:

> First of all he had to dezambofy himself. His hair wasn't a major problem; he dyed it with peroxide and had it straightened. As for his skin, he tried mixing starch, rice powder and talcum from the chemist's until he found the ideal combination; but a dyed and powdered zambo is still a zambo. He needed to know how the North American gringos dressed, talked, moved and thought [...] With hair that was now straightened and bleached, a pair of blue jeans and a loud shirt, Roberto was on the brink of becoming Bobby.

Such low self-esteem appears to have been widespread among Afro-Peruvians, and many of them likewise opted to whiten themselves, albeit in a less obvious way, either by passing themselves off as belonging to other racial groups or by marrying into them, thereby hastening their decline as an ethnic group.

The African Heritage: the *Marinera*
Though Afro-Peruvians became acculturated and came to think of themselves as Creoles rather than as a distinct community, they still

retained traditional forms of cultural expression like music and dance. These underwent an evolution as they adopted European instruments like the guitar and the harp and learned European musical techniques, but that in its turn won them greater social acceptance. Blacks were also popular as teachers of music and dance and they introduced variants to fashionable European dances and adapted African dances to Creole tastes. As a result, though dance associated with blacks was often condemned by the ecclesiastical authorities as lewd and obscene, a process of cultural syncretism between African and Spanish-Creole traditions gradually took place. Perhaps the main example of that process is what came to be coastal Peru's most popular dance form, the *marinera*.

The dance was originally known as the *zamacueca* and variations of it were to be found all along the Pacific coastal region from Piura in the north to Chile in the south, but during the War of the Pacific (1879-83) the Peruvian version was renamed *marinera* as a tribute to the heroics of the nation's navy and to distinguish it from the enemy's version known as the *cueca* or the *chilena*. The dance is to all intents and purposes a re-enactment of the mating ritual, with the man and woman facing each other, each of them flourishing a handkerchief and completing slow circles. The *zamacueca* derived from dances brought from Africa by black slaves but it was also influenced by Spanish dances like the *fandango*, with which it has a clear affinity, and its double ancestry is evident in the instruments that accompany it, since the music is provided by a combination of guitars and the *cajón*, a wooden box with a circular hole in the face which originated as an improvised substitute for the traditional African drum. Because it was thought of as an African dance and therefore uncouth and because its movements were regarded as indecent, respectable society disapproved of the *zamacueca*. Significantly, in Felipe Pardo y Aliaga's play *Frutos de la educación* (The Fruits of Education, 1830), the English businessman Don Eduardo—who is presented as a model of the European civilized values which Peruvians should seek to emulate—breaks off his engagement to Pepita when he catches her dancing it. At the same time, as a series of Pancho Fierro's paintings shows, it came to be accepted by all sectors of society as their national dance. One depicts an uninhibited version of it as danced by lower-class blacks, while in another an army officer and an elegantly dressed lady perform a more genteel version.

The extent to which the *zamacueca* infiltrated the whole of Creole society is illustrated by one of Fierro's more humorous works set in a room of a hospital run by nuns and featuring one of the nursing sisters dancing with her patient, a wounded army officer, with his bed in the background. Later, in its new guise as the *marinera*, the dance was to be celebrated as an expression of Creole identity in the work of twentieth-century painters like Julia Codesido, Teodoro Núñez Ureta and Víctor Humareda.

As the case of the *zamacueca* suggests, African music underwent a process of creolization. Even so, in the late 1950s a movement emerged that sought to win recognition of blacks' contribution to Peruvian culture by reconstructing and reviving almost forgotten Afro-Peruvian musical genres. The pioneer of the movement was historian José Durand, but the main force behind it were Nicomedes Santa Cruz and his sister Victoria, who researched black musical traditions and produced the first commercial recordings of Afro-Peruvian music. As a result of their efforts, leading singers like Eva Ayllón incorporated Afro-Peruvian genres into their repertoire. Likewise, in the field of literature, Gregorio Martínez has sought to promote black pride by writing the history of Afro-Peruvians in the novels *Canto de sirena* (Siren Song, 1977) and *Crónica de músicos y diablos* (Chronicle of Musicians and Devils, 1991).

Rímac

At the northern end of Jirón de la Unión a stone bridge, the Puente de Piedra, leads over the river to the district of Rímac, which, because the

bank on that side is lower, is also known as Abajo El Puente (Below the Bridge). The bridge dates from 1610 and replaced an earlier structure, part of which had collapsed in 1607 when the river was in spate. Until several decades after independence this was the only bridge strong enough for vehicular traffic, the others being precarious wooden structures. A second bridge, the Puente Balta, was built around 1870. Named after the modernizing president of the period, it is an iron structure that was considered at the time to be a great feat of modern engineering. Since then various other bridges have been added to meet the demands of modern traffic.

Over time the Puente de Piedra has undergone many changes, as a result both of modifications and of damage caused by earthquake and fire. In its heyday there was an arch at the south side and on the bridge itself the walls had semicircular insets with seats. More than just a crossing, the bridge was a focal point for the community, a place where people would go on summer evenings to socialize and enjoy the cool by the river. According to Ricardo Palma, it was also a place where young men and women gathered to eye one another up:

> *In the colonial period it was almost impossible to walk over the bridge on moonlit nights. This was everyone's rendezvous. Both pavements were taken over by elegant young men who, as they took relief from the midsummer heat in the breeze from the river, feasted their eyes on the young women who came out to breathe the cool air, embalming the atmosphere with the sweet perfume of the jasmines which they wore in their hair.*

The area on the other side of the river—known as San Lázaro after a hospice and church established in 1563 for black slaves suffering from leprosy— developed into a humble lower-class district peopled mainly by blacks. The land beyond it, however, was to become a space for repose and recreation. As the city's population grew, groups of monks seeking peaceful conditions more propitious for meditation and strict observance of the rules of their order founded retreats away from the urban hustle and bustle. One of these was the monastery of Los Descalzos, a Franciscan retreat established in 1592 at the foot of the Cerro San Cristóbal. In 1611 the viceroy inaugurated a promenade, the Alameda de los Descalzos, leading from the edge of San Lázaro to the monastery. Modelled on the promenade in Seville, it consisted of a central carriageway adorned with fountains and flanked by two tree-lined avenues with stone benches. Here Lima's high society would come to circulate on foot, on horseback or in carriages. In the 1850s the promenade underwent a renovation inspired by a desire to emulate the great capitals of Europe, which were regarded as models of urban civilization and progress. It now featured gardens enclosed by iron railings, marble benches, iron urns and statues of Greek and Roman figures representing the signs of the zodiac and the months of the year.

The promenade was part of the route of one of Lima's great annual rituals, the excursion to Amancaes, a plateau behind the Cerro San Cristóbal, which derived its name from a yellow flower—a kind of narcissus—which grew there in profusion thanks to the moisture from the winter mist. Though the excursion took place on St. John's Day (24 June), the festival was more pagan than religious in character, since it was essentially a celebration of the renewal of life symbolized by the blossoming of the flowers. Crossing the bridge over the Rímac and following the Alameda de los Descalzos, people of all classes flocked to Amancaes on horseback, in carriages or on foot. There, on a vast meadow of flowers, they sang, played music, danced, ate and drank before returning to the city in the evening in boisterous and drunken good humour, most of them carrying bunches of flowers. In time, as the event grew more and more popular, it became the practice for traders to set up stalls to sell food and drink to the excursionists. Gradually the festivities were extended till the end of July, and by the early twentieth century what had started out as a simple excursion to the countryside had become a series of organized events such as festivals of folk music and horse-riding displays. But as the city expanded and became modernized and people found other diversions, Amancaes' popularity waned and in the 1950s the area was settled by squatters and built up.

The eighteenth century was to see the construction of two new promenades in the Rímac area. Situated near the start of the Alameda de los Descalzos and at a right angle to it, the Paseo de Aguas was opened in 1768. Modelled on Rome's Piazza Navona, it was conceived as a system of aqueducts, fountains and waterfalls fed by the river and ending in an artificial lake, but the project was never actually completed and the water feature was restricted to miniature ponds. Even so, with its ornamental colonnade, its greenery and its wide paths, it was an attractive amenity, as was the Alameda de Acho, sometimes called the Alameda Nueva, a second tree-lined promenade running along the river towards the bullring. The latter no longer exists, having fallen victim to urban development and replaced by a road. But in the latter part of the eighteenth century and throughout the nineteenth, the complex formed by the three promenades was a select recreation area for the capital's elites. The role of the *paseos* is described in the memoirs of William Bennet Stevenson, an Englishman who spent over twenty years in the region between 1804 and 1827:

> *To these public paseos such numbers of the fashionable inhabitants resort on Sundays and other holidays, particularly in the afternoons, that as many as three hundred carriages may sometimes be counted: the richer tradesman parades in his calesa, drawn by one mule; the nobleman in his coach and two; the titled of Castile in a coach and four; and formerly, the Viceroy in his coach and six; he being the only person in Lima, excepting the Archbishop, who enjoyed this*

distinction. Gentlemen seldom go in the coaches, so that the beauty
of Lima have the temporary privilege of riding alone and nodding
without reserve to their amorous galanes, who parade the side walks.

In fact, contrary to a widespread myth, Viceroy Amat did not build
these promenades to indulge his mistress. Rather they were part of a
project to embellish the city in the manner of Paris and Bourbon
Madrid, and that involved developing Rímac as a select area where the
wealthy few could mingle with their own kind instead of having to
share public space with the plebeian masses, as had hitherto been the
case. During this period, too, the city's elites began to build country
homes for themselves in the rustic part of Rímac. The one surviving
example is the Quinta de Presa (Jirón Chira 344), a house constructed
in the classical French style, with a garden at the back laid out
symetrically in the French manner.

Nineteenth-century paintings of people strolling in Rímac's
promenades, such as the German Johan Moritz Rugendas' *Promenade
in the New Alameda* (1842), feature females dressed in the *saya y manto*,
the traditional street dress of Limeñan women from the early viceregal
period down to the Republican era. The *saya* was an overskirt, worn
tight at the waist and raised to show off feet and ankles. Throughout
the colonial period the skirt was tight-fitting, showing off the figure
but making it difficult to walk; after independence it was replaced by
a more comfortable flared skirt. The skirt was usually complemented
by a shawl thrown over the shoulders. The *manto* was a thick veil
fastened to the back of the waist; from there it was brought over the
shoulders and head and drawn over the face so closely that all that was
left uncovered was a small triangular space sufficient for one eye to
peep through. Wearers of the outfit were known as *tapadas* (veiled
women).

The *saya y manto* was unique to Lima to the extent that, according
to Ricardo Palma, it was not worn even in Callao. Moorish in origin,
the *manto* allowed women to circulate freely around the city without
fear of molestation. Yet if it was initially an emblem of female modesty,
it came to serve a quite different purpose, functioning as a disguise that
freed women from social constraints and allowed them to engage in
playful flirting or to conduct secret liaisons, as Max Radiguet noted in
the 1840s:

The saya y manto, *a costume which was originally designed to serve ideas of chastity and jealousy, has come through one of life's contradictions to act as a cover for diametrically opposite customs; its uniformity makes the city one vast salon of intrigues and ingenious manoeuvres that mock the vigilance of the fiercest Othellos. With such elements scandals, merry adventures and burlesque misunderstandings cannot fail to occur.*

The colonial authorities made repeated attempts to ban the *saya y manto* as immoral, but Lima's women refused to be dictated to in matters of fashion and it persisted until the second half of the nineteenth century. Then, as the country began to modernize, it was abandoned in favour of the styles of London and Paris. In fashion now were voluminous flounced skirts over hooped petticoats; high-necked dresses, blouses or jackets with lace sleeves; complicated hair styles with thick curls and long ringlets, topped by hair-nets or plumed hats; and as accessories parasols, gloves, fans and shawls.

Another of Rímac's landmarks is the bullring, the Plaza de Acho. Opened in 1768, the arena continues to function and, though it has undergone renovation, it is one of the city's best-conserved historical buildings. Bullfighting has always been popular in Lima and remains so to this day. The city's first bullfight was held in the Plaza Mayor in 1540 and Francisco Pizarro himself took part, killing one of the bulls. Thereafter it became the custom to stage bullfights in the main square as part of the public festivities that were a regular feature of colonial life.

The Plaza de Acho was a product of the ideology of the Age of Enlightenment, which informed official thinking in the latter part of the eighteenth century, as the project of promoting a more rationally ordered society involved the creation of dedicated spaces for public entertainments that had previously been held in the open. A display covering the history of local bullfighting can be seen in the nearby museum, the Museo Taurino. The bullring is overlooked by the Mirador de Ingunza, a now-dilapidated belvedere dating from 1869. Ingunza, it seems, was a wealthy gentleman who built a holiday home in the area and, since he was a bullfight fan, he had the tower incorporated so that he could have his own private grandstand.

Another building of historical interest is the Backus and Johnston Brewery, founded in 1890 by two American entrepreneurs who recruited a German expert to take charge of the brewing process. The brewery is in itself a symptom of how Peruvian life was changed by independence from Spain. Hitherto Peruvians had lived within the confines of the Spanish empire, isolated from contact with other nations. Following independence, foreign merchandise flooded into the country, foreign businessmen established themselves in the city and foreign immigrants came to settle. Beer is one example of how foreign influence dramatically altered Peruvians' traditional life-style. Nowadays Peruvians pride themselves on the quality of their beer and think of it as a local tradition, but in fact the production and consumption of beer took off only from the late nineteenth century onwards.

The location of the brewery in Rímac in the last decade of the nineteenth century is also indicative of how the character of the area was changing. It had traditionally been the area where the city's rich took their recreation and led their public lives. But in the latter nineteenth and early twentieth centuries these elite communities moved away from the city centre to new homes on the southern edge of the city, and the area around the Parque de la Exposición replaced Rímac as the main public recreation space. Rímac, like other parts of the city centre, became increasingly the preserve of the proletariat and by the end of the nineteenth century it had become a slum area inhabited mainly by poor blacks. In 1907 Abelardo Gamarra described the once-elegant Alameda de los Descalzos as being in a sorry state of dereliction and frequented only by coloured down-and-outs:

> *Today the only people you see passing along that desolate, dilapidated promenade are beggars, the idle and ne'er-do-wells, who gather with their tins and their old dogs to receive food from the monks at the monastery [...] the black man bloated with rum, the scruffy black woman, the poor young boy degraded by the begging to which he is reduced, groups of these beings squatting in the gutters, waiting for their meal or grumbling about the lack of it; that's what animates this scene of desolation and neglect.*

Today the Rímac district remains somewhat seedy and run-down, but its historic sites have been restored to something of their former glory and are an essential part of the tourist circuit.

The River, the Bridge and the Promenade

Adjoining the Puente de Piedra on the south bank of the river is a modern promenade built in the 1990s on the site of the former Polvos Azules market, which was destroyed by fire. The Alameda Chabuca Granda commemorates one of the legendary figures of Creole popular music, singer and songwriter Chabuca Granda (1915-83). Granda's greatest hit, "La flor de la canela" (The Pick of the Bunch/Cinnamon Flower), nostalgically evokes the area formed by the old bridge, the river and the Alameda de los Descalzos as a symbolic space reflecting the core of the city's Creole identity and an emblem of a Lima that is in the process of disappearing:

Let me recount it, Limeñan,
Let me tell you the glory
of the enchantment evoked by the memory
of the old bridge, the river and the promenade.

The song especially celebrates the grace, beauty and infectious humour of a mulatto woman—the title plays on the double sense of the phrase "flor de la canela", cinnamon being a term often used to describe mulatto women on account of their supposed hot blood—who epitomizes the traditional image of Limeñan womanhood:

Jasmines in her hair and roses on her face,
jauntily walked the cinnamon flower,
scattering wit, and as she passed she left behind
the aromas of the posy she wore on her breast.
Her tiny feet carried her from the bridge to the promenade
along the pavement which vibrated to the rhythm of her hips,
she gathered the laughter of the breeze from the river
and cast it into the wind from the bridge to the promenade.

The song dates from the 1950s and its popularity can be attributed to its celebration of Creole heritage at a time when the Creole population felt their identity threatened as the city around them was changing beyond recognition as a result of rapid modernization and the influx of Andean migrants. Like all nostalgic evocations of the past, it is rose-tinted and glosses over the social inequalities of Lima's history by incorporating into an idealized image the Afro-Peruvians who were marginalized in the real world. Yet by opting to privilege a mulatto woman as the protagonist of her song, Granda acknowledges that what has come to be accepted as Creole popular culture has been shaped in large part by the black population of slum areas like those of Rímac.

Colonial Literature

In Jirón Amazonas, on the south bank of the river to the east of the Plaza Mayor, is a book lover's paradise, the Feria del Libro. Visiting this market, one tends to take for granted that books, and all that they signify, are available to everyone. Yet a very different picture is suggested if one makes the short journey to the monastery of San Francisco, one of whose treasures is a magnificent seventeenth-century library housing a collection of 25,000 leather-bound books and 6,000 parchments dating from the fifteenth to the eighteenth century. Enclosed as it is within the walls of the monastery, the library points to the fact that throughout the colonial period book learning was the preserve of a small elite.

Though Spanish Peru was born of military conquest, the most powerful instrument of colonization was the written word. The advantages that knowledge of writing gave the Spaniards over a native population whose culture was oral are highlighted by Ricardo Palma in "Carta canta" (Letter Speaks), a historical anecdote set in the early decades of the colonial period. Two Indians belonging to an *encomienda* some distance from Lima are entrusted by the steward with the task of delivering a consignment of melons to their master in the city, with a covering letter. On the way they are tempted to sample the melons, but are afraid that the letter, which they believe to be a spirit, will spy and inform on them. So they hit on the idea of outwitting it by placing it behind a wall so that it cannot see them and proceed to devour two of the melons. Naturally, when they get to Lima, their master discovers the shortfall by reading the letter and has them punished, thereby confirming the Indians' belief that the letter is able to speak.

The story shows how ignorance of writing disadvantaged the Indians in their relations with the Europeans. Firstly, as is indicated by the patronizing tone of the narrative, it led to their being stereotyped as intellectual inferiors and natural subordinates. And, secondly, the

Indians' perception of writing as magical was metaphorically true in that, in a manner similar to modern computer technology, it empowered the Spaniards by enabling them to communicate across distance and to store and access information.

Contrary to the myth that the conquistadors were a gang of illiterate thugs, the men of Pizarro's expedition seem to have been a fairly representative cross-section of Spanish society. The core of the group was made up of petty gentry and upper plebeians, and not only are at least 76 of the total of 168 reckoned to have been functionally literate, but they also included ten notaries. Following established practice, Pizarro used writing to legitimize the expedition's actions in his report to the king, the *Verdadera relación de la conquista del Perú* (True Report of the Conquest of Peru, 1534), compiled by his secretary Francisco de Jerez. The report purports to be a factual account of the conquering expedition up to the capture and execution of Atahualpa, but despite its plain, unvarnished style it is very much a public relations exercise aimed primarily at earning royal endorsement but also, since it was clearly intended for publication, at shaping public opinion.

Likewise, the royal authorities were alert to the value of the written word as a medium of political propaganda. Pedro Sarmiento de Gamboa's *Historia de los Incas* (History of the Incas, 1572) was commissioned by Viceroy Francisco de Toledo, who, to consolidate Spanish authority, sought to destroy the influence of the surviving Inca elite, and it sets out to validate Spain's right to dominion in Peru by demolishing the Incas' claim to be legitimate rulers of the country.

Books played a crucial role, too, in the evangelization of the natives, as reflected by the fact that the first work printed in Peru—a catechism translated into Quechua and Aymara (1584)—was designed as a tool to aid priests in their missionary work. Books were also the work tools of the clerics, lawyers and administrators who ran the Church and the colonial bureaucracy. And they were a means whereby the colony's small elite reading public kept abreast with developments in Spain and shared membership of a Hispanic cultural community. This sense of *hispanidad* lies behind the "Epístola a Belardo" (1621), a poetic epistle addressed to Lope de Vega by one of his Peruvian admirers under the name of Amarilis, in which, employing a style reminiscent of much of Lope's own verse, she expresses her admiration for the genius of the great Spanish poet and dramatist and declares herself platonically in love with him. As Amarilis' text suggests, most of the writing produced in the colony itself followed Spanish models and helped to create a local culture that was an extension of that of the mother country.

Yet, as we have already seen in Buenaventura de Salinas y Córdova's *Memorial* (1630), books could also articulate a growing Creole consciousness. At times, too, they could be a vehicle for voicing criticism of the Spaniards' treatment of the natives, as Pedro Cieza de León does in his *Crónica del Perú* (Chronicle of Peru, 1553), where, while never questioning Spain's right to dominion, he accuses the settlers of betraying their country's imperial mission by devastating a once-ordered kingdom. Representatives of Peru's subaltern groups also adopted the written word as a medium for fighting the cause of their people. The son of a conquistador and an Inca princess, the self-styled Inca Garcilaso de la Vega, Peru's first *mestizo* writer, authored *Comentarios reales* (Royal Commentaries, 1609), a history of the Inca empire designed to promote a positive image of pre-Hispanic civilization and thereby to raise the status of Indians and *mestizos* in the eyes of the dominant Spaniards. Felipe Guaman Poma de Ayala, a minor provincial chieftain, conceived his *Nueva corónica y buen gobierno* (New Chronicle and Good Government, 1615) as a letter to the king. A monumental history accompanied by some 398 pictorial illustrations, it constructs an image of pre-Columbian Peru as a stable, ordered world, catalogues the evils of Spanish colonial rule and makes recommendations to the monarch for the future good government of his overseas domains. But the fate of his manuscript—sent to Philip III, it languished in oblivion until it was discovered in the twentieth century—suggests that access to writing did not necessarily guarantee subalterns a hearing.

In colonial times poetry was the most prestigious of the literary genres. Much of the verse produced was circumstantial. As part of the celebration of major public events the colony's leading men of letters strove to outdo one another in hyperbolic eulogies of the imperial order and the colonial authorities. Such eulogies were characterized by displays of ingenuity involving extravagant conceits and technical virtuosity. An example is a poem composed by Pedro de Peralta Barnuevo in 1724 congratulating Viceroy José de Armendáriz, the Marquis of Castelfuerte, on his organization of the festivities to celebrate Luis I's accession to the throne. The poem defies translation, since all 247 words of its 15 stanzas begin with the initial letter of the viceroy's surname:

Alto Armendáriz, afectuoso alabas
austral Alcides, al amado Atlante,
armoniosos acentos, animado,
ardiente, anhelo, apacible aplaudes.

Less ephemeral was the work of Diego Dávalos y Figueroa, whose *Miscelánea austral* (Southern Miscellany, 1602-3) includes some fine sonnets in the Petrarchan style, and Diego de Hojeda, whose *La Cristiada* (The Christiad, 1611) is considered to be the best sacred epic in the Spanish language. But the most interesting poetry of the colonial era is a current of satirical verse, cultivated mainly by Spanish immigrants who for one reason or another became disenchanted with their adopted homeland. Thus, Mateo Rosas de Oquendo took his leave of the viceroyalty with a "Sátira a las cosas que pasan en el Perú, año de 1598" (Satire of What's Happening in Peru, 1598), in which he curses the ten years he has wasted in the country and takes his revenge by mocking local society and customs. Later, in *Lima por dentro y fuera* (Lima Inside and Out, 1797), Esteban de Terralla Landa was to pen a poetic epistle in the same vein warning his fictional correspondent of the woes which lie in store for him should he be foolish enough to set foot in Peru.

The major colonial poet was Juan del Valle Caviedes (1644-98). A substantial part of his output is made up of love lyrics and religious and philosophical poems, but the best of his work are his satires. Born in Spain, he emigrated to Peru at a early age and, from the little that is known of his life, it seems that he attempted various business projects, which were largely unsuccessful, as a result of which he periodically found himself in financial difficulties. His experience was that of a member of the lower sectors of the settler community and his view of colonial Lima was clearly coloured by his modest social position. He presents it as a society whose tone is set by the viceregal court, a parasitic society where success is achieved by cultivating an appearance that impresses and by pandering to those in positions of wealth and power. The sonnet "Para labrarse fortuna en los palacios" (How to

Make Your Fortune at Court), for example, ironically lists the qualifications necessary to gain favour at the viceregal court:

> *To find grace and favour at Court*
> *what's needed is a spoonful of the liar,*
> *a spoonful and a half of the vile flatterer,*
> *and two generous spoonfuls of clown.*
>
> *Add three spoonfuls and a smidgen of tattle-tale*
> *and four more of pimping go-between,*
> *then heap five big ones of gossip,*
> *belittling others for their work and their actions.*
>
> *You must be one continuous amen to every word*
> *spoken by the Lord or Viceroy whom you serve*
> *and the more nonsensically he prattles and prates*
>
> *the more loudly should ring your applause,*
> *and if you persist with this charade*
> *you'll have at Court everything you'll ever wish.*

The principal target of Caviedes' satire is the medical profession, whom he lambasts as quacks deluding and exploiting a gullible public by projecting an air of knowledge and authority that disguises criminal incompetence. Singling out well-known doctors by name, he sets about demolishing their public image, not only by exposing their quackery, but by the strategy of ridiculing their physical peculiarities:

> *Ramírez, with his bulging face*
> *and powerful neck of a bull,*
> *is only a miserable butcher*
> *who puts on airs of Avicenna.*
> *And when he has filled the house*
> *to the roof with scraps and leavings*
> *of his deeds of judicious dash,*
> *the common herd in their ignorance*
> *say that he's a fount of learning*
> *because he's fat and wears spectacles.*

Caviedes is not just criticizing the primitive state of medical science in the colony. Doctors are portrayed as exemplifying the principal defects of society at large and are represented as frauds who rise to positions of prestige and affluence, not because of their knowledge and competence, but because of their ability to impress and deceive. They are also depicted as parasites on the social body, growing fat by gulling the public. More than that, by suggesting that more people die at the hands of doctors than from disease, Caviedes implies on a wider scale that the ills of colonial society are due primarily to the ineptitude of its elites, who owe their positions not to merit but to their skill at cultivating the image required to impress and win favour.

The Cementerio General
One of Lima's most interesting sites is the Cementerio General Presbítero Matías Maestro (Jirón Ancash, cuadra 17), which is laid out as a kind of mini-city with wide central avenues and narrower side-streets. Opened in 1808, it came to be regarded as one of Lima's most beautiful public spaces, and in the nineteenth century people would go there to stroll and to look at the monuments. The cemetery is interesting not just because it houses the tombs of famous politicians and intellectuals, but because it conveys a sense of the affluence of Lima's Republican elites. Just as prosperous families of the time made public display of their social eminence by constructing elegant mansions and sporting expensive clothes in the latest European fashions, so too they built impressive mausoleums as symbols of their status and to that end they recruited the services of some of the nineteenth century's finest sculptors. Among the best examples are the mausoleum of the Elmore family and the monument to Francisco Girbau.

Though most of the tombs date from the Republican era, the cemetery is also a monument to the spread of the rationalist, scientific thinking of the Enlightenment in the latter part of the colonial period. Traditionally the dead had been buried in crypts underneath the city's churches, but enlightened thinkers headed by Hipólito Unánue, Professor of Anatomy at the University of San Marcos, argued that such a practice was unhygienic and constituted a hazard to the health of the population. Accordingly, they proposed the construction of a public cemetery beyond the city limits, a proposal which, apart from the issue of public health, also reflected a desire to assert the primacy of the civil authority over the Church by building a state cemetery. For its time and place the project represented a radical innovation and it was carried through in the face of strong opposition from traditionalists.

The cemetery is named after its architect, the Spanish cleric Presbyter Matías Maestro (1766-1835). A controversial figure in the history of the city's public art, Maestro headed a reaction against baroque ornamentation that was to see neoclassicism impose itself as the dominant style. An architect, sculptor and painter, he enjoyed official support and formed a team of artists and artisans around him to undertake commissions entrusted to him by the civil and ecclesiastical authorities. In particular, he set about renovating the interior of the city's main churches and in the cause of modernization baroque reredos, pulpits and sculptures were jettisoned in favour of others in an austere classical style, which was regarded as a more fitting expression of religious sentiment. The type of reredos favoured by Maestro consisted of a single unit curved at the top and supported by Ionic columns, a good example being that of the church of San Pedro. Some exteriors were likewise renovated in the neoclassical style, as in the case of the main doorway of the church of Santo Domingo. Most of Maestro's ecclesiastical work took the form of renovating existing buildings, but the church of Santo Cristo (Plaza las Maravillas, Barrios Altos) was constructed entirely on the neoclassical model, the Ionic columns and smooth pediment of its doorway conveying a sense of harmony and proportion that reflects the rationalist spirit of the era.

The Amantes del País

As the spirit of the Enlightenment took hold, the Sociedad Académica de Amantes del País (Academic Society of Lovers of the Country) was founded in the late 1780s by a group of Lima intellectuals, foremost among whom were José Rossi y Rubí, Hipólito Unánue and José Baquíjano y Carrillo. Modelled on similar societies in Spain and the colonies, it was set up as a forum for the promotion and dissemination of knowledge, its main purpose being to contribute to the progress of Peru by improving understanding of the country and exchanging ideas for its development. As a vehicle for reaching a wider public, the Society founded the *Mercurio Peruano* (Peruvian Mercury), a journal which appeared twice weekly between 1791 and 1794. The prospectus lamented the current lack of knowledge about the country and argued that in order to flourish Peru needed information: data on commerce, mining, arts, agriculture, fishing, manufactures, botany, mechanics, religion and public decorum.

Setting the tone of the publication, the first article "Idea general del Perú" (A General Idea of Peru) consists of a succinct description of the physical geography of the country, of the various peoples who make up its population, and of its economic resources. Over the following four years the various numbers of the *Mercurio* were to flesh out that initial thumb-sketch by studying in greater length and depth different aspects of the country's reality. In the same spirit Hipólito Unánue later published five annual *Guías* or Guides (updated each year, 1793-97), providing systematic information on the viceroyalty's geography, history, economy, natural resources, population, educational institutions and public organization and including maps and statistical tables.

The pages of the *Mercurio* contain nothing that could be construed as critical of the imperial order. That is hardly surprising given the climate of the times, for the rebellion of Túpac Amaru II in Peru itself (1780-81) and revolution in North America and France made the colonial authorities wary of anything that smacked of subversion. Indeed, the Bourbon monarchy's determination to strengthen and maintain its control over the viceroyalty manifested itself visibly in military constructions that not only served the practical function of reinforcing the capital's defences, but were designed to be imposing symbols of the power of the state. The most important was the Castillo del Real Felipe, a fortress overlooking the port of Callao, completed in the 1770s, while in the city itself military barracks, the Cuartel de Santa Catalina (Av. Nicolás de Piérola 1577), were built in 1806 as a headquarters from which subversion could be controlled and suppressed. In any case, though the Amantes del País saw themselves as modernizers, their agenda did not extend to challenging the imperial system. They did not simply regard themselves as members of a Spanish nation spanning the Peninsula and the Americas, but they also occupied positions of influence and prestige in the colony and had close links with the viceregal authorities. Unánue, for example, was named the colony's Chief Medical Officer and acted as adviser to several viceroys. Moreover, their commitment to promoting the progress of the colony through the spread of modern ideas and useful knowledge was in line with the modernizing philosophy of the Bourbon regime, and both the Society and the *Mercurio* enjoyed official patronage.

Nonetheless, the Amantes del País articulated a growing Creole consciousness and they gave shape to the concept of Peru by defining it as an entity. Peru was the territory contained within the frontiers marked by the reorganization that had separated New Granada and Buenos Aires from the original single viceroyalty. Within those frontiers Peru was the sum of the towns and regions described in the pages of the *Mercurio*. Peru was also a human community made up of the various races who inhabited its territory. Historically, they traced Peru's origins back beyond the Conquest to the foundation of the Inca empire, thereby recuperating the pre-Hispanic past as part of their heritage. Unánue's *Guía*, for instance, states that "the Empire of Peru" was "founded by Manco Capac in the middle of the eleventh century... and subjected to Spanish domination in 1533." Reinforcing the point, a chronological table of the country's monarchs lists 14 Incas followed by a series of Spanish kings from Charles V onwards. Yet the Amantes del País tended to see themselves as standing in relation to the ancient Peruvians in much the same way as contemporary Spaniards stood in relation to the early Iberians: for them the Incas were barbaric ancestors with whom they could never truly identify but who gave their country a historical continuity stretching back to the earliest times. And recognition that Peru was a multiracial society did not imply any sense of racial equality, for they saw natives and blacks as natural subordinates. Nonetheless, as suggested by one article which describes the jungle tribes as "our barbarians", the other races were still considered as fellow countrymen, even if they were viewed with condescension. The Amantes del País thus began to conceptualize a nation and by defining the country they were also in a sense staking it out as their own. Even though the majority of Lima's Creoles did not favour separation from Spain, the psychological climate for such a separation was already being created.

Part Four
CAPITAL OF THE REPUBLIC

Monuments to the Heroes of Independence

Lima's major civic festival is Fiestas Patrias, when Peru's independence is commemorated and celebrated with parades and festivities and solemn ceremonies reaffirming commitment to the ideals on which the Republic was founded on 28 July 1821. On that occasion General José de San Martín and his entourage, the town council and members of the clergy had paraded through the city on a route that symbolically formed the L of Lima and Liberty. The procession started out from the Plaza Mayor, where the Act of Independence was officially signed and the declaration made publicly, and it subsequently made three halts to repeat the declaration—in the Plaza de la Merced, the Plaza Santa Ana and the Plaza de la Inquisición—before returning to the main square, where the birth of the new nation was celebrated with a thanksgiving in the cathedral.

The choice of site for the final declaration was loaded with significance. For if the service in the cathedral signalled that the patriots regarded the Church as one of the pillars of the new Republic, they were also keen to signal a break with the despotism and intolerance which the Inquisition represented. In the evening the Plaza Mayor was illuminated and the celebrations continued into the night with fireworks and dancing. All social groups participated in the festivities, including the city's blacks, whom the water-colourist Pancho Fierro depicts parading with flags and musical instruments, hoping no doubt that the new regime would improve their lot, as indeed it eventually did when slavery was abolished in 1854.

A somewhat more jaundiced view of Peruvian independence was voiced later in the century by Manuel González Prada. Such was the colonial mentality of Lima's Creoles, he claimed, that they would never have broken free from Spain if San Martín and Bolívar had not granted them their independence in much the same way as President Castilla later emancipated the country's black slaves:

Without Bolívar, Sucre, San Martín and Arenales, without those who came from outside to give us freedom, who knows if to this day we'd be vegetating under Spanish domination! Incapable of manumitting ourselves by the action of our own arms, we Limeñans (and all Peruvians) are the freed men of Colombia and Argentina. Argentinians and Colombians did for us what Don Ramón Castilla later did for the blacks.

There is an element of unfairness in that judgement, since Lima was the headquarters of a formidable royalist army numbering some 70,000 men. Nonetheless, the fact remains that the majority of the Creole elite did not actively campaign for independence, since they had a vested interest in the maintenance of the old order and feared a breakdown of the social controls that kept the black and indigenous masses in their place, and they joined the bandwagon only after a chain of events made it clear that independence was inevitable—the collapse of political legitimacy in Spain with the capture of the royal family by the French and the imposition of Joseph Bonaparte as king; a domino effect caused by a growing independence movement in other parts of the continent and the successes of the patriot armies.

Consequently, it is foreign liberators rather than local patriots who are commemorated in Lima's main monuments to the Republic's founding fathers. Dating from 1859 and located in front of the Congress building, in the square bearing his name, is a statue of Bolívar on horseback on top of a marble pedestal with reliefs representing the battles of Ayacucho and Junín. In 1921, on the centenary of independence, San Martín was honoured by the construction of a new square named after him. In the middle stands an equestrian statue on a pedestal representing the Andean *cordillera*, which he crossed to liberate Chile and Peru. On the sides of the pedestal are two friezes: one is an allegory of the Declaration of Independence; in the other fraternity between Peru and Argentina is symbolized by two embracing soldiers. Yet, though overshadowed by the liberators, a number of Peruvians also played a leading role in the struggle for independence and in 1924 they, too, were given their monument when, to house and honour their remains, the former church of San Carlos (Av. Nicolás de Piérola, cuadra 12) was refurbished and inaugurated as the Panteón de los Próceres (Pantheon of the Notables).

The founders of the Republic were also commemorated in painting by José Gil de Castro (1785-1840), a number of whose works can be seen the Museo Nacional de Antropología, Arqueología e Historia. Though born in Lima, Gil de Castro grew up in Chile, where he made his name as portrait-painter of the local elite. Joining San Martín's army of liberation, he subsequently became the Peruvian government's official painter and as such he created the public image of the new nation. Inevitably, of course, his subjects include the great Liberators, San Martín, Bolívar and Sucre. Bolívar, for example, is depicted standing erect with his hand on his breast, in a classic Napoleonic pose which identifies him as the personification of republican ideals. He also portrayed a number of eminent Creole patriots like Archbishop Francisco Javier de Luna Pizarro and Generals Luis José de Orbegoso and José de La Mar, who made a substantial contribution to the independence movement and who were to become the ruling class of the new Republic.

Among the most interesting of such portraits is that of Mariano Alejo Alvarez, a lawyer who campaigned for the rights of Creoles and who rose to become Chief Justice of the Supreme Court. Alvarez is painted standing in the library of his house alongside his eleven-year-old son. His rigid stance and austere clothing project the image of a strict patriarch and upright citizen, and in his hand he holds a book entitled *The Duties of Man*. Painted in an identical pose, the son is a faithful reflection of the father, who thereby takes on the status of a role model passing on to a new generation the civic and moral virtues on which the Republic was founded.

Another of Gil de Castro's subjects was José Olaya, a humble Indian fisherman from the seaside village of Chorrillos. In 1823 Congress had been forced to take refuge in the fortress of Callao when the Spaniards temporarily reoccupied the capital. Swimming to and from the fortress, Olaya acted as messenger between Congress and the patriots in the city. Eventually he was captured, but even so he contrived to swallow the letters he was carrying to prevent them falling into the hands of the enemy. The Spaniards then subjected him to brutal torture to force him to reveal the names of those involved in the patriot cause, but he maintained a stubborn silence, whereupon he was executed by firing squad. Shortly after his death Gil de Castro painted an imaginary full-length portrait of him holding in his right hand the messages entrusted to him and which he safeguarded at the cost of his life. The Olaya portrait forms a stark contrast to Gil de Castro's other work, since whereas his subjects are usually presented in dark clothing in sombre interiors, Olaya wears a white costume and head-scarf which make him stand out and throw his Indian features into relief. The painting is an exceptional example of patriotic iconography in that the elevation of a humble Indian to the status of national hero represents an attempt to project an image of the new Republic as embracing all of Peru's peoples and races. Even so, the fact that Gil de Castro's later work consists of a gallery of figures like Alvarez shows that the indigenous masses continued to be marginalized in a nation run by the Creole elites.

Indeed, in "Túpac Amaru relegado" (Túpac Amaru Relegated, 1964), poet Antonio Cisneros suggests that it was common practice to write the country's Indians and mixed races out of history. Satirizing the standard version of national history that was still being taught in Peruvian schools in the 1950s, the poem focuses on the portraits of the so-called liberators which figured in textbooks and decorated public buildings, reflecting the image of the nation which the Creole elites set out to promote. The real heroes of the struggle for independence, the poet insinuates, were the Indian and *mestizo* masses who shed their blood on the battlefields, but it was the Creole military leaders directing operations from the sidelines who were to go down in official mythology as the founders of the nation. Symbolic of that doctoring of history are the martial whiskers sported by the generals, for in their portraits they acquired ever more heroic proportions as myth-making blew them up into national heroes:

> *There are liberators*
> *with long sideburns*
> *who saw the dead and wounded brought back*
> *after the battles. Soon their names*
> *were history and the sideburns*
> *growing into their old uniforms*
> *proclaimed them founders of the nation.*
>
> *Others with less luck have taken up*
> *two pages of text*
> *with four horses and their death.*

The second stanza shows the reverse side of the Creole version of history by alluding to its treatment of one of the precursors of independence, José Gabriel Condorcanqui, who in 1780 led an abortive Indian insurrection under the name Túpac Amaru II. According to Cisneros, the standard textbooks allotted him a mere two pages, thereby reducing him to the status of minor historical figure, and those two pages focused on the crushing of his insurrection, highlighting his horrendous execution (he was pulled apart by four horses). Inviting us to read between the lines, Cisneros implies that the reason for this downgrading of Túpac Amaru is that he was a *mestizo* and a champion of Indian rights. What the poem exposes, in other words, is the Creole elites' defence of the traditional social hierarchy through the propagation of a mythology which promoted white models and marginalized figures who might serve as models for other racial groups. It was not until 1968 that Túpac Amaru was incorporated into the pantheon of the heroes of Peruvian independence when the populist military government headed by General Juan Velasco adopted him as a symbol of a revolution that aimed to create a more inclusive and equitable society.

Congress, the major institution bequeathed to the nation by the founders of the Republic, stands in Plaza Bolívar—formerly Plaza de la Inquisición but symbolically renamed to signal the triumph of liberty over despotism—on the site of the old University of San Marcos, where its first sessions were held. Housing the Senate and Chamber of Deputies, the present building, dating from the 1920s, is constructed in a French classical style intended to reflect the dignity of the institution and to define it as heir to the European liberal tradition. Though in practice Peruvian democracy has tended to be presidentialist in character, with parliament playing a secondary role, the Congress building embodies a democratic ideal to which Peru has always aspired but to which all too often it has failed to live up. After attending a session of the Senate in the early 1830s, Flora Tristan offered a damning assessment of Peru's politicians, whose impressive eloquence she dismissed as empty rhetoric disguising a lack of civic spirit:

> *The dignity of their bearing, their sonorous voices, the accentuation*
> *of their words, their imposing gestures, all combine to captivate the*
> *audience [...] pretentious, bold of word, they deliver with assurance*

pompous speeches which exude self-sacrifice and love of the fatherland,
while every single one of them thinks only of his own private inter-
ests and nothing for this fatherland, which, moreover, these bluster-
ers would be incapable of serving. In this assembly there is nothing
but constant conspiracies to appropriate the resources of the State;
that goal lies concealed in the depths of everyone's thoughts; virtue
colours every speech, but the basest egoism is revealed in their actions.

The early Republic was continually destabilized by conspiracies, coups and rebellions, and between 1821 and 1845 there were no fewer than twenty-four changes of regime. Subsequently the country was to become more stable but throughout Peru's history as an independent republic constitutional rule has been repeatedly interrupted by periods of dictatorship. In "Descripción de monumento, plaza y alegorías en bronce" (Description of a Monument, a Square and Allegories in Bronze, 1964) Antonio Cisneros' ironic description of a fictional square mischievously points to Peru's failure to live up to the ideals enshrined in its public monuments:

The horse, a liberator
of green bronze whitened
by birdshit.
Three fat girls:
Country, Liberty
and, a little tilted,
Justice. [...]
Almost daily too
assault troops,
black truncheons, green helmets
whitened by birdshit.

The statue of the Liberator is flanked by symbolic figures representing the ideals of the Republic which he founded, but the fact that Justice is in a slightly recumbent position, as though bending over backwards to let itself be violated, suggests that the country's rulers have never hesitated to manipulate the values they profess to revere. The end of the poem echoes the opening lines to establish a link between the Liberator and the riot police posted in the square to control political expression, the implication being that what he fathered was, ultimately, an undemocratic state run by the same old elites. The birds' droppings that deface both the statue and the helmets of the police imply only too clearly that official mythology and the reality it covers up are worthy of contempt.

Monuments to the Heroes of Later Conflicts

Other public monuments commemorate later conflicts in which Peru was involved. The Plaza Dos de Mayo and the imposing monument standing in the middle of it celebrate a victory that did much to boost Peru's self-esteem. In 1866, when a dispute with Spain escalated, a gung-ho Spanish fleet bombarded Callao but was driven off by Peruvian shore batteries. Symbolically located on the site of the old gateway to the city on the road from Callao, the memorial—the work of two Frenchmen, the architect Guillaume and the sculptor Gugnot— was inaugurated in 1874. Constructed in marble and bronze, it consists of an elegant classical column topped by a sculpture of Victory holding aloft the palm of triumph. The pedestal features six bas-reliefs with scenes of the battle and an allegorical representation of American solidarity in the shape of statues of four female figures personifying Peru and the neighbouring countries who supported her (Ecuador, Bolivia and Chile). The monument stands as a statement of Peruvian national pride, but its classical style clearly demonstrates that the Peru envisaged by the Creole elites was one constructed on the European model.

Peru's next military conflict was to prove a disaster. Its origin was a long-standing dispute between Chile and Bolivia over the Atacama Desert. Chilean business interests had moved into the area to exploit its nitrate resources and in 1879 a disagreement over export taxes due to Bolivia escalated, leading to Chile's military occupation of the region. In 1873 Peru, fearing Chilean encroachment into its own southern provinces, had signed a secret defensive pact with Bolivia and it was now drawn into the war. It was a conflict for which it was ill prepared and, following the defeat of its navy at Angamos in October 1879, the Chileans were able to land an army which by June 1880 had occupied the southern provinces of Tarapacá, Tacna and Arica, despite heroic resistance at Arica. The Chileans then advanced on Lima and after considerable bloodshed the defence lines at Chorrillos and Miraflores were overrun in January 1881 and the capital occupied. In the interior

General Andrés Cáceres led a resistance campaign, but in the end the Peruvians were forced to bow to the inevitable and accept Chilean terms for peace. Under the terms of the Treaty of Ancón (1883) Peru lost its three southern nitrate-rich provinces, though Tacna was eventually restored to it in 1929.

An account of life during the occupation has been left by German travel writer Hugo Zöller, who visited Lima in December 1883:

> *In those sectors of the territory which were under Chilean occupation for several years, such as Callao and Lima for example, they intro-duced a regime that was excessively rigid, perhaps even despotic and dictatorial [...] The whole administration rested in hands of the Chileans [...] Not a single Peruvian newspaper appeared in Callao or Lima. The inhabitants received their news only through the three news-sheets edited by the Chileans [...] During the first ten months of Chilean domination only a military justice system existed in Lima [...] A great inconvenience for the populace was that for a long time there was not even minimal policing. The insecurity then must have been very great, and even during my stay no-one went out wearing a gold watch, particularly at night, and no-one went out into the street without a revolver. If I went into a Peruvian shop, I was warned about drunken Chilean soldiers. [...] On two occasions, following brawls that had broken out between soldiers and civilians, Lynch, the Chilean Supreme Commander, had flagrantly innocent Peruvians shot merely to inspire fear. [...]*
>
> *Meanwhile, the best of Peruvian society fumed with indignation and no Chilean officer was ever seen in their most elegant club (the Club de la Unión). Near the hills there is a handsome promenade which used to be much frequented, but since 1881 it has been closed and not a single person shows himself there. Of the numerous army of occupation only Lynch and a few other top commanders visited Peruvian families. The other officers appeared to make up for the lack of social pleasures with good eating and drinking [...] There was no theatre, no concerts, no decent café [...] no museum, no attractive shop.*

For the city's inhabitants the occupation was a painful experience. Most families had at least one relative who had been killed in the war or was fighting with the resistance. Food was in short supply because of a fall in agricultural production and the priority given to the provisioning of the victorious army. Punitive indemnities were exacted from the leading citizens. Public buildings such as the National Library, the University of San Marcos and the Palacio de la Exposición (today's Museo de Arte) were taken over by the troops as improvised barracks. Museums, libraries and educational institutions were sacked and their collections and equipment transported to Chile, and when Ricardo Palma was appointed Director of the National Library after the occupation he found that only 738 of its 56,000 books were left. Reduced to impotence by a severely applied martial law, Limeñans nonetheless found ways of expressing resistance. It became the fashion, for example, for brides to marry in black as a sign of mourning for their country, and social life virtually ceased, as citizens shunned public spaces and withdrew into their homes, whose doors remained ostentatiously closed to the occupiers.

Yet if the defeat was a humiliation for Peru, the war also produced heroes who salvaged national pride and monuments to them are part of the Lima landscape. The first of the heroes was Admiral Miguel Grau, who managed to keep a vastly superior Chilean fleet at bay for four months with his obsolete monitor *Huáscar* before meeting his death at Angamos. Grau's home (Huancavelica 172) has been preserved as a museum and in 1946 a monument was erected to him in the square that bears his name. Other martyr-heroes were thrown up by the battle of Arica. Colonel Francisco Bolognesi, commander of the besieged clifftop garrison, rejected a Chilean invitation to surrender and was executed when it was overrun, while Alfonso Ugarte preferred to ride his horse off the cliff top and into the sea rather than surrender. A monument to Bolognesi stands in the square named after him, while Ugarte is commemorated by a statue located in San Isidro (Av. Javier Prado Oeste, cuadra 16). The house where Bolognesi was born (Cailloma 125) is a museum commemorating those who fought in the battle. Parque Reducto on Avenida Benavides in Miraflores marks one of the defensive positions where resistance to the invaders was fiercest, while the Parque de la Reserva, adjoining the National Stadium, was opened in 1929 to commemorate the civilian reservists who fought in the defence of Lima. A statue to Cáceres stands in the Parque Cáceres in Jesús María.

Pancho Fierro: Scenes of Everyday Life
In the early years of the Republic, recalled Ricardo Palma, there was no perceptible change in the way the people of Lima lived and behaved:

> *Colonial life did not disappear with the last rifle-shot on the battle-field of Ayacucho. In the matter of customs [...] everything, but everything, endured, without the slightest divergence, as in the days of the colonial period. Nothing had changed. The only thing that was lacking was the viceroy.*

Confirmation that this was so is to be found in the work of the self-taught mulatto water-colourist Pancho Fierro (1807-79), examples of which can be seen in the Museo de Arte and the Museo del Banco Central de Reserva.

Fierro produced a corpus of some 1,200 paintings—most of it dispersed in private or foreign collections—documenting scenes that were part of the daily life of Lima's streets, where all races and classes mingled. There are, of course, signs in his work that times and fashions have changed: the insignia of the Republic is displayed on the platform in the Plaza Mayor where a crowd has gathered to watch the draw of the national lottery; a man selling lottery tickets from a desk in the street is wearing a top hat. Yet in the latter picture the female customer is wearing the traditional *saya y manto* and has her face partially covered in the time-honoured manner. Indeed, overall, the paintings suggest that Lima still retained much of its colonial character. The image of a sleepy little town is evoked by a municipal guard dozing on his horse as he does his rounds. The city's lack of public amenities is humorously alluded to in a picture entitled "Cubriendo una necesidad" (Covering a Need), which shows a man using his cloak to conceal a woman while she hunkers urinating. The basic nature of public services is likewise illustrated by a series in which a black *aguador* (water carrier) delivers water to houses, waters the streets to control the dust and, as another part of his duties, kills a stray dog. Processions featuring Indian dancers or blacks dressed up as devils are a continuation of colonial practice. The continuing importance of the Church is suggested by the presence of priests wearing black cassocks and wide-brimmed clerical hats or a sacristan going round the neighbourhood soliciting alms. Provisioning of the city, too, seems to have followed the colonial pattern: stalls dispense Creole food and drink; a market trader offers an array of fruit for sale; donkeys bring firewood, fodder, pisco, butter, fish and tamales into the city from the outlying districts; a whole gallery of itinerant street vendors, mostly blacks and Indians, ply their wares: milk, fruit, cheese, poultry, *mazamorra* (a custard made from corn, sweet potato flour and fruit), ices, *bizcochos*, sweets, flowers, baskets, candles etc.

But Fierro's work does not merely document daily life but offers an image of the nation incorporating people of all social classes. The upper classes are represented, for example, by a lady being driven through the streets in her calash and by a gallery of eminent doctors and lawyers. All the same, Fierro had a marked predilection for members of the lower orders—blacks, Indians, people of mixed race—and seems consciously to claim for them recognition of their place in national society. In that respect, it is significant that alongside paintings of army officers on horseback he should have devoted two to ordinary foot-soldiers with their *rabonas*, the female camp followers who accompanied their men on campaign. These works invite the viewer to acknowledge the debt which the country owes not only to the rank and file who made up its armies but to their female partners, who, though regarded as loose women by respectable society because their relationships were unformalized, acted as porters, cooks and nurses as well as providing their men with emotional support and comfort. Marginalized in the literature of the time, the lower orders are given in Fierro's art a presence corresponding to that which they had in real life, where they constituted the majority of the population. A succession of images of ordinary people going about their daily business makes it clear that the city could not have functioned without their contribution. And paintings such as those depicting the *zamacueca* demonstrate that the culture of the subaltern peoples was making its mark on Creole culture.

Foreign visitors like American Charles Samuel Stewart in 1829 were shocked by the spectacle of poverty and decay that greeted them on their arrival in the city:

> *Rarely have I felt such great surprise as I did on entering the first street after passing through the city gate. Instead of the "splendid city" which since childhood I had read about with such wonder, I was tempted to fancy myself in Timbuktu and I could not help exclaiming: if this is "the City of the Kings" how the mighty are fallen! or:*

how the credulous have been deceived! Single-storey houses built of mud, with huge doors and windows exposing filth and poverty to the gaze [...] everything presented a ruinous and pitiful appearance.

Lima had been brought to a sorry state by a combination of destruction, deterioration and neglect caused by the upheavals of the struggle for independence and the political instability which followed. The wars had devastated the economy, governments ran up a huge foreign debt and in the period up to 1840 budget deficits were chronic.

Later, however, the country was two enjoy two periods of relative political stability, the first from the mid-1840s till around 1880 and the second from 1895 to 1930. During those periods, too, the economy flourished and resources were available to invest in development. The great aspiration of the country's elites was to drag Peru out of its backwardness and turn it into a modern nation on the model of Europe. As a central part of that project they embarked on the modernization of Lima with the aim of making it a capital worthy of an independent republic.

Desamparados Station

Following a three-week visit at the end of 1947, English writer Christopher Isherwood observed that, away from the Plaza Mayor, "central Lima resembles the duller parts of nineteenth-century Paris." The model for the new Lima *was*, in fact, Paris, which in Peru, as in other Latin American countries, was regarded as the cultural capital of the world. But though many of the buildings in the centre show a very marked French influence, the style tends to be eclectic rather than slavishly imitative. And if they struck Isherwood as dull, it is because they are mostly commercial edifices which replaced many of the old mansions in the city centre as business activity increased with the expansion of the economy. Even so, some of them are very impressive, such as the premises of Peru's oldest newspaper *El Comercio* (Miró Quesada 300) or the Banco Central de Reserva (Ucayali 299; now a museum), both of which date from the 1920s and have a sober, austere majesty and solidity.

Whereas such edifices stand as a break with the past, two of Lima's finest buildings, located in the vicinity of the Plaza Mayor, blend in with the old city while simultaneously reflecting the modernity of the epoch. Both establishments exemplify the project of creating an infrastructure for development: the Central Post Office (Conde de Superunda 199), opened in 1897, and Desamparados Railway Station, built in 1908 and situated by the river behind the Presidential Palace. They also illustrate a characteristic feature of building during this period, the displacement of traditional local materials like adobe and *quincha* by modern materials. The Post Office has a luminous glass-roofed arcade, while the station's interior features iron structures and stained-glass windows adorned with allegorical decorations. At the same time, both buildings have handsome neoclassical façades, painted in warm colours and harmonizing with the environment of the area.

Flanking the large clock above the station entrance are two allegorical figures symbolizing industrialization and progress in the shape of a locomotive and a cog-wheel. The railway was the nineteenth century's great symbol of progress, and as the terminal of the Central Railway—it replaced the original terminal, which was located in today's Plaza San Martín—Desamparados is the starting-point for one of the world's great railway journeys. Climbing from sea level to heights of some 15,000 feet, the line links Lima and La Oroya, where it forks, with one branch leading to the mining town of Cerro de Pasco and the other to the Andean market town of Huancayo. Unfortunately, passenger services were discontinued some years ago—though it is rumoured that plans are afoot to reinstate them—and the line is now used only by freight trains. Even so, the station remains a monument to the railway era.

Peru's first railways were two local lines constructed in the 1850s and linking Lima to Callao and Chorrillos. Yet the railway was seen, above all, as the means by which Peru's isolated rural regions could be opened up for development and linked to outside markets. The leading advocate of investment in railroad construction was the politician Manuel Pardo, who in 1862 articulated his vision of the benefits which it would bring the country:

> *What easier, quicker, more powerful way is there of increasing national production and with it the wealth both of private individuals and of the state? [...] If in European countries the role of the railway track comes down to facilitating and activating communications between two points of their territory, in Peru its mission is to create*

those relations which do not exist between places isolated from one another; in Europe the railways facilitate traffic and commerce and by so doing they foster industry and increase the value of property; in Peru they will create it all: commerce, industry, and even property, because they will give value to that which today is valueless.

Furthermore, the growth of material wealth brought by the railways also entails a veritable growth of civilization, the moral and intellectual improvement of the nation whose territories have suddenly been enriched by the locomotive.

A few years later President José Balta (1868-72) recruited the American entrepreneur Henry Meiggs to undertake an ambitious railroad-building programme which eventually culminated in two major lines: the aforementioned Central Railway and the Southern Railway, linking Mollendo, Arequipa, Puno and Cuzco. Given the ruggedness of the Andean terrain, both lines are remarkable feats of engineering.

Unfortunately, however, the construction of Peru's railways also involved a sorry story of incompetence, irresponsibility and corruption. The programme proved to be much more expensive than had been anticipated, partly because of logistical difficulties, partly because costs were inflated by swindles and kickbacks. To finance the scheme the government raised some £36 million in foreign loans, contributing to the build-up of a massive debt which brought the country to bankruptcy in 1876. As a result, the project was left paralysed and it was not until the first decade of the twentieth century that it was eventually completed. Moreover, the cost of its completion was such that the Peruvian Corporation, a company formed by British creditors, was given control of the railways for a period of sixty-six years as part of a settlement of Peru's foreign debt.

The Guano Republic

The fiasco of the railways is symptomatic of Peru's mishandling of the wealth generated by the guano boom. The demand for fertilizers in the wake of Europe's nineteenth-century agricultural revolution proved to be a bonanza for Peru, since it had rich guano resources on the islands off the coast. In the four decades from 1840 to 1880 around eleven million tons were mined, transported and sold to European and North American markets. Under the "consignment" system established for the commercialization of guano, the state auctioned off to private merchant houses rights of extraction and marketing in return for loans or advances on future profits. The trade was dominated mainly by foreign houses, such as the British company Antony Gibbs and Sons in the 1840s and 1850s and the French firm Dreyfus after 1869. A ditty circulated in London making fun of the source of the Gibbs' wealth:

The House of Gibbs made their dibs
selling the turds of foreign birds.

The Gibbs dynasty could afford to laugh it off, since the profits of the guano trade laid the foundations for what was to become one of London's most prestigious merchant banks, and William, who took over the family business in the 1840s, amassed a huge personal fortune which enabled him to purchase an enormous country estate— Tyntesfield, near Bristol, now owned by the English National Trust, on which he built a magnificent gothic mansion.

Yet it was by no means the case that Peru was ripped off by rapacious foreign merchants. Peruvian syndicates controlled the market in the 1860s, but on the whole governments preferred to deal with foreign houses, which they regarded as more enterprising and trustworthy. Even when they did not control the market, local merchants prospered as agents of foreign companies. Most of the income from guano went into the state treasury, since on average the government retained 60 per cent of the sale price, and it is estimated that during the guano era revenue totalled approximately £80 million, about eighty times the 1850 budget. Like the Arab oil emirates of the latter twentieth century, Lima was awash with money.

In the main the government channelled guano revenue into worthy projects designed to foster national development, but it did so on scale which it simply could not afford and its outgoings were boosted by a culture of cronyism and corruption. Worse, the country's prosperity rested on shaky foundations, since it was dependent on a finite resource. By 1869 guano revenue had come to represent 80 per cent of government income and as reserves began to run out, revenue from the trade fell 35 per cent from £4 million in 1869 to only £2.6 million in 1875.

Theoretically the wealth generated by guano should have enabled Peru to diversify its economy by providing the capital to develop other areas of economic activity. Instead, the abundance of money actually hindered such development by making imports cheap and increasing the cost of labour, and investors found it more profitable to purchase government bonds than to risk their money in new enterprises. At the same time, the government shied away from unpopular fiscal policies that would have put its finances on a sound footing, with the result that the state ended up receiving in taxation from each citizen only one-fifth of what it was spending per head of population. In other words, Peru was guilty of living beyond its means. The elites spent heavily on conspicuous consumption, and an avalanche of foreign imports led to a severe balance-of-payment problem, with the country consuming from abroad three times what it produced. The government, too, consistently overspent, financing its projects with foreign loans, and it went on borrowing heavily even as income was declining, so that by 1872 the servicing of the foreign debt was consuming S/13.5 million out of the total guano income of S/15 million. It is hardly surprising, then, that by 1876 things had come to such a pass that Peru was forced to declare a moratorium on its debt repayments.

The affluence and extravagance of the guano era are evoked in Ricardo Palma's "El baile de La Victoria" (The Dance at La Victoria), which describes a dinner dance given by President José Rufino Echenique to Lima's elites. The opulence of the occasion, Palma tells us, was unmatched in the history of the city:

> *No! Never has there been given in Lima, since it was founded by Don Francisco Pizarro in 1535, a dance greater in magnificence than that which, on the evening of Saturday 15 October 1853, the President of the Republic, General Echenique, offered Congress and the well-bred citizenry.*

Some 1,300 guests attended the event, and the display of wealth took its most ostentatious form in the dresses and jewellery worn by the women, with the wives of men enriched by the guano boom outshining those of the old elite.

The backdrop to Palma's story is the Consolidation, a scheme initiated by President Ramón Castilla in 1850 to consolidate the internal debt by issuing bonds to those who claimed reimbursement for unpaid loans. During the presidency of his successor Echenique the state admitted under the scheme claims for compensation for damages incurred in the wars of independence and subsequent conflicts. Upward of $25 million was transferred from the state to private citizens, creating, as Palma puts it, men of substance out of nothing:

> *God raised man out of nothing, but President Echenique surpassed him with his Consolidation, raising many men—very many—out of nothing, that is, out of humble poverty to arrogant opulence.*

The Consolidation did not, in fact, turn paupers into millionaires, but further enriched the elites who had already profited from the guano boom and the expansion of the state financed by it. Yet it certainly was the most blatant example of the culture of cronyism and corruption which characterized the era. Many of the claims for compensation from the state were unfounded and the scheme came to be viewed as a massive fraud whereby Echenique doled out public money to his cronies. Both the opulence on display at the president's dinner dance and the corruption which funded it reflect the way in which Peru's elites squandered the fruits of the guano boom and wasted the opportunity to use it as a springboard for development.

Two nineteenth-century novels indirectly evoke the climate of the guano era through the story of the moral and economic downfall of a young woman blinded by the false glamour of a life of opulent ostentation. In Luis Benjamín Cisneros' *Julia* (1861) the idyllic romance of the lovers Andrés and Julia is cut short when the latter, succumbing to the corrupting influence of the society around her, forsakes her unpretentious fiancé to marry a dashing young man-about-town, only to come to grief when her husband squanders his fortune on gambling and deserts her after absconding with his company's funds. Likewise, the eponymous protagonist of Mercedes Cabello de Carbonera's *Blanca Sol* (1889) has been brought up to expect to be indulged, pampered and admired and regards it as her destiny to occupy a dazzling position in high society and to bask in its adulation. This ambition she achieves by cynically marrying for money. Completely subjugating her weak spouse, she squanders his fortune on expensive clothes and lavish entertainments until she becomes the leading light in the social firmament. She indulges, too, in a series of flirtations, mainly to glory in the homage paid to her by society's most desirable males and in the notoriety it brings her. In the end, when her extravagance brings her husband to bankruptcy and her seeming infidelity drives him out of his mind with jealousy, she finds herself ostracized by the society that had formerly paid court to her. Julia and Blanca Sol could thus be said to personify the Creole elites who, instead of prudently managing the guano bonanza and investing it in a programme of viable development, misused and squandered it and ended up paying the inevitable price.

The Teatro Segura

Lima is relatively well off for theatres. In addition to some fine small establishments like the Club de Teatro (28 de Julio 183, Miraflores) and the Teatro Canout (Petit Thouars 4550, Miraflores), cultural institutions such as the Alianza Francesa (Arequipa 4595, Miraflores), the Catholic University's Centro Cultural PUCP (Camino Real 1975, San Isidro) and the Instituto Cultural Peruano Norteamericano (Angamos Oeste 160, Miraflores) regularly stage theatrical productions. But the city's major theatre is the handsome Teatro Segura, located in the Historic Centre (Huancavelica, 265). It is so partly by default, since the magnificent Teatro Municipal (Ica, 377), the primary locale for drama, ballet, opera and symphonic concerts, was severely damaged by fire in 1998 and still awaits reconstruction. Even though it took second place to the Municipal, the Teatro Segura was always a prestigious theatre in its own right and it is particularly important because of the history attached to it and because it houses a museum documenting the theatrical and musical life of the city.

Opened in 1909, it stands on the site of the Teatro Principal, the nineteenth century's foremost playhouse. Theatre had been popular in Lima since colonial times, but the affluence of the guano era generated demand for high-class entertainment and in the second half of the century the city had no fewer than four establishments. In keeping with the prevailing view that Europe was the home of true culture, foreign artists and companies were brought over to entertain and uplift the local public. The Principal specialized in Italian opera, which had caught on with Lima's middle classes as high culture at its most sublime, and its visiting divas were the object of the kind of hero-worship now accorded to pop stars. In 1853, for instance, the famous Italian soprano Biscaccianti was accompanied from her hotel to the theatre by a cheering crowd of over 2,000 people.

The theatre is named after Manuel Ascencio Segura (1805-71), the major local dramatist of the nineteenth century and the country's best playwright to date. During the colonial period Peru had produced very little in the way of home-grown drama and virtually nothing of any quality. Segura's contemporary, Felipe Pardo y Aliaga (1806-68), who had spent his formative years in Spain, was dismayed by the poverty of the local theatre and in his newspaper reviews compared it unfavourably to the productions of touring European companies. He himself wrote three plays aimed at raising its level by adapting European models to national themes, but he lacked the technique to translate good intentions into good theatre. By contrast, Segura was highly critical of the cultural inferiority complex which led Peruvians to overvalue everything foreign and to deride the works of their own countrymen. The author of thirteen plays depicting the middle-class world to which he belonged, he not only won popular success but demonstrated that it was possible to create a genuinely national theatre of quality.

Though he thought of himself as a moralist whose purpose was to "correct the customs, abuses, excesses with which our land is unfortunately plagued," Segura's talent was above all that of a perceptive observer of the social scene, and his plays are memorable mainly for their lively and entertaining depiction of Limeñan customs and types. Not only did he lay the foundations for a Peruvian theatrical tradition, but by portraying the Creole middle classes to themselves he contributed to the creation of a sense of national identity, albeit one that was exclusively urban-based.

Segura's plays are also an invaluable resource for understanding the urban middle classes' perception of the events and processes that shaped their daily lives. Their dissatisfaction with the military's dominance of public life is conveyed by the one-act *El Sargento Canuto* (Sergeant Canuto, 1839), where the arrogance of the military is personified by the eponymous protagonist, the suitor of Don Sempronio's daughter Jacoba. Put off by the way he struts and swaggers around, swollen up with self-importance, Jacoba has repulsed him again and again, but he keeps pursuing her, unable to conceive that she could fail to be besotted by his manliness and that she should choose instead to bestow her affections on Pulido, a mere boy without prospects. Impervious to her feelings and wishes and determined to have his own way, he goes about his courtship as a kind of military campaign which, by a process of attrition, will eventually break down her resistance. As is suggested by Don Sempronio's words of encouragement to him, a parallel is insinuated between Canuto's campaign to win Jacoba and the coups by which the military regularly seized the presidential palace: "Take her, lad; no coward/gets to enter the palace." Acting as a mouthpiece for civilian opponents of military rule, Jacoba's sister declares that for a husband she wants a man who will treat her properly rather than a soldier who will dominate her: "I don't want generals;/what I'd like is a civilian/who'll love me and treat me right." And in the end Canuto is thwarted by the resolute opposition of Jacoba and Pulido, and when the latter stands up to his bullying tactics the sergeant's much vaunted courage proves to be mere bluster. Such a dénouement was, of course, one which ordinary citizens hoped to see re-enacted on the public stage.

A grievance repeatedly voiced in Segura's work was that the honest, conscientious middle classes tended to be overlooked in appointments to government posts, which went instead to well-connected opportunists who lacked all sense of patriotism and civic virtue and were cynically concerned to pursue their own self-interest. In *La saya y manto* (1841) Don Mariano is depicted as a man completely devoid of moral sense or political principles and willing to serve any government that will give him a job: "To me it's all the same/if we're ruled by Don Andrés,/Basilio or Buggins./I show respect, devotion/to him who offers me a post;/to him who doesn't I denigrate him/as much as I can and I detest him./Expediency is the voice/that commands my patriotism." Mariano eventually succeeds in obtaining the post he has been scheming for. Don Bonifacio, on the other hand, an honest and decent man who had been promised a position as a reward for his past services, finds himself passed over. Whether or not it was true that unscrupulous opportunists came off best in the scramble for government posts, the text makes it clear that in the difficult economic climate of the early decades after independence the public administration came to be viewed in much the same way as the Church had been in the colonial period: as a career offering security and status. In the event, changing economic circumstances were to open up new opportunities for the middle classes, since the income generated by the guano boom enabled the government to expand the state bureaucracy.

The eagerness with which many Peruvians embraced European styles and habits as status symbols is caricatured in *Ña Catita* (1845) in the figure of Don Alejo, a rich man-about-town who shows off his superior taste by sporting foreign fashions, putting on foreign airs and interspersing his speech with foreign words. He urges Don Jesús to catch up with the times by abandoning his traditional Spanish cape in favour of an English overcoat: "You're off on a *promené/*from what I see./But with a cape…! Who nowadays wears/such Spanish clothing?/[…]/ Get yourself a Lord Ragland,/which is dress *comm'il faut.*" Later he tells Doña Rufina that only foreigners know how to make clothes: "Disabuse yourself… in Lima/they'll never make anything of quality./That's why, madam,/I only let foreigners dress me./*Hubí* makes my frock coats…/[…]/*Monsieur Prugue* my waistcoats…/[…]/The German my boots."

As noted earlier, Segura laid the foundations for a national theatre. Unfortunately, no one emerged after him to build on those foundations and it was not until the 1940s that Peruvian theatre underwent a revival. Since then new playwrights have come to the fore and a number of fine plays have been produced, the best being Juan Ríos' *Ayar Manko* (1952), Julio Ramón Ribeyro's *Vida y pasión de Santiago el pajarero* (Life and Passion of Santiago the Birdman, 1960), Sebastián Salazar Bondy's *El rabdomante* (The Water-diviner, 1965) and Alonso Alegría's *El cruce sobre el Niágara* (The Crossing of Niagara Falls, 1958). On the whole, however, Peruvian dramatists have failed to match the achievements of the country's poets and novelists in terms of both quantity and quality.

The National Library and Ricardo Palma

The National Library was created by Liberator San Martín in 1821 as part of a policy of promoting education and learning. It was installed in the old Jesuit Colegio del Príncipe and amassed an impressive collection for its time, but it was plundered by the Chileans following their occupation of Lima. It later made a remarkable recovery but was burned down in 1943. Dating from the 1940s, the present building (Av. Abancay, cuadra 4) was designed to combine Peru's different cultural traditions, with a façade decorated with pre-Hispanic motifs and an interior patio evoking the atmosphere of a colonial cloister. Its most important holding is the collection of manuscripts dating back to the sixteenth century.

Various of the country's leading intellectuals have held the post of Director, but the name most associated with the Library is that of Ricardo Palma (1833-1919), who was responsible for rebuilding its holdings after the departure of the Chileans. The foremost literary figure of the nineteenth century, Palma was the creator of the *Tradiciones peruanas* (Peruvian Traditions), a collection of chatty anecdotes recounting episodes from the nation's past in a humorous, colloquial style. From 1872 onwards he produced over five hundred such stories embracing every period of Peru's history from Inca times to the mid-nineteenth century and covering regions of the interior as well as the cities of the coast.

Palma sought to give his fellow countrymen an awareness of their history and to create a sense of nationhood rooted in the heritage of the past and shaped, above all, by the colonial experience. Engaging his readers' interest by focusing, not on great events, but on the minutiae of history—crimes, illicit love affairs, feuds, unusual or miraculous happenings etc.—he then uses the stories as a pretext for incorporating basic instruction in national history and as a vehicle for commentaries aimed at shaping his public's perception of the national past. Since the vast majority of the traditions are set in the colonial times, he has often been accused of creating a nostalgic mythology that idealizes the colonial past as a lost Golden Age. In fact, he was very much a nineteenth-century liberal and he frequently congratulates himself and his readers on their good fortune in not having been born in the benighted colonial era, and he is critical of the conquistadors and the feudalistic class hierarchy introduced by the Spaniards. Moreover, the traditions are very much linked to the present in that they invite parallels with contemporary history. The feuding between the conquistadors is seen as foreshadowing the power struggles of the nineteenth-century military *caudillos*, while his satire of colonial society's obsession with lineage and titles has as its real target the oligarchic families who constituted the Republic's "aristocracy".

Nonetheless, the title "Peruvian Traditions" is somewhat misleading, for these vignettes' vision of the country is very much Lima-centred. Not only are most set in the capital but the relationship of complicity between the narrator and his readers usually involves a recognition of their common condition as Limeñans. Palma writes as the spokesman of Lima's middle classes, promoting them as the backbone of the country and expressing their disenchantment with a republican regime that has defrauded their expectations. Again and again he points out that in many ways independence has changed nothing, since government continues to be unrepresentative, autocratic and corrupt. Thus, a story about arbitrary abuse of authority in colonial times invites the readers to sympathize with the victim by drawing a parallel with their own experience in the present:

> *Don Gabriel made a fuss and protested till the cows came home; but it's well known that, then as now, protesting is a waste of time and breath and that anyone who has a little bit of power will do as he wants with those of us who weren't born to govern but to be governed.*

In particular, Palma expresses the middle classes' resentment at the perceived dominance of national life by the same old oligarchy. "Un litigio original" (A Curious Litigation) revolves around an incident in the seventeenth century involving two noblemen whose coaches came face to face in a narrow street. Neither would give way, each of them claiming that his lineage entitled him to precedence. Eventually the dispute was referred to the viceroy, who in his turn referred it to the king for arbitration. Meanwhile, the coaches remained in place and by the time a ruling came back from Madrid they had disappeared, perished by the weather and looted by the public. Recounting the episode with mock seriousness, Palma undermines the prestige of the Republic's dominant classes, who were perceived—erroneously—as a hereditary elite. The whole story is based on an ironic contrast between noble credentials and pettiness of conduct, subtly suggesting that the Creole aristocracy lacks the qualities to constitute a true elite and merely perpetuates arbitrary hierarchies and class distinctions. Clearly implied in the ending is that, like the coaches, they are an anachronism destined to disappear in the natural order of things, swept away by the lower orders who see no reason to respect outmoded hierarchies.

The latter episode is also the subject of the painting "El pleito de las calesas" (The Dispute of the Calashes) by Teófilo Castillo (1857-1922), the leading painter of the early twentieth century. Castillo recorded his admiration for Palma in a famous portrait he did of him and, inspired by the writer's example, he produced a series of paintings evoking scenes from colonial times, such as "La procesión de Corpus Christi" (Corpus Christi Procession), "Los funerales de Santa Rosa" (Santa Rosa's Funeral) and "El santo de la abuelita" (Grandmother's Saint's Day). Castillo cultivated what might be called a neo-impressionist manner and, in his exteriors particularly, swirls of colour seem to envelop the scene evoked in the mists of times past. His works have a solemnity that contrasts with Palma's ambivalent treatment of the past, but painter and writer coincide in their concern to give Peruvians a sense of their colonial heritage.

The Escuela Nacional de Bellas Artes

Lima's most important art museums are the Museo de Arte (Paseo Colón 125) and the Museo del Banco Central de Reserva (Ucayali 299), while the Palacio Municipal also houses a fine collection of paintings. Yet the most significant building in Peru's art history is the Escuela Nacional de Bellas Artes (Ancash, cuadra 6), whose creation owes much to the aforementioned Teófilo Castillo.

In the nineteenth century the majority of Peruvian artists received their training in Europe, funded by government scholarships aimed at boosting intellectual and cultural life by enabling promising young Peruvians to study abroad. Such was the case of the so-called academic painters—Francisco Laso (1823-69), Ignacio Merino (1817-76) and Luis Montero (1826-69)—whose art contributed to the process of nation-building that was going on at the time. Montero's "Los funerales de Atahualpa" (Atahualpa's Funeral), a large-scale work which hangs on the landing of the grand staircase of the Museo de Arte, and Merino's "Proclamación de la Independencia" (Declaration of Independence) re-create key episodes in the nation's history. Laso's "Santa Rosa" portrays the saint, one of the great emblems of Peruvian identity, in a state of a mystic ecstasy. Merino depicts typical Creole merry-making in "Jarana en Chorrillos" (Carousal in Chorrillos). Laso also incorporates Peru's non-European peoples into the national family. Two of his best-known works depict Indians in typical costume: in "Indio alfarero" (Indian Potter) a potter stands holding in his hands one of his ceramics as if it were a votive offering, while "El haravicu" (The Story-teller) shows a group of peasants listening to a story-teller. "La lavendera" (The Washerwoman) features a graceful black woman hanging up washing on the roof terrace of a Lima house. By applying techniques learned in Europe to local themes, these painters sought to dignify Peru's people and their history, bestowing on them the status associated with the subjects represented in the great tradition of European painting. The result is that while the paintings are technically accomplished, their subjects—particularly in the case of Indian characters—come across as examples of a classical ideal of beauty and dignity rather than as true-to-life Peruvians. The women bemoaning the death of their lord in Montero's painting, for instance, resemble Roman matrons rather than Inca princesses. Ironically, despite their good intentions, what such paintings project, in the end, is the Creole elites' Eurocentric view of the nation.

As art critic for local journals Castillo campaigned for the establishment of a national art school to train the country's artists, and his dream came to fruition in 1917. The School was housed in a refurbished colonial convent and retains its layout, with classrooms surrounding a central patio. Constructed in the so-called neo-Peruvian style, the modern façade is a synthesis of Hispanic and indigenous decorative elements; the composition of the huge stone portal evokes the Spanish baroque but its ornamental details derive from pre-Hispanic cultures. Daniel Hernández (1856-1932), who had made a successful career for himself in Europe, was invited to return to Peru to run the new School. Hernández's own work is fairly conventional, but he had a solid mastery of technique and disciplined work habits and in the role of Director he was to prove extremely effective.

If Hernández ensured that new generations of painters received a solid training, it was a young teacher at the School, José Sabogal (1888-1956), who inspired them with a new concept of painting. Around him emerged a group of artists—Julia Codesido (1892-1979), Camilo Blas (1903-85) and Enrique Camino Brent (1909-60)—who sought to create an authentically national art inspired by the country's landscape and its people. Sabogal and his followers privileged Andean scenes featuring rugged landscapes, Indian villages and peasants in indigenous costumes. Sabogal favoured vivid colour contrasts and strong outlines exaggerating his subjects' features with the evident intention of magnifying the Indian, as can be seen in famous works like "Plaza serrana" (Andean Village Square), "La Santusa" (Santusa) and "Varayok de Chincheros" (Community Leader of Chincheros). His protégés operated within the same parameters but they had their own distinctive trademark. Camino Brent, for instance, had a taste for architectural structures and for group scenes emphasizing the generic rather than the individual, good examples being "Claustro del Cusco" (Cusco Arcade) and "La familia del Collao" (The Family from Collao).

The great merit of Sabogal and his group is that they produced an art that broke with the narrow Lima-centred view of the nation. Though it has often been criticized—with some justification—for presenting an external view of the Andean world that tends to lapse into the picturesque, the movement came to be known as *indigenismo* (Indigenism) because of its privileging of the Indian as a subject. That term, however, is something of a misnomer, since they did not just paint Andean scenes and types, but depicted people and customs from all over Peru, thereby offering a pluralist view of the nation as a country made up of diverse regions, people and cultural traditions. Sabogal's work includes typical scenes from the capital such as the procession of El Señor de los Milagros; images from the jungle region such as "Ánforas de Amazonas" (Amphorae of the Amazon Region), which depicts two woman carrying amphorae on their head; and scenes from the northern coast, like "Mujer en el desierto" (Woman in the Desert), featuring a woman trudging across a sandy landscape with a pitcher of water on her head, and "Caballitos de totora" (Reed Boats), showing fishermen at sea on their traditional curved, peapod-shaped reed boats known as "little horses". Among Codesido's best-known works are portrayals of Limeñan women. Illustrating her characteristic use of elongated, angular shapes, "Morena limeña" depicts a coquettish mulatto woman and "Tapadas limeñas" features a group of females with their faces covered in the traditional manner.

Other graduates of the School kept their distance from Sabogal's group but pursued essentially the same ambition of creating a national art depicting Peru's landscapes and peoples. Their painting came to be known as neo-Peruvian, a term signifying a willingness to recognize and celebrate all of the country's peoples and cultural traditions that might equally well have been applied to Sabogal and his followers. In reality, the only significant difference between the two groups was one of style, for the neo-Peruvians shunned the exaggerated stylization which the so-called *indigenistas* made their hallmark. Foremost among them was Jorge Vinatea Reinoso (1900-31), who as well as a painter was a magazine illustrator and political cartoonist. His work covers a range of themes similar to that of Sabogal: traditional Limeñan festivals like the Paseo de Amancaes and the procession of El Señor de los Milagros; Andean scenes in "Atardecer en el Titicaca" (Nightfall over Lake Titicaca), "Procesión serrana" (Andean Procession) and "Plaza de Chucuito" (Chucuito's Main Square); and various depictions of his native Arequipa. As opposed to Sabogal, however, all of his paintings are characterized by his delicate and subtle use of colour.

From the 1940s onwards there were to be new developments on the Lima art scene. A second art school was set up when the Catholic University founded its own Escuela de Artes Plásticas. Art galleries, too, began to spring up and the city now has a number where temporary exhibitions are regularly held, perhaps the best being that of the Instituto Cultural Peruano-Norteamericano (Av. Angamos Oeste 160, Miraflores). The country has also produced some fine modern artists, only some of whom can be mentioned here. Unfortunately, though, Lima lacks a museum with a permanent collection of modern art. Samples of the work of major artists can be accessed on websites such as the Sophia Virtual Gallery (www.terra.com.pe/sophia/rep-txt.shtml).

After 1940 there was a reaction against the type of art represented by Sabogal, which had come to be regarded as provincial in its emphasis on local themes and as subordinating art to thematics. Accordingly, younger artists sought to "modernize" Peruvian painting by evolving new forms of pictorial expression which would bring it into tune with developments in the international art scene. Sérvulo Gutiérrez (1914-61) first made his name in the early 1940s with a series of sculpturesque female nudes like "Los Andes", where the human figure seems to be part of the surrounding mountain landscape. In the 1950s he abandoned that line in favour of what was to become his defining style, a kind of hallucinatory expressionism based on swirling plays of colour. Among his best works in that manner are his portrait of Santa Rosa de Lima and various landscapes, still lives and figures of Christ.

Other major figures are Jorge Eduardo Eielson (b. 1924), Tilsa Tsuchiya (1929-84), Gerardo Chávez (b. 1937) and Carlos Enrique Polanco, but Peru's greatest and most internationally famous painter is undoubtedly Fernando de Szyszlo (b. 1925). Szyszlo's work has gone through several phases. In the 1950s he cultivated abstract expressionism, leaving his pictures untitled so as not to influence the viewer's perception of the work. Then, in the late 1950s, he started producing titled abstracts whose titles pointed to their Peruvian subject-matter. In particular, he created a series of thirteen pictures inspired by a famous sixteenth-century Quechua poem lamenting the death of the Inca Atahualpha and the destruction of the Andean universe, each work in the series bearing as title a line from the poem. The second is called "Watupaqurcan suncollaymi" (My heart had a premonition) and has a red background covered by vigorous black brushstrokes, creating an atmosphere of sombre disquiet. Later, from the mid-1960s onwards, he began to cultivate a kind of neo-figurativism based on suggestion and allusion, so that one can detect in his work evocations of Peruvian landscapes—particularly that of the coast—and pre-Hispanic culture. "Travesía" (Crossing) features what can be identified as the head of a sacrificial victim sculpted on the wall of the temple of Sechín, while "Noche estrellada" (Starry Night) reworks the image of the flying shaman which is a recurrent motif in Paracas textiles.

Szyszlo is an artist who consciously set out to take Peruvian art out of its provincialism and place it within the western mainstream. At the same time his evolution confirms that contact with the wider western world made him aware that his identity was rooted in Peru and that part of his heritage as a Peruvian was the non-western culture bequeathed by the great pre-Hispanic civilizations. Yet, as an artist, Szyszlo has always been concerned first and foremost to give expression to the human condition. Not all of his works refer to Peru. A later series entitled "La habitación número 23" (Room 23) consists of variations on the theme of a desolate hotel room, a metaphor for the rootless condition of modern man. Those which do evoke Peru's pre-Hispanic past do so not merely as a means of defining his cultural identity, but to signal the unchanging nature of human experience and of man's response to the world in which he lives.

The Casa Courret: European Influences

In colonial times Lima's up-market shopping street was Calle Mercaderes. After the renaming of streets in the Republican period, Mercaderes became the third block of the Jirón de la Unión, which throughout the nineteenth century and the greater part of the twentieth was the city's main street and as such the location of its fashionable

shops and cafés. Two buildings in particular are monuments to the street's former splendour.

The Casa Courret (no. 463), whose neo-rococo façade features wrought-iron balconies and whimsical masonry work reminiscent of Gaudí, is a fine example of the *art nouveau* style which was one of the expressions of the elegant modernity that the city began to embrace in the latter half of the nineteenth century. It was the premises of Lima's most prestigious photographer, the Frenchman Eugenio (Eugène) Courret. Courret's work, an archive of which is held in the National Library, constitutes a photographic history of the period, portraying people dressed in the fashions of the time and recording the city's streets and buildings as they were then. Courret ran a flourishing business (he had branches in other parts of the city) and not only was he in demand for portraits but his photographs were used for visiting cards, postcards and as series of collectable cards distributed as a marketing ploy with products such as soap, perfume, sweets and cigarettes.

The Casa Courret is only one architectural example of how European immigrants established themselves as part of Lima society. Another is located in the once fashionable district of Barrios Altos (Junín 1201) to the east of the Historic Centre. The Quinta Heeren was a self-contained suburban neighbourhood built by Oscar Heeren, a successful German businessman who married into one of Lima's top families. Begun in 1890, the project took several decades to complete. It was modelled on a type of housing complex that was widespread throughout the Austro-Hungarian empire in the nineteenth century and, in the words of art historian Juan Manuel Ugarte Eléspuru, the visitor "has the impression of being transported by the magic carpet of the imagination to Prague, Cracow or Bratislava." Terraced houses look on to a small square adjoining the grounds where the main residence is situated. Constructed in the Austrian neoclassical style, it is characterized by its rectilinear symmetry, the simplicity of its form being compensated by a play of the dark colours of the frames and pillars against the light ochre of the walls. Marble sculptures embellished the square and illumination was provided by elegant street lamps. Though now overgrown, the grounds were neatly laid out gardens with ornamental ponds, a collection of exotic plants, a Japanese garden and a small zoo and included a tennis court and a space for horse-riding. The Quinta was an elite residential area, but it also housed several foreign embassies and artists like Teófilo Castilla established studios there. Its bucolic quiet and romantic atmosphere also made it a favourite spot for young lovers. Reflecting the general pattern of inner-city decline that followed the elites' abandonment of the old centre, the Quinta is now much deteriorated but efforts are now being made to preserve and revitalize the area.

Europeans constituted a significant presence in nineteenth-century Lima. Some were merchants and entrepreneurs seeking to take advantage of the new trading opportunities created by the opening up of Peru to international commerce. Others were immigrants attracted by the economic opportunities which Peru seemed to offer, particularly during the guano era. Among the Creole elites there was a consensus that such immigration should be encouraged, as in line with the assumptions of the time it was believed that national development was hindered by the fact the bulk of the country's population was made up of racially and culturally inferior Indians, blacks and people of mixed race and that an influx of Europeans would raise its cultural level and foster progress. In many quarters, too, it was felt necessary to shake off the negative influence of the Spanish colonial legacy, and immigration from more progressive European countries was seen as a means of revitalizing Creole society. Such was the view expressed by Manuel Atanasio Fuentes in 1876:

Immigration will give robustness to our anaemic nature, energy to our character, positivism to our calculations, new horizons to the efforts of each and every one and, if I might put it that way, fierceness to our race.

Yet in comparison with neighbouring countries like Argentina, Brazil, Chile and Uruguay, attempts to attract immigrants proved largely unsuccessful. In the period up to 1880 a mere 20,000 Europeans opted to settle in Peru and of these the vast majority were concentrated in the Lima-Callao area, the main reason being that the landowning regime prevailing in the interior—large estates employing a servile labour force—afforded little opportunity for small farmers. In 1876 foreigners in Lima numbered 15,368 out of a total population of 100,156, with the main European communities consisting of 2,949 Italians, 1,416 French, 724 Spaniards, 442 Germans and 417 Britons.

Nonetheless, Europeans exercised an influence that was disproportionate to their numbers.

The Italians formed by far the largest European community, and by 1863 there were 341 Italian businesses in the capital. Many went into the retail trade, running bars and general stores, but others became small farmers in areas close to Lima or set up factories producing textiles, leather goods, food products and drinks. Italian immigrants prospered to such an extent that in 1889 their business community pooled its capital to found what was to become Peru's largest commercial bank, the Italian Bank, later renamed the Banco de Crédito. Italians have also left their mark on Peru in many different ways. The naturalist Antonio Raimondi (1826-90), who taught courses at the University of San Marcos, published important books based on research carried out on travels around the country and he founded the Botanical Gardens adjoining the Faculty of Medicine on Avenida Grau. A few blocks away along Jirón Huanta a statue of him stands in the Plaza Italia. There is no such monument to Pedro D'Onofrio, who founded an ice-cream business at the start of the twentieth century, but his name lives on in the ubiquitous carts and tricycles which sell D'Onofrio ice-cream in the city's streets and parks.

Because of the prestige enjoyed by Europeans the influence of the immigrant communities brought about a change in Limeñans' lifestyles and eating habits. The custom of drinking tea was learned from the British, as were formal table manners and the use of cutlery. As we have seen, the production and consumption of beer took off after American entrepreneurs founded the Backus and Johnston Brewery in Rímac in 1890. Thanks to the Italians, pasta has become a staple food and numerous other European dishes have widened and varied the local diet. The Creole elites founded gentlemen's clubs like the Club de la Unión and the Club Nacional in imitation of the British community's Phoenix Club (1879). The Lima Cricket Club, founded in 1859, was likewise the model for local sports clubs and, indeed, the popularization of sport was due largely to British influence. Today many descendants of European immigrants are prominent figures in national society, as is indicated by the European surnames of major writers like the poets Emilio Adolfo Westphalen and Carlos Germán Belli and the novelist Alfredo Bryce.

The Palais Concert

The Jirón de la Unión's most fashionable café was the Palais Concert (no. 706), now a cultural centre. Opened in 1913, it became the emblem of the so-called *Belle Époque*, the period when Lima was flourishing and undergoing modernization on the French model. It had a confectionery and bar, two public rooms containing a hundred tables, magnificent chandeliers hanging from the ceiling, and walls covered with mirrors in *art nouveau* style. A female orchestra played Viennese waltzes and German *lieder*. Among its regulars was writer and journalist Abraham Valdelomar (1888-1919), who adopted the public persona of a dandy in the manner of Oscar Wilde and was known by his journalistic pen-name, El Conde de Lemos. One of his witticisms highlights the Palais' status as the city's most prestigious meeting-place, but it also points to the capital's small-town character and to the concentration of wealth, education and influence within a very narrow circle: "Peru is Lima; Lima is the Jirón de la Unión; the Jirón de la Unión is the Palais Concert; therefore Peru is the Palais Concert."

The Palais was also an indicator of how Lima society was beginning to change as the city took on a modern form. In addition to the European music then in vogue, the orchestra also played fashionable pieces by Peruvian composer Daniel Alomía Robles, famous for his arrangements of traditional Andean melodies adapted to urban tastes and western instruments, of which the best-known is "El cóndor pasa" (The Condor Passes). Popular music as such—and particularly Andean popular music—was still looked down upon as culturally inferior, of course, but this was nonetheless a sign that public taste was ready to accept what was deemed to be sophisticated national music.

Among those who frequented the Palais were people like Valdelomar, young men of humble provincial origins who had come to the capital to be educated and to make their way in the world and who, in their different ways, were pressing for a more open society. Valdelomar was the founder of *Colónida* (1916), a literary magazine which, though it lasted for only four issues, served as a rallying point for a group of young writers dedicated to bringing fresh blood to the country's literature. His dandyism, though in a sense yet another example of the aping of European fashion, was more than exhibitionist posturing. It was a way of challenging the closed social hierarchy of the so-called Aristocratic Republic, an assertion that the true aristocrats were not the affluent Creole bourgeoisie but talented people of whatever origin. His best works are two collections of short stories which manipulate a discourse of nobility to challenge the racial and cultural assumptions which validated the hegemony of the coastal elites. In the title-story of *El caballero Carmelo* (The Light-brown Knight, 1918), which evokes his childhood in the little fishing community of Pisco, the eponymous champion fighting cock is depicted as a paladin symbolizing the natural dignity and nobility of the humble folk of rural Peru. *Los hijos del sol* (Children of the Sun), published posthumously in 1921, reworks Inca legends to re-create the sumptuous magnificence of the pre-Columbian past and thereby questions prevailing prejudices about the backwardness of the Indian.

Valdelomar was only one of many provincials who came to Lima in search of education, and by 1919 students from the provincial middle classes had come to constitute a substantial majority of the University of San Marcos' intake. Several of these were to go on to make their mark on the life of the nation. Julio C. Tello (1880-1947) became the founding father of Peruvian archaeology, while Víctor Raúl Haya de la Torre (1894-1979) founded the reformist Alianza Popular Revolucionaria Americana (APRA), which in the 1930s became Peru's first mass political party. Peru's greatest poet, César Vallejo (1892-1938) followed the provincial's traditional route to self-improvement by moving from the small Andean village of Santiago de Chuco to Trujillo and from there to the capital in 1918. In Lima he published two volumes: *Los heraldos negros* (The Black Heralds,1919) and *Trilce* (1922). The latter was to revolutionize poetry in the Spanish language by means of a style based on defamiliarizing techniques, but at the time it was too innovative for Lima's conservative literary environment and received a lukewarm reception. In the same year Vallejo opted to leave Peru and settled in Paris, winning international recognition with his posthumously published *Poemas humanos* (Human Poems) and *España, aparta de mí este cáliz* (Spain, Take This Cup From Me).

A number of the poems of Vallejo's first two books convey the provincial's experience of the capital, expressing the loneliness and homesickness felt by the poet in the big city through the persona of a defenceless boy adrift in a frightening world. *Trilce* XIV summarizes the reaction of the recently arrived provincial, overawed and intimidated by the alien environment in which he now finds himself:

Here's my explanation.
This lacerates me with earliness.
That manner of going about on trapezes.
Those toughs as brutish as they're phoney.
That rubber which sticks the quicksilver to the inside.
Those buttocks seated upwards.
That can't be, been.
Absurd.
Madness.
But I've come from Trujillo to Lima.
But I'm earning a wage of five soles.

Another poem contrasts the green, fertile valleys of the northern highlands with the valley of Lima, arid and shrouded in grey mist. While the first landscape is identified with the love dispensed by his mother, the latter serves as an image of the unwelcoming environment of the city:

Oh valley without mother height, where everything sleeps a horrible half-tone, without cool rivers, without inlets of love.

Being provincials was not the only disadvantage the likes of Valdelomar and Vallejo had to contend with. The former bore slight but unmistakable signs of African ancestry, while the latter was a *cholo*, a *mestizo* with pronounced Indian features. Part of the colonial legacy was that Lima was a profoundly racist society and those who were visibly non-whites were looked down on as inferiors. In practice, the situation was somewhat more complex, as Ernst Middendorf noted in 1893. Since few Peruvians were wholly white, the category of white embraced people of mixed race who looked European and even those who did not were accepted as honorary whites if they had achieved social status:

In Peru whites include all those who, in the colour of their skin, the shape of their face and the texture of their hair, are preponderantly of European descent. But there are very few Peruvians of purely European origin, since in the course of time black and Indian blood has also infiltrated completely white families, however much their members might wish to resist accepting the existence of such a mix. In addition to these white Peruvians, there are a fair number of people whose skin can in no way lay claim to that colour, but who would be offended [...] if they were not considered to be white: people who because of their wealth, their political influence or their talent would never, out of courtesy, be ranked among the mestizos, even though they have more of the native than of the Spaniard.

Nonetheless, whiteness remained the yardstick, and if racial origins could be disregarded—at least publicly—in the case of those who had established themselves socially, no such exception was made for those who were struggling to make their way in the world. And mixed-race provincials often brought baggage with them in the form of an internalized sense of inferiority instilled in them by generations of social conditioning. The personas adopted by the two writers can be seen as a reflection of that situation, in that Vallejo's defenceless boy personifies the insecurity of the *cholo* while Valdelomar's aristocratic dandy is an over-the-top reaction to the experience of feeling looked down upon.

Neither writer nor any of their contemporaries speak directly of racism in their work, but their experience is re-enacted by Martín Villar, the protagonist of Miguel Gutiérrez's novel *La violencia del tiempo* (The Violence of Time, 1991). As a scholarship student at Lima's Catholic University in the 1960s, Martín is representative of the provincial under-classes who are beginning to break down traditional barriers by gaining access to higher education. But his patrician teachers and classmates treat him with undisguised contempt as an upstart who has forgotten his station and he himself is plagued by a sense of inferiority which makes him ashamed of his *cholo* features and his cheap provincial clothing:

Young Villar felt himself blush as he compared his suit of coarse cash-mere and unmistakable small-town tailoring with the elegant, sober outfits of genuine English cloth, cut and finished by genuine famous London tailors, and worn by spruce, athletic young men, fair-haired or at least white or with a slightly brownish complexion.

To come to terms with his complexes, Martín researches and writes a novel about the history of the Villars, a family of rural labourers. The text revolves obsessively around a skeleton in the family cupboard, which he discovers to have been the humiliating public beating administered to his great-grandfather by the local white landowner. Recalled again and again, that episode functions as a metaphor for the mortifying experience of social inferiority that is the heritage of lower-class *mestizos*.

The Barrio Chino: Asian Immigrants

Not all immigrants were European. While Lima has always looked westwards towards Europe for its cultural models, geographically it faces eastwards across the Pacific towards Asia and by 1875 Peru had recruited around 100,000 Chinese "coolies" for labour on coastal plantations, the guano islands and railroad construction. Though such immigration was opposed by those sectors of the elite who believed that the infusion of yet another non-western people would further debilitate the nation, it was a response to a labour shortage on the coast, particularly after the abolition of slavery in 1854. Initially the Chinese had a hard time of it. Fleeing poverty and famine in their own country, they found themselves living and working in appalling conditions in a state of virtual servitude; and when, at the end of their period of indenture, they made their way to Lima and other cities, they were frequently victims of racial prejudice, sometimes involving violence. They nonetheless established a presence in the capital, and Lima became home to the largest Chinese community in South America, while over the country as a whole the current Chinese-Peruvian population is estimated to be close on one million. The *barrio chino* (Chinatown), located near the Central Market and centred around Calle Capón and Jirón Parura, was already a flourishing community by the 1880s. One of the characters in Fernando de Trazegnies' *En el país de las colinas de arena* (In the Land of the Sand Dunes, 1995), a semi-fictional account of Chinese immigration, observes a scene of oriental animation:

> *Great was his astonishment when he arrived at Calle Capón and saw hundreds of Chinese, some with pigtails and walking with little hops, others already westernized and rushing in both directions, in front of crowded small shops piled high with products from the Far East and in which old men with slanted eyes, dressed in the traditional*

*manner and seated gravely behind their counters, attended to their
customers in Chinese. And alongside these small establishments dealing in food and cheap goods there were also some large business houses
which imported articles in silk, lacquer and marble as well as tea. It
was unbelievable that barely four or five blocks from the elegant
house of his master, located in an aristocratic European district, one
could feel oneself transported to the commercial zone of any city in the
Celestial Empire.*

Later, when news of a thriving Chinese community spread, big
Chinese merchant houses based in Hong Kong and San Francisco
established branches in Lima and Chinese businessmen came to try
their fortune in Peru. Though initially immigrants tended to gravitate
towards the *barrio chino*, the Chinese did not confine themselves to
their own quarter but established themselves in other districts as the city
expanded. Until recently a feature of every neighbourhood was "el
chino de la esquina", the corner shop run by Chinese. Another beloved
Limeñan institution is the *chifa*, the Chinese restaurant, several of
which are to be found in every neighbourhood, though the best are
generally reckoned to be located in the *barrio chino* itself. Many
Chinese integrated by marrying local women and their descendants are
to be found in virtually every walk of life. Among those who prospered
are the Wong brothers, who turned their father's corner shop into
Lima's biggest supermarket chain. One of the most interesting works of
fiction of recent times is Siu Kam Wen's *El tramo final* (The Last
Stretch, 1985), a collection of short stories portraying the Chinese
community from the inside.

Not all Asian immigrants were Chinese, for as the recruitment of
Chinese coolies became more difficult, the booming coastal sugar
plantations turned to Japan as a source of labour. Between 1899 and
1923 around 18,000 Japanese workers arrived in the country and on
completion of their contracts many of them invested their savings in
setting up on their own. Later, between 1924 and 1936, a second, more
numerous wave of immigrants came with the intention of establishing
their own businesses. Many became small farmers but others gravitated
towards the city. Curiously, one of the activities where the Japanese
distinguished themselves was hairdressing, and in 1924 Lima had no
fewer than 130 Japanese hairdressing establishments. Though the

Japanese have tended to be more inward-looking and reluctant to intermarry than the Chinese, they too have made their impact in many different areas of national life. Elected President in 1990, Alberto Fujimori dominated the political scene for a decade. The Museo Amano, the country's best collection of pre-Columbian textiles, is a foundation bequeathed by Japanese collector Yoshitaro Amano; one of the leading poets of the 1970s generation, José Watanabe, is the son of an immigrant Japanese farming family; and Tilsa Tsuchiya, one of Peru's major painters, had a Japanese father and a part-Chinese mother.

The Casona de San Marcos

To the east of the Plaza San Martín is the Parque Universitario (Av. Nicolás de Piérola 1222), a small park constructed in 1919 as part of the urban development of the early twentieth century. It is so called because it is located in front of the building which at that time was the cloisters of the University of San Marcos, America's oldest university. The Casona (large house) represents an intermediate phase in the University's history. Founded in 1551, San Marcos was initially run by the Dominican order and held its classes in the monastery of Santo

Domingo until 1576, when it moved into its own premises on the site currently occupied by the Congress building. In the late 1860s and early 1870s it transferred to the Casona, where it was based for close on a century. In the 1960s, as a result of the expansion of student numbers, it relocated to the Ciudad Universitaria, a modern campus in the suburbs in the direction of Callao. The Casona now functions as the University's cultural centre and is also used for ceremonial events.

Colonial San Marcos was one of the pillars of the established order, producing the educated elites who manned the colony's main institutions. Its most famous scholar, Pedro de Peralta Barnuevo (1664-1743), was twice rector of the University, Professor of Mathematics and Peru's Chief Cosmographer and Chief Engineer. The author of over sixty works, he was known in Europe for his scientific treatises on medicine and astronomy and for an almanac which he produced yearly, but he also authored *Lima fundada* (The Foundation of Lima, 1732), an epic poem on the Spanish conquest of Peru, and several plays, including an adaptation of Corneille's *Rodogune*. A man of vast erudition, Peralta kept abreast with scientific and literary currents in the world through correspondence with leading intellectuals in Europe and was a precursor of the Enlightenment thinking that was to take root in Peru later in the century. Yet he was very much a transitional figure, cultivating a literary style that was characteristically baroque in its predilection for extravagant conceits and a diction as far removed as possible from everyday language. A loyal colonial who proudly regarded Peru as the jewel in the Spanish crown, Peralta enjoyed the patronage of several viceroys and was regularly entrusted with responsibilities such as the organization the city's mourning for the death of King Luis I.

Among the paintings in the Casona's art gallery is a portrait of Peralta by Cristóbal de Aguilar, one of a trio of portrait painters who came to prominence in the first half of the eighteenth century—the others being Cristóbal Lozano and José Díaz—and whose work marks a significant evolution in Peruvian art. Hitherto painting had dealt almost exclusively with religious themes, and the rise of portraiture signalled a move towards a more secular society. Inevitably, many of these portraits were of viceroys, such as Lozano's painting of the Conde de Superunda, but others, such as that of Peralta, depict eminent members of the Creole elite, suggesting that this was a society with a growing sense of local civic pride. Peralta is seen standing in his study surrounded by the books he wrote and pointing to a globe of the world, a symbol both of the prodigious breadth of his learning and of the international reputation he enjoyed.

The Casona began life in 1605 as a Jesuit training college but was closed in 1767 when the Jesuits were expelled from Spain and its territories. As part of a policy of reforming education, which had been dominated by scholasticism, it was reopened as a college of higher education, the Convictorio de San Carlos, and a new curriculum was introduced with emphasis on practical subjects like mathematics, the natural sciences, physics, history and geography. San Marcos, too, began to adopt a new approach to learning in line with Enlightenment thought. Standing in the Parque Universitario is a statue of Hipólito Unánue (1755-1833), the University's Professor of Anatomy, who exerted a great influence on the development of medical studies and the creation of a scientific consciousness. A leading member of the Sociedad de Amantes del País, he published numerous articles on scientific subjects in the *Mercurio Peruano* and was instrumental in the establishment and organization of the country's first medical school, the Escuela de Medicina de San Fernando in 1811.

In the years leading up to independence San Carlos was to become a focus for criticism of the colonial regime and was closed down in 1817 by Viceroy Pezuela on the pretext of the deterioration of the building's fabric. A few decades earlier San Marcos had been made aware that the colonial authorities were not prepared to tolerate anything that smacked of subversion. In 1781 Law Professor José Baquíjano y Carrillo—whose portrait also features in the Casona's art gallery—delivered the customary eulogy to incoming Viceroy Agustín de Jáuregui. After a florid account of Jáuregui's service to Spain in various military capacities, he focused on his accomplishments as Captain General of Chile, where he had pursued a successful Indian policy marked by humanity and justice, and he then went on to praise his concept of public office, which was based on an understanding of the need to take account of the will of the people. The oration provoked no immediate reaction and was even printed and put into circulation. Subsequently, however, it was denounced as seditious, its praise of Jáuregui being interpreted as a veiled attack on imperial practice. The tract was proscribed and all available copies confiscated and Baquíjano himself was officially reprimanded and forced to make a grovelling apology.

A major turning-point in San Marcos' history was the university reform of 1919. Since its relocation in the Casona the University had gradually evolved with the times. In 1875 a Faculty of Political and Administrative Sciences was founded, which introduced courses in economics and commerce, and intellectuals of the so-called generation of 1900, heavily influenced by European positivism, propounded practical knowledge as the path to development. Yet it still remained very much the domain of the elites, as made clear by the fact that at different times two prominent members of the ruling Partido Civil held the position of Rector. By 1919, though, students from the provincial middle classes had come to constitute a substantial majority of San Marcos' intake and they successfully agitated for a reform of the institution's internal structure to allow student participation in its government and to make merit the prime criterion for teaching and administrative appointments. They also demanded a university more responsive to the needs of the population as a whole, and as a reaction to the changing character of San Marcos a private Catholic university, the Pontificia Universidad Católica del Perú, was established in 1917 as a more traditional and more select alternative. Thereafter the Católica came to be the preferred choice for the offspring of the country's elites, while, as access to university education widened, San Marcos took on an increasingly proletarian character and became a hotbed of left-wing political militancy. In Mario Vargas Llosa's *Conversación en La Catedral* (Conversation in The Cathedral, 1969), a novel set mainly in the late 1940s and early 1950s, the wealthy, upper-class Zavala family are dismayed when their rebel son Santiago rejects the accepted career path of studying at the Católica and opts instead to enrol at the state university, which in their eyes is "a nest of *cholos*" and "a nest of subversives".

These quotations point to two defining features of San Marcos' history since the 1919 reform. On the one hand, the University became increasingly politicized, and boycotts, strikes, public demonstrations and confrontations with the police became endemic. While this meant that student activists often played an important role in campaigning on social issues and in resisting dictatorship, it also had the negative effect of causing serious disruption to teaching. In Vargas Llosa's novel Santiago Zavala's father warns him that "in San Marcos you didn't study anything... they just played politics, it was a nest of Apristas and

Communists, all the grumblers in Peru gather together there." These words voice a concern shared by many people, since the activities of the militants disrupted the education of fellow students who simply wanted to study and obtain a qualification. One of the reasons for the subsequent appearance of an array of private universities is precisely that there was a market for institutions where education could be pursued in a non-politicized environment.

San Marcos also experienced a massive increase in student numbers as a result of widening access to education. Whereas in 1940 Peru had a mere 3,370 university students, by 1995 the number had risen to 372,908. And while students had traditionally tended to come from middle-class backgrounds, the majority of San Marcos' undergraduates are now working-class, many of them the children of migrants from the provinces. The growing demand for higher education led to a proliferation of new universities. Until 1955 Peru as a whole had only five universities, but the 1960s saw an expansion of the educational system and by 1968 the number of institutions of higher education had risen to thirty and by 1985 there were 46. In addition to the state University of San Marcos and the private Catholic University, Lima now has two major technological universities—the Universidad Nacional Agraria and the Universidad Nacional de Ingeniería—as well as an number of private universities such as the Universidad Cayetano Herredia, the Universidad del Pacífico, the Universidad de Lima, the Universidad Federico Villareal, the Universidad Ricardo Palma, the Universidad Inca Garcilaso de la Vega, and the Universidad San Martín de Porres. Unfortunately, the expansion of higher education has not been matched by an expansion of occupational opportunities and in modern-day Peru academic qualifications are no guarantee of employment. As a result, in recent years the country has suffered a brain drain as university-trained professionals have emigrated, mainly to the United States, to find the career opportunities unavailable to them at home.

Despite the growing number of universities, the most prestigious academically are still San Marcos and the Católica, which have adjoining campuses in the Ciudad Universitaria. The Católica, once elitist and conservative, has moved with the times and is now a progressive institution with a high reputation for teaching and research. San Marcos went through a bad spell in the 1980s and early 1990s when it was infiltrated by Shining Path activists and the government sent in the military to dislodge them. Since then it has reorganized and put its house in order, and teaching and research now take precedence over politics.

La Colmena and the Plaza San Martín

The plan for the modernization of Lima involved the construction of an avenue intersecting the city west to east, from the Plaza Dos de Mayo to present-day Avenida Abancay. Originally known as La Colmena after the development company responsible for the project, it was later renamed Avenida Nicolás de Piérola but is still usually referred to by the original name. It was constructed in three phases, the first of which was completed in 1907, the last in 1919. The first stretch was developed as high-class apartment buildings. Between it and the second stretch a new square, the Plaza San Martín, was constructed in 1921 to commemorate the Independence Centenary. Featuring a monument to the Liberator in the middle, it has an essentially classical layout and is given architectural coherence by the replication of arcades and façades on the north and south sides. The neocolonial style of most of the surrounding buildings was intended to give the square a distinctively Peruvian character.

Between the 1920s and the 1960s the area around the Plaza San Martín was the heart of Lima, having replaced the Plaza Mayor as the city centre. Close by to the east was the University. To the north and west were the shops, cafés, bars, restaurants and cinemas of the Jirón de la Unión and La Colmena. The arcades of the square itself were full of bars, cafés and night clubs, one of which is described as it was in the 1950s in Mario Vargas Llosa's novel *La tía Julia y el escribidor* (Aunt Julia and the Scriptwriter, 1977):

Javier had chosen the Negro-Negro to end the evening because it had a certain intellectual-bohemian atmosphere—on Thursdays they gave little shows, one-act plays, monologues, recitals, and it was a favourite gathering place for painters, musicians and writers—but besides that it was also the darkest boîte in Lima, a basement in the arcades of the Plaza San Martín that had twenty tables at most, with a décor we thought was 'existentialist'. It was a night spot that, the few times I had been there, gave me the illusion that I was in a cave in Saint-Germain-des-Prés.

Three of the square's buildings are of particular interest. Like most inner-city establishments, the neocolonial Hotel Bolívar is today struggling to survive, but in its day it was chic and exclusive. Built in 1924 to bring the city into line with other capitals by giving it a large luxury hotel, it had 200 sumptuously furnished rooms. Its public rooms were likewise luxuriously furnished and decorated, with chandeliers, alabaster lamps and Belgian carpets. A former *maître d'hôtel* of the London Ritz was recruited to run it and a Swiss chef appointed to take charge of the cuisine. It had a Palm Court where afternoon tea dances were held and a cabaret entertained diners in its famous restaurant, as Mario Vargas Llosa's novel describes:

I'd never been to the Bolívar Grill and it seemed to me the most chic and elegant place in the world, and the supper we had the most exquisite meal I'd ever tasted. An orchestra played boleros, paso dobles and blues, and the star of the show was a French girl, as white as snow, who caressed each syllable of her songs while seemingly masturbating the microphone with her hands.

International music stars like Pérez Prado were signed up to play at the Bolívar and it became famous for its *pisco sour*, a local aperitif consisting of pisco (a grape-based spirit) mixed with lemon juice, syrup, egg white and crushed ice and served with a splash of bitters. Over the years many world-famous foreign visitors have stayed at the Bolívar, including Robert Kennedy, Richard Nixon, Charles de Gaulle and Ava Gardner. It also became a fashionable social centre for Lima's elites and it was there that the most prestigious functions were held.

The Teatro Colón and Peruvian Cinema

One of the square's most elegant buildings, the Teatro Colón is a monument to the emergence of cinema as a new form of popular entertainment. Cinema caught on very early and from the end of the nineteenth century onwards silent films were shown, first in marquees and then in movie theatres, but the opening of the Colón in 1929 coincided with the advent of talkies and it was there that the first sound-film was shown. The Colón's days as a film theatre are past, but cinema remains one of Lima's favourite spectacles. Reflecting the country's level of development, most of the films shown are foreign, produced mainly in Hollywood but also in Europe and in other Latin American countries like Mexico. Yet though the Peruvian film industry cannot realistically hope to compete with the foreign giants, film-making has been going on in the country since the days of silent movies. In the period between 1927 and 1933 fourteen feature films were made and regular production continued until the 1940s. After that various factors combined to paralyse activity, but legislation introduced in the early 1970s to encourage film production led to a renaissance. Armando Robles Godoy anticipated the renaissance with *La muralla verde* (The Green Wall, 1970), which won recognition at a number of foreign festivals. Since then Peru has produced several fine films, the most notable being Federico García's *Tupac Amaru* (1984); *Gregorio* (1985), a collective production by the Grupo Chaski; and Alberto Durant's *Malabrigo* (1986) and *Alias "La Gringa"* (1991).

Peru's leading and most internationally successful director is undoubtedly Francisco Lombardi, whose best works are *La ciudad y los perros* (The City and the Dogs, 1985), an adaptation of Mario Vargas Llosa's novel of the same name, and *La boca del lobo* (The Lion's Den, 1988). Both films illustrate Lombardi's favourite strategy of developing situations of extreme violence in enclosed environments in order to bring out social conflicts and the depths to which human beings are capable of descending. The first is set in a military college where a young cadet is murdered and another tries to bring his killer to justice, only to be blackmailed into capitulating to a cover-up. The second is set in an Andean village where a small army detachment has been posted to counter the incursions of Shining Path guerrillas. Culturally estranged from the villagers they are supposed to be protecting and increasingly unnerved by the activities of the unseen guerrillas, they progressively lose their human decency and take out their anguish and frustration on the locals. *La boca del lobo* is, in the view of most critics, Peru's most accomplished film.

The Club Nacional: Meeting-place of the Elite

Adjacent to the Teatro Colón is another handsome building, the Club Nacional. In the mid-nineteenth century Lima's elites began to form gentlemen's clubs on the English model. Founded in 1855, the first and most important of these was the Club Nacional, which met in different places before moving to its present premises in the 1920s. A decade later the Club de la Unión was founded in the Plaza Mayor, where it shares the same block as the Palacio Municipal. Of the two the Club Nacional was always the more select and exclusive. Upper-class intellectual Víctor Andrés Belaúnde recalled that in the early decades of the twentieth century membership of the Club was a prerequisite for anyone who was anyone in Lima:

> *In that period there were no evening spectacles that could compete with the Club Nacional, which provided its halls and rooms for animated talks on social, literary and even political themes. Many members regarded it as an elegant custom to take tea in the Club in order to discuss the news of the day with friends [...] I rated the Club Nacional the foremost and most animated meeting-place in Lima. A good Limeñan had to follow family tradition and belong to the Club Nacional from an early age.*

And it was said that the most important political decisions were taken not in the Presidential Palace or in Congress but within the walls of the Club Nacional.

Until 1919 the club was the domain of the *civilistas*, the inner circle of the Partido Civil, Peru's first modern political party, which had come into being in the late 1860s as a focus for all those opposed to military rule but which came to represent the interests of the coastal elites. The *civilistas* first gained power in 1872 when Manuel Pardo was elected to the presidency and from 1899 they ran the country for a twenty-year period. That era came to be known as the Aristocratic Republic, as the *civilistas* were regarded as the country's aristocracy; and so they were in the sense that they constituted a small unrepresentative elite distinguished not just by wealth but by culture and education. Democracy was limited, since the electoral law of 1895 had excluded illiterates, and as a result *civilista* governments were voted in by a small minority of literate male electors who made up only about four per cent of the total population. Elite families were bound together by ties of marriage and their children rubbed shoulders at school and university. José Pardo emulated his father Manuel by becoming president in 1904 and again in 1914, leading Manuel González Prada to denounce the nepotism of Peruvian politics, where a group of related families constituted a kind of mafia:

A José Pardo y Barreda in the Presidency, an Enrique de la Riva Agüero as Head of Cabinet, a Felipe de Osma y Pardo in the Supreme Court, a Pedro de Osma y Pardo as City Mayor, a José Antonio de Lavalle y Pardo as Public Prosecutor, portend a Felipe Pardo y Barreda in the Legation in the United States, a Juan Pardo y Barreda in Congress and all the other Pardos, Pardo y Lavalle, Pardo y Osma and Pardo y de la Riva Agüero wherever they can be fitted in.

Half a century later Sebastián Salazar Bondy complained in the essay *Lima la horrible* (Lima the Horrible, 1964) how it was a measure of Peru's failure to modernize and democratize itself that the capital was still home to the same dominant elites who ruled in colonial times, an oligarchy of Hispanic families whose wealth derived initially from ownership of land but who subsequently branched into banking, commerce and industry and effectively controlled the social, political and economic life of the nation. Seeing themselves as a hereditary aristocracy, those old ruling families were convinced of their divine right to lord it over the masses and resolutely resisted all forms of social change:

There they are, rich and prosperous, just as Cieza de León saw them three centuries ago, gentlemen and ladies of the Great Families living in the lap of luxury [...], with virtually the same old ideas of the last century or the one before, terrified by words like revolution, agrarian reform, trade unionism etc., but entirely convinced that, apart from some superficial changes, the world, their world, will never end.

In fact, few of the oligarchy could trace their origins back to colonial times and in one of his essays González Prada mocked the newspapers' habit of referring to Lima's high society as if it were a hereditary aristocracy, claiming that they were merely a gang of opportunists who had enriched themselves during the guano era.

Here the only dividing line is that drawn by money and the only nobility we have is the gang formed by the descendants of the profiteers enriched by the Consolidation, guano and nitrates. [...] On their coat of arms the profiteer nobility should display a hand thrust into a bag.

Though some descendants of old colonial families figured in their ranks, the *civilistas* were actually a new elite which had emerged in the 1850s and which was formed by those who had profited from the guano boom and the accompanying expansion of the state, subsequently going on to build on their fortunes by investing in economic activities like sugar, cotton, mining, banking, insurance, real estate and manufacturing. At the core of this elite was a small group of prominent families allied by marriage, but it continually renovated itself by incorporating prosperous European immigrants and successful local entrepreneurs.

For sixty-odd years the Club Nacional was the meeting-place of the most powerful and influential men in the country. The oligarchy's monopoly of public affairs was eroded when President Augusto B. Leguía (1919-30) eliminated the Partido Civil as a political force and staffed an expanded bureaucracy with members of the rising middle classes. Even so, they retained their economic power and from 1930 until the 1960s regained effective control of the state, on some occasions by supporting conservative military rulers (Sánchez Cerro, Benavides, Odría) and on others by getting one of their own (Manuel Prado, 1939-45 and 1956-62) elected to the presidency. Throughout that period, though, the oligarchy came under increasing challenge, and eventually the pressure for socio-political change became so strong that in 1968 the military, to forestall the threat of Marxist revolution, intervened and implemented reforms which effectively broke their hold on the country. That is not to say that members of Peru's old elites have ceased to have influence, but they are no longer a dominant oligarchy, and though the Club Nacional continues to be a prestigious gentlemen's club, it is no longer a place where political decisions are made.

Turn-of-the-Century Writers

The era spanning the Aristocratic Republic and the years leading up to it is illuminated in different ways by the work of four major writers of the period. José Santos Chocano (1875-1934), who spent most of the period abroad, became a celebrity throughout the Spanish-speaking world with works like *Alma América* (Soul of America, 1906) and *¡Fiat Lux!* (1908) and on his return to Lima in 1922 he was ceremonially crowned as the country's national poet by President Leguía. Chocano saw himself as the voice of Spanish America, affirming its pride in itself in face of the encroachment of the Anglo-Saxon North. The vision of America presented in his poetry is, above all, one of nobility and grandeur. Poems like "Ciudad colonial" (Colonial City) recall the graceful elegance of Lima's days of glory as the viceregal capital of South America, and others, such as "La tierra del Sol" (Land of the Sun), evoke the sumptuous splendour and majesty of the Inca empire. More commonly he adopts an epic tone to re-create scenes from the Conquest, celebrating the courage and exploits of the conquistadors, as in "Los caballos de los conquistadores" (The Horses of the Conquistadors), or recounting the equally heroic deeds of famous indigenous warriors. A similar sense of the noble and grandiose marks compositions describing the awesome immensity of the American landscape and the magnificent creatures that inhabit it. Thus, perched above the world in the solitary splendour of a snow-capped Andean peak, the majestic bird of "El sueño del cóndor" (The Condor's Dream) embodies his grandiose conception of his continent. Underlying this repeated emphasis on nobility and grandeur is an elitist view of the nation, which becomes particularly evident in "Blasón" (Escutcheon), where the poet boasts of his descent from two equally noble races, the Incas who created a mighty empire and the Spaniards who achieved the epic feat of conquering it:

When I feel myself Inca, I render homage
to the Sun and am given the sceptre of his royal power;
when I feel myself Spanish and sing of colonial times,
my verses are like crystal trumpets.

My rich imagination comes from old Moorish stock:
the Andes are of silver, but the lion is of gold;
and I fuse the two races in myself with epic din.

My blood is Spanish and Incaic its pulsation,
and were I not a poet, I might have been
a white adventurer or an Indian emperor.

By claiming descent from noble ancestors, Chocano identifies himself with the ruling classes and his celebration of miscegenation is ultimately a celebration of Peru's new elites, who had long since ceased to be mainly white and were made up primarily of people who were ethnically of mixed race but culturally westernized. Hence, while Peru's Indian heritage is appropriated as a prestigious emblem of national identity, it is relegated to a vanished past and the unassimilated indigenous masses are effectively written out of the poem.

By contrast, Clorinda Matto de Turner championed the cause of the Indian masses, denouncing their oppression and exploitation in *Aves sin nido* (Birds without a Nest, 1889), the most famous novel of the period. Set in a fictional Andean community, the novel depicts the systematic extortion and abuse to which the Indian peasantry are subjected at the hands of the local notables headed by the governor and the parish priest. In their troubles the hard-pressed Yupanqui family turn for help to Fernando and Lucía Marín, a cultured and humanitarian couple from Lima, who embody the liberal, progressive spirit of a modernizing elite committed to the country's development (these attributes are indicated by the fact that Fernando is a working capitalist, the managing director of a mine in which he is the major shareholder). Clearly implied by the couple's protection of the Yupanqui family is that modernization opens up for the Indian masses the prospect of a life of dignity in a humane and liberal society. The sequel novel *Herencia* (Heredity, 1895) recounts the story of Margarita Yupanqui, whom the couple adopt and who moves with them to Lima, where she fits into society as if to the manner born. The novel thus tells us that, just as she is rescued from poverty and abuse by being adopted into the Marín family, so too the redemption of her race will be brought about by its assimilation into the national family, the underlying assumption being that the future of the Indian masses lies in their becoming westernized and thereby ceasing to be Indians. In that regard it reflects the thinking of the coastal elites, who advocated the integration of the indigenous masses into the mainstream of national life, since they saw the pre-capitalist rural economy presided over by the conservative Andean landowning oligarchy as an impediment to the country's progress and recognized that a free work-force was an essential prerequisite for industrial development. In practice, though, the coastal oligarchy found themselves in a contradictory position, since to maintain control of the state they were obliged to cultivate the support of the regional elites, the price of which was to give them a free hand to rule as they pleased in their own localities.

The leading dissident of the period was Manuel González Prada (1844-1918). In the aftermath of the humiliating defeat by Chile he lambasted the nation's leaders and institutions in a series of speeches and essays which were reprinted as *Páginas libres* (Free Pages, 1894). Peru had lost the war, he argued, not just because of the corruption and incompetence of its leaders but because its armies were made up of Indian conscripts dragooned into fighting for a country in which they had no stake. Peru was a sick organism and would never be made healthy until the oligarchy, the Church, the military and all the other institutions of the past were destroyed, until Lima's stranglehold on the nation was broken, and until the *mestizo* proletariat and the Indian peasantry were incorporated into the nation as equal citizens. His later thinking, articulated in *Horas de lucha* (Times of Struggle, 1908), evolved in the direction of anarchism and, indicting capitalist society as based ultimately on force, on the latent aggression of the haves against the have-nots, he concluded that resort to force was justified in order to overthrow it. González Prada was an iconoclast rather than the creator of a coherent political ideology, but his diagnosis of Peru's ills was to be the starting-point for twentieth-century radicalism.

A radical of a different kind was poet José María Eguren (1874-1942), who lived totally committed to his art and in the 1910s and 1920s created a distinctive body of verse in the Symbolist manner, employing a poetic language which, though apparently simple, is rich in suggestion and dense in meaning. His poetics are defined in "Peregrín cazador de figures" (Peregrine the Hunter of Images), where he presents himself in the guise of Peregrín, who, from a lonely belvedere, peers into the night and explores a dark, mysterious landscape, representative of the world of the imagination, whose secrets he seeks to apprehend intuitively and to capture in symbolic figures:

In fantasy's belvedere,
amid the sparkle of perfume
tremulous with harmony;
in the flame-consuming night;
while the unfledged duckling sleeps,
the Orphic insects swamp one another
and glow-worms smoke;
when the sylphs sport stripes and braid
and moths of cork flit through the air
or the grizzled vampires lisp
or the resolute hunchbacks patrol;
through the night of nuances,
dead eyes and long noses;
in the distant belvedere,
across the plains;
with eyes of diamond
Peregrine the hunter of images
gazes from the dark heights.

Eguren was the first of a remarkable number of major poets which Peru produced in the course of the twentieth century, making its poetry one of the richest in Latin America.

The *Canción Criolla*

In the late nineteenth and early twentieth centuries, as Lima became a modern city and the elites moved to elegant new housing in the outskirts, the majority of lower-class Limeñans lived in overcrowded slum conditions in areas around the old city centre. In some cases several families occupied a single building subdivided into apartments with shared communal facilities. Another typical form of local housing, dating back to colonial times, was the *callejón*, a row of small, badly lit and poorly ventilated one- or two-roomed houses leading off from a narrow uncovered alleyway and housing between 50 and 200 people, all sharing a single water-stand. Other members of the working class had moved to new industrial zones like La Victoria and Vitarte located beyond the old city limits, where they lived in poor-quality factory housing that was little improvement on the slums of the centre. From those lower-class districts emerged a form of popular music known as the *canción criolla* and in those districts there are still a number of social clubs-cum-*peñas* devoted to keeping that tradition alive: Centro Musical Pedro A. Bocanegra (Jirón Chancay 575); Centro Musical Unión (Jirón Tayacaja 641); La Valentina (Cuadra 9, Avenida Iquitos, La Victoria).

After Independence the term "Creole" evolved and came to designate not just the descendants of the Spanish settlers but the people and culture of coastal Peru (as opposed to the Andean region) and of Lima in particular. In contrast to the high culture of the elites, that culture was popular in character, a hybrid that had grown out of the intermingling of Hispanic and Afro-Peruvian traditions. The *canción criolla* is essentially dance music, but it came to be called song because it was accompanied by lyrics popularized through radio and records. It comprises various genres, but the one which came to be virtually synonymous with it was the *vals* (sometimes called *valse*). As the name suggests, the *vals* was a popular adaptation of the Viennese waltz, which was fashionable among Lima's upper classes at the turn of the century. It appropriated the rhythm of the waltz, adapted it to local instruments and styles and put lyrics to it. It was, in essence, a creolization of European music.

The *canción criolla* enjoyed its heyday from the mid-1930s to the mid-1970s, reaching large audiences through shows in the city's theatres, nightclubs and *peñas*, through radio and records and, later, through television and cassettes. Star performers such as singers Jesús Vásquez and Lucha Reyes, the group "Los Morochucos", guitarist Oscar Avilés and singer-songwriter Chabuca Granda were feted as national celebrities. At the level of the state it received official recognition when the government inaugurated an annual Day of the *Canción Criolla* in 1944, as groups were invited to play at the presidential palace and the country's highest honours were conferred on top artists. The *canción criolla* came to be seen as an expression of national identity both by the public and by officialdom, and when stars went on international tours they were regarded as ambassadors for Peru. It is an indication of the extent to which the *canción criolla* became associated with Peruvianness that as late as the 1985 elections, when Alan García sought to shed APRA's sectarian image and to re-brand it as the party of all Peruvians, he adopted the nationally loved *vals* 'Mi Perú' (My Peru) as his campaign song in place of the traditional Aprista *Marseillaise.*

The *canción criolla* grew out of festivities in lower-class neighbourhoods and was composed and performed by musicians who were usually workmen or artisans without formal training. Lyrics and tunes circulated by oral transmission, though specialized journals known as *cancioneros* later appeared which published them in printed form. Songwriters did not bother to register authorship of their work since at that time it had no commercial outlet, and many songs of the period which remain classics to this day are of unknown authorship. Significantly, the first artist to adopt a more entrepreneurial approach was not a member of the lower orders but a middle-class *aficionado* of popular music. Alejandro Ayarza, known as "Karamanduka", not only copyrighted his songs but formed a group called "La Palizada", which performed at public functions. In 1912 Ayarza staged a musical show entitled "Música Peruana" and from then on the *canción criolla* no longer operated merely on an amateur basis but was performed by semi-professional groups for public entertainment in the city's theatres and public places.

The 1920s saw a renovation of the *canción criolla* as the so-called Old Guard was replaced by a new generation who adapted it to the more cosmopolitan tastes of the period. Felipe Pinglo (1899-1936), in particular, widened its appeal by transforming it into a minor art form. Pinglo had been born and brought up in the cultural traditions of

Lima's popular neighbourhoods and he always remained very much part of that scene, regularly composing for and performing at local *fiestas*. Pinglo authored many of the great classics of the Creole canon but, though like other artists of the period he registered authorship of his songs and had his music performed at public concerts, he never made a living from his art and instead remained a semi-professional all his life, working as a clerk during the day. He is remembered by an ornate headstone in Lima's Cementerio General.

The *canción criolla*'s big breakthrough came in the mid-1930s with the growing influence of broadcast radio, when stations began to feature it on their programmes and it caught on with the listening public. From then on, its history is closely linked to the development of an entertainment industry. Songwriters and performers became professionals earning a living from their work and not only were they now reaching a mass audience at home, but top names exported their work abroad through record sales and concert tours. Yet despite its commercialization, the *canción criolla* never became mass culture in the manner of western pop. It was not subject to the rapid vicissitudes of fashion characteristic of the western music scene and classics authored by the Old Guard and by Pinglo and his generation remained perennial favourites. Not all the new songwriters were professionals, as the tradition of the lower-class amateur persisted, and one of the great hits of the 1940s, "Alma, corazón y vida" (Soul, heart and life), was written by Adrián Flores Alván, a building worker who had no interest in turning professional. Many of the top singers such as Lucha Reyes and Jesús Vásquez came from humble backgrounds, and in their professional careers they were merely carrying on the cultural tradition in which they had been brought up. At the same time, the tradition of partying remained very much alive among the lower classes, and in popular neighbourhoods the *canción criolla* continued to be played, sung and danced to in the time-honoured manner.

The roots of the *canción criolla* lie in the *jarana*, a boisterous party involving eating, drinking, singing and dancing to the accompaniment of guitars and the *cajón*, a wooden box improvising as a drum. Such an event was an escape from the dreary humdrum of working-class life. The *vals* might seem out of place in this atmosphere, since it is typically a maudlin lament bewailing the life-devastating suffering occasioned by love unrequited, frustrated or betrayed, a classic example being "Hermelinda":

> *Listen, my beloved, to the voice of my song*
> *which springs from my lyre like a desolate strain.*
> *In the evil of your absence, fearing a thousand misfortunes,*
> *my soul is sick and my heart wounded.*
> *For me the birds no longer sing their love*
> *nor does the morning dawn emit its perfume*
> *nor the timid stream, fleeing among the flowers,*
> *reflect your fleeting face in its mirror.*

Yet in the context of the *jarana* the *vals* was far from being as tragic as it sounded. All those involved knew that they were hamming it up, wallowing in self-pity while enjoying a convivial evening. The *vals* functioned as catharsis, as a means of exorcising sorrows while having a good time.

Nonetheless, the *vals* expressed genuinely felt emotions. Although its repertoire consists mainly of love songs, the lyrics were a vehicle whereby the lower classes verbalized their experience of life. In many cases, songwriters thought of themselves as poets. The singer frequently presents himself as a troubadour and, as "Hermelinda" demonstrates, composers sought to give their songs an air of refinement by shunning vulgar everyday speech and employing a flowery language modelled on the fashionable poetry of the period. One of the charms of the *vals*, in truth, is that it often combines the ridiculously pretentious with flashes of genuine poetry.

In general terms, its prevailing tone of anguished despair would seem to be a response, not just to the love situation evoked, but to the hard conditions of working-class life. The *vals* perpetuates traditional gender relations in that a male voice addresses a silent woman, but he is never master of the situation, since she either rejects him, toys with him, abandons him or betrays him. Typically the male is beset by lack of self-belief, by doubts as to his ability to succeed, as in "Hermelinda":

> *To calm the doubt that grows agonizingly*
> *think of me, Hermelinda, think of me.*

The lyrics usually convey a spirit of defeatism and fatalism as the man passively resigns himself and acknowledges his impotence by frequent allusions to the all-powerful influence of destiny in human life. The *vals* suggests, by extension, that Lima's lower classes had little faith in their ability to control their lives or to improve their condition and that their response was to retreat into a fatalistic acceptance of their lot. Some of Pinglo's most popular songs highlight the unfairness of life and invite us to empathize with the suffering of the poor. His greatest hit, "El plebeyo" (The Plebeian), questions social inequalities and class barriers by evoking the anguish of a man of the people frustrated in love because his beloved is an unattainable social superior. Yet the treatment of social injustice is entirely sentimental and devoid of political consciousness, reflecting the fact that, though the 1910s saw the beginning of organized labour militancy, the bulk of Lima's working classes had still not become politicized because they were employed mainly in small-scale enterprises and isolated from one another.

Perhaps the most significant development from the 1930s onwards was the adoption of the *canción criolla* by Lima's middle classes, who found in it an expression of their sense of themselves as Peruvians. That was true not just of the less educated sectors of society but even of writers and intellectuals. In the 1930s, for example, the writer César Miró, then living in Paris, opted to express his homesickness for Peru through the medium of the *vals*, composing in the process one of the canonical works of the genre, "Todos vuelven" (Everyone returns). So pervasive was the popularity of the *canción criolla* that though educated Limeñans often ridiculed it as mawkishly sentimental and comically pretentious, they usually ended up singing it when they got together socially. An example of that ambivalence is to be found in the work of Blanca Varela, one of the leading poets of the 1950s generation. As made clear by the title of the collection *Valses y otras falsas confesiones* (Waltzes and Other False Confessions, 1972), she regarded the *vals* as shallow posturing. Yet the book's opening poem, written on her return to Lima after a long period of residence in the United States, is entitled "Valses" and is interspersed with lines and phrases from well-known songs, expressing her love-hate relationship with her native city in a manner that echoes the *vals*. The nucleus of the poem consists of a sequence of songs in which, in the time-honoured tradition of the *vals*, the personified city is the object of sentimental declarations of affection or maudlin recrimination, the two strands coming together in the concluding lines:

> *I don't know if I love you or hate you*
> *for I've come back*
> *only to name you from within*
> *from this sea without waves*
> *to call you mother without tears*
> *shameless*
> *loved at a distance*
> *remorse and caresses*
> *leprous toothless*
> *mine*

Here the poet's status as a child of Lima, shaped by its cultural environment, manifests itself in the fact that she cannot help herself from indulging in the Creole sentimentality which the *vals* epitomizes.

Though the *canción criolla*'s repertoire consists predominantly of love songs, other themes emerged from the 1950s onwards. The line of social criticism initiated by Pinglo was carried on by Chabuca Granda, the top songwriter of the period. Her "Bello durmiente" (Sleeping Beauty), born of her dismay at the emergence of yet another representative of the oligarchy as president in the 1956 elections, depicts Peru as a handsome sleeping prince whom she longs to bring awake with a kiss, while her "María Sueños" (Maria the Dreamer) poignantly evokes the underdevelopment in which the Peruvian people continue to live. Likewise, Alicia Maguiña's "Indio" (Indian) evokes the degradation of the country's once-great indigenous people, expresses solidarity with their suffering and consoles them and herself with the prophecy that one day they will regain their human dignity.

The history of the *canción criolla* is also linked to the increasingly massive process of migration from the provinces to the capital. The arrival in Lima of singers and composers from the northern coastal provinces enriched and renewed the *vals*, since they brought to it a jaunty playfulness which contrasted strongly with the traditional mournfulness of the Lima variety. The northern style was incorporated into the *canción criolla*'s repertoire because Limeñans could identify with it as a variant of coastal culture. In contrast, though some attempts were made to introduce an Andean flavour, the *canción criolla* was largely impervious to Andean influence. The one major exception was Luis Abanto Morales. Abanto became a big star with a distinctive style marked by the use of Andean instruments and a tone of sadness typical of Andean music, and in *valses* like "Cholo soy y no me compadezcan" (I'm a *cholo* and don't feel sorry for me) he gives expression to the experience and perspective of the Andean migrants.

Another growing trend was the nostalgic evocation of the old Lima which was fast disappearing. The classic example is Chabuca Granda's "La flor de la canela", which evokes the old bridge over the Rímac leading to the Alameda de los Descalzos as the heart of Creole Lima. Significantly, "La flor de la canela" was the most popular *vals* of all time, for it expresses Limeñans' yearning to cling to their sense of identity as their city was changing around them as a result of modernization and migration from the countryside.

The *canción criolla* flourished in an era when Lima was relatively isolated from the outside world and had a more or less cohesive Creole identity. From the 1960s onwards, as new modes of communication expanded horizons and as culture became increasingly international, Lima's middle-class youth turned to western pop and to Latin American tropical music like *salsa*. At the same time, as Andean migrants moved into the capital and Creoles found themselves outnumbered in what had been their city, the *canción criolla* became the music of a minority, overtaken in popularity by the Andean music of the migrants and the *chicha* of their offspring. It still has its enthusiasts, but it is a type of music that is past its sell-by date and is now a minority interest. More generally, there is a flourishing Creole musical tradition that continues to renovate itself but, given the changes that Lima has undergone, it can never dominate the musical scene as the *canción criolla* did in its heyday.

The Parque de la Exposición
During the guano era the Creole elites' commitment to the idea of modernization manifested itself, above all, in the Great Exhibition held

in 1872 on the model of that staged in London in 1851, though on a much more modest scale. The aim was both to show the world how much Peru had advanced and to attract foreign investors. Among the features of the Exhibition were a display of modern machinery, a Chinese pavilion, a botanic garden and a collection of pre-Columbian antiquities. As a site for the Exhibition a park—the Parque de la Exposición—was landscaped in what was then the city's outskirts, in the area which today flanks the Paseo Colón. It consisted of a complex of gardens adorned with arbours, fountains and statues and included a zoo and an artificial lake with a Japanese bridge leading to an island in the middle.

In its heyday the Parque—or more exactly the Parques, since after the area was divided by the construction of the Paseo Colón the smaller part closer to the city became known as the Parque Neptuno—occupied an area of about fifty acres and in the decades following the Exhibition it was the capital's most popular recreation spot. People of all social classes went there to stroll around the gardens, cycle, row on the lake, visit the zoo, practise sports, listen to concerts, watch air balloons, acrobatics and theatrical performances; and the restaurant at the zoo became one of the city's favourite eating places. While the official ritual of Independence Day continued to take place in the area around the Plaza Mayor, the Parque became the site where celebrations were held. These included displays of gymnastics, shooting competitions, concerts by military bands and, as the centre-piece, a military parade.

The Parque de la Exposición represents important developments with regard to the city's social life. Firstly, it was part of a policy of channelling public diversions away from streets and squares into a dedicated space and of turning the Plaza Mayor into a site reserved for official ceremonial. Secondly, within that dedicated space organized activities replaced public diversions which traditionally had been largely unregulated and often chaotic. In short, for the Creole elites modernization involved not only building modern amenities but fostering what were perceived as more civilized forms of social behaviour.

As a result of urban development, today's Parque is much diminished in size, but it remains a pleasant oasis of green amidst the city bustle. In recent years it has been renovated, while some features of the Exhibition survive, such as the Moorish and Byzantine pavilions and the fountain of Neptune. It also features some later additions. The Centro de Estudios Histórico-Militares (Centre for the Study of Military History) was originally the Peruvian pavilion at the 1900 Paris Exhibition and was subsequently dismantled and reconstructed on its present site. The Chinese Monumental Fountain and the Museo de Arte Italiano were both donated to the city in 1921 to commemorate the Independence centenary. The latter came with a collection of 200 paintings and sculptures by contemporary Italian artists, but the museum is used mainly for temporary exhibitions and has only a few Italian works on display. Still the centre-piece of the Parque is the Exhibition's main pavilion, the Palacio de la Exposición, which, in keeping with architectural practice of the period, combines an iron framework with a stately classical façade. The Palacio now functions as the Museo de Arte de Lima, housing an important collection of Peruvian paintings from the viceregal and Republican periods as well as a collection of pre-Hispanic ceramics and textiles. Information on the museum and a sample of its holdings can be accessed on its website (www.museoarte.perucultural.org.pe).

The Estadio Nacional

On the Paseo de la República, just beyond the Parque de la Exposición, stands Peru's national football stadium, opened in the 1920s and rebuilt in the 1950s. The stadium is yet another sign of how lifestyles changed as the city became modernized. The late nineteenth and early twentieth centuries saw the growing popularity of sport, a trend encouraged by the country's elites as a means of fostering the health and well-being of the population. Like most innovations of the time, this development was largely the result of European influence. By 1865 British residents had formed the Lima Cricket and Lawn Tennis Club, which later became the Lima Cricket and Football Club as football gained popularity in Britain. In time Peruvian members were admitted, and in 1892 a football match was played in public between teams representing the two countries. Emulation of European customs later led members of the Lima elite to found their own club, the Club Unión Cricket, where tennis, cricket and later football were played. As early as 1875 the Club de Regatas had been founded in Chorrillos, where the well-to-do practised water sports like rowing and swimming, and to this day its installations remain a feature of the Lima coastline. Such clubs were highly exclusive, membership of the elites being a prerequisite for admission, and clubs like the Regatas are still an enclave of Lima's privileged few.

Football, on the other hand, was appropriated by the masses and became the working-class sport *par excellence*. Football provided a cheap form of recreation, since it could be played on waste ground with an improvised ball, and it had the further attraction of being a team game with a strong social dimension. By 1912 around twenty clubs had sprung up. Some of these were sponsored by employers as a means of promoting good labour relations and encouraging workers' loyalty to the company. Others appeared spontaneously at neighbourhood level, founded by the players themselves and kept going by their subscriptions, as was the case of Alianza Lima, which originated in one of city-centre neighbourhoods and later moved to the new industrial district of La Victoria. Such clubs became social institutions enabling young men to bond on and off the field, and they also became a focus for a sense of local community, since each time the team played it was felt to be representing the neighbourhood. To this day football remains the sport of the people at a grassroots level, where it is played by thousands of young men in matches between scratch teams on waste ground or in inter-district championships contested by amateur neighbourhood teams.

The institutionalization of football came with the establishment of the Peruvian Football Federation in 1922 and the opening of the Estadio Nacional, whose original stand was donated by the British colony on the occasion of the Centenary of Independence. The capital's football fans have always given their allegiance to one or other of the city's two arch-rivals, Alianza Lima and Universitario de Deportes, while Rímac and Callao have their own local teams, Sporting Cristal and Sport Boys respectively. Traditionally, Alianza, composed mainly of players from the largely black, working-class neighbourhood of La Victoria, was perceived as "the people's champion" and enjoyed huge support among the lower echelons of society, while Universitario, which was founded by university students, was seen as representative of the Creole middle and upper classes. Over the years that distinction has become ancient history but the rivalry between the teams remains as strong as ever.

In a society where they were disadvantaged, football was a sphere where it was possible for Afro-Peruvians to triumph. Blacks were thought to bring a special flair to the game, and many of country's legendary stars, such as Alejandro Villanueva and José María Lavalle, were coloured. Even so, they were often treated as second-class citizens. In 1929, when the Federation selected a national team to compete in the South American Championship in Argentina, it relegated blacks to the role of reserves and picked only "whites" to avoid giving a negative image of the country abroad. The structure of Peruvian football, in general, mirrored socio-economic hierarchies. Until the 1960s the championship was exclusively Lima-based, and presidents of the Federation were drawn from the country's elites. Since then football has come to reflect—and has contributed to—the process of social change taking place in the country. Nowadays all teams are racially mixed, and even Universitario, traditionally the club of the Creole middle classes, now attracts supporters from among the ranks of Andean migrants. Football offers the image of an egalitarian and multiracial society in a country still divided by prejudice and inequality. It has also helped foster a sense of national identity, and large radio and television audiences followed the national team's fortunes in the final stages of the World Cup competition in 1970, 1978 and 1982.

Paseo Colón

In 1870 President José Balta had the city wall demolished, an act both functional and symbolic, since it signalled that psychologically as well as physically Lima had broken free of the stifling restrictions of the past and was now ready to grow and develop. In practice, the planned development did not take place until several decades later, since it was hindered first by economic crisis and then by the War of the Pacific. Yet, though it was carried out in a piecemeal fashion, a grand design lay behind the development plan, involving the creation of a city of grand boulevards flowing into squares on the model of Haussmann's design for nineteenth-century Paris. As we have seen, one element in the design was La Colmena, an avenue intersecting the city with a square, the Plaza San Martín, in the middle. Another was a series of avenues forming a ring road along the route of the old city walls. The first stretches, corresponding to present-day Avenida Alfonso Ugarte and Avenida Grau, were completed under Balta, but were left unlinked because of reluctance to drive a road through the Parque de la Exposición. The link was eventually made in 1900 with the opening of the Paseo Colón. A trio of squares with monuments—Dos de Mayo, Bolognesi and Grau—joined the avenues together.

Originally named 9 de Diciembre, the central link in the chain came to be known as the Paseo Colón following the erection of Italian sculptor Salvatore Revelli's statue of Columbus. The history of the statue illustrates a change that was taking place in the concept of urban living. It actually dates from 1860 and was originally located in one of the elites' traditional promenades, the Alameda de Acho, but was subsequently moved to its present site, which became the fashionable promenade in the early decades of the twentieth century. Throughout the colonial period, in keeping with the thinking which equated civilized living with the urban, life had revolved around the city centre. Now, as the centre became increasingly crowded, the wealthy moved to exclusive areas on the edge of the city where they no longer had to rub shoulders with the lower orders and could combine the comforts of modern living with access to green spaces. Today the once elite housing of the Paseo Colón area is in a sorry state of neglect and is occupied mainly by small shops, offices and private academies of one kind or another. Nonetheless, the elegance of that housing is still evident, as is the very marked French influence on the architectural style. A fine example is the Quinta Alania (Paseo Colón 393), a condominium with four spacious apartments accessed through a huge arched gateway and topped by Parisian-style attics. *Art nouveau* decorative motifs are featured in the ironwork of the gate and on the caryatides supporting the arch.

As the Quinta illustrates, a feature of the period was the spread of high-class communal housing. Particularly fashionable were up-market rented apartments in buildings constructed by banks and insurance companies, such as the Edificio Rímac, completed in 1924. Located in the Paseo de la República and looking on to the Parque de la Exposición, it houses a series of three- and four-storey apartments with elaborate Second Empire façades crowned by attics. Equally impressive is a complex of apartment buildings ringing the Plaza Dos de Mayo.

It is significant that the statue of Columbus is given pride of place in what at the time was the most select area of the capital, for it encapsulates the Eurocentric view of the nation that lay behind this process of urban development. It shows Columbus holding a cross and standing protectively over the huddled figure of a naked Indian woman personifying savage America. Peru, the monument suggests, will raise itself up to the level of a civilized nation by embracing the European progress introduced to America by Columbus.

The Monument to Manco Cápac

Yet by the 1920s Peru's indigenous heritage was beginning to be acknowledged, and a relatively short distance away, off the Avenida 28 de Julio, a statue of the first Inca was erected in 1926 in the Plaza Manco Cápac. The Inca stands on a granite pedestal pointing into the distance, as though announcing the future nation that was to grow out of the empire he founded. The base features four bas-reliefs depicting the religion, the festivals and work activities of the Inca people and, above them, two condors and two llamas as emblems of the Andean world. Significantly, though, this monument was not an initiative of the Creole elites but was an Independence Centenary gift from the Japanese community, apparently reflecting the belief that the ancient Peruvians were of Asian origin.

Despite any such belief, most Limeñans were not yet ready to shed their prejudices with regard to the Indians and their culture and, as Mario Vargas Llosa's *La ciudad y los perros* (The Time of the Hero, 1963) records, local humour has not always treated the monument respectfully, one joke being that the Inca is directing customers to the red-light district in La Victoria: "The stone Inca that loomed against the sky reminded him... of what Vallano said once: 'Manco Cápac is a pimp, he's pointing the way to Huatica Street.'"

Even so, the monument is an indication that change was in the air. As noted earlier, after the War of the Pacific writers like Manuel González Prada and Clorinda Matto de Turner had sought to open the eyes of the urban public to the plight of the Indian masses and to the need to incorporate them into the nation. In 1909 Pedro Zulen formed the Asociación Pro-Indígena (Pro-Indian Society) to educate the public about the conditions in which indigenous people lived and to promote social reform. Interest and pride in the indigenous past was stimulated by American archaeologist Hiram Bingham's discovery of the long-lost Inca city of Machu Picchu in 1911 and by Julio C. Tello's pioneering work in pre-Inca archaeology. The paintings of the so-called *indigenista* group headed by José Sabogal accorded a place in national society to an indigenous peasantry who had traditionally been marginalized and countered prevailing prejudices with regard to the Indian by propagating a positive image of Andean culture. In Cuzco there was a resurgence of Andean nationalism among middle-class intellectuals such as Luis E. Valcárcel and José Uriel García, who challenged the coastal elites' western model of the nation and proposed the construction of a new national identity rooted in the autochthonous tradition. Valcárcel's *Tempestad en los Andes* (Tempest in the Andes, 1927) argued that Peru was an essentially Andean nation, since its civilization originated in the sierra and from there spread to the coast, and that despite centuries of domination by Lima, the Andean people had kept their ancestral culture alive. In messianic language Valcárcel announced the coming of a new era in which the Andean people, rousing themselves from passiveness and availing themselves of western technology, would re-establish themselves as the hegemonic force in the nation.

The 1920s and 1930s also produced a body of fiction describing the experience of the Indian peasantry, culminating in the classic *indigenista* novel, Ciro Alegría's *El mundo es ancho y ajeno* (Broad and Alien is the World, 1941), an account of the process whereby traditional Indian communities were destroyed by the expansion of the large estates in the late nineteenth and early twentieth centuries. But the major portrayer of Andean Peru was José María Arguedas (1911-69), who ranks with Mario Vargas Llosa as one of Peru's two leading novelists. An ethnographer as well as a writer, Arguedas saw himself as an intermediary between the indigenous Quechua-speaking Andean world and westernized urban Peru. As a scholar he made collections and translations of Quechua literature and folklore and published important literary and anthropological studies. In his fiction he set out to correct stereotyped images of the Indian and simplistic views of Andean society, highlighting in particular that traditional Quechua culture has been both resilient and adaptable, assimilating western influences without losing its distinctive identity, and that such is its strength that it has exercised a profound influence on the mentality of the Andean elites. His great achievement was to convey convincingly the magical-religious thinking of the Andean people through a literary style which captures in Spanish the flavour of Quechua. Some of Arguedas' works—the stories of *Agua* (Water, 1935); the novel *Los ríos profundos* (Deep Rivers, 1958)—draw on his personal experience to depict the clash of Peru's two main cultures through the predicament of a young boy torn between them, while the *Yawar Fiesta* (Bloody Fiesta, 1941) and *Todas las sangres* (All the Bloods, 1964) paint broad overviews of Andean society.

The Casa del Pueblo

Though dating only from the 1940s, the Casa del Pueblo in Avenida Alfonso Ugarte (no. 1012) is a building of major historical significance. As the headquarters of APRA (Alianza Popular Revolucionaria Americana), Peru's first—and indeed only—mass political party, it stands as a symbol of opposition to everything represented by the Club Nacional in the Plaza San Martín. Indeed, Peru's history from 1930 to the 1960s was dominated largely by the struggle between APRA and the Peruvian oligarchy.

Founded in 1924 with the declared aim of radically transforming Peruvian society, APRA terrified the ruling establishment with its strong performance in the 1931 presidential elections. Unlike the communists, who were never more than a sect, it demonstrated an ability to organize a mass movement and acquired a mystique that made it a focus for the hopes and aspirations of millions of ordinary Peruvians. More than just a political party, it was a messianic movement. Its rallies, charged with ritual and symbolism, were like revivalist meetings, and party propaganda likened its charismatic leader, Víctor Raúl Haya de la Torre, to Christ. Its anthem, sung to the tune of the *Marseillaise*, called upon Peruvians "to embrace the New Religion", promising them that through the party they would attain their "longed-for redemption". It also had its credo, which was recited communally at rallies: "I believe in APRA all powerful...; I believe in Víctor Raúl Haya de la Torre, Founder-Director of our great Party, which was conceived by the work and grace of the Patriotic Spirit;... I believe in the triumph of the Sacred Cause... and that only *Aprismo* will bring salvation to Peru and that we will enjoy one day a better life." A standard greeting exchanged by party members was "Seasap", an acronym for its most famous chant—"Solo el aprismo salvará al Perú" (Only Aprismo will bring salvation to Peru). Being an Aprista was a way of life, and children born into an Aprista family were brought up in the faith and in their turn passed it on to their own children.

One of APRA's great strengths was its organization and discipline. Throughout the country it established an extensive network of grassroots committees, organized on hierarchical and military lines. It also blended politics with social and family life by opening community centres (*casas del pueblo*) in working-class neighbourhoods. There, as well as a wide variety of recreational activities, cheap food was available in the "people's restaurants", free medical and legal services were provided by party professionals, and night schools offered pre-university courses as well as training in a range of trades. APRA was also extremely effective at infiltrating party loyalists into unions, the state bureaucracy, schools, universities and the lower ranks of the armed forces.

APRA drew strength from the experience of long years of persecution, particularly under the regimes of military strongmen Luis M. Sánchez Cerro, Oscar R. Benavides and Manuel A. Odría. Demonized by the right-wing press, which claimed that its goal was to set up a totalitarian, one-party state, APRA was outlawed for most of the period between 1933 and 1956 and was effectively driven underground. Its leaders were jailed or forced to go into hiding or exile. Haya de la Torre himself spent five years holed up in the Colombian Embassy following Odría's seizure of power in 1948 and spent other periods in exile. But it was ordinary Apristas who bore the brunt of the crack-down. In 1932 over a thousand were massacred by the army in Trujillo following an uprising provoked by the arrest and deportation of party leaders. Apristas were regularly rounded up, jailed and tortured. Others were penalized by being dismissed from their job. For years Aprista families struggled to survive without their menfolk. Yet that shared experience of persecution had the effect of instilling in them a fierce sense of loyalty and a conviction that they would inevitably prevail, and party mythology likened them to the early Christians by referring to those years of repression as their time in the catacombs. And on those occasions when the party was eventually legalized and its leaders allowed to return from exile, it gave proof of its strength by staging mass rallies of up to 200,000 supporters.

There is, however, a less admirable side to APRA's history. Though it argued with some justification that it was merely responding to state repression, it itself was guilty of resorting to violence. It had its own strong-arm brigade, the *búfaloes* (Buffaloes), which served as a bodyguard but also engaged in acts of intimidation and terrorism. The 1932 Trujillo massacre was retaliation for the Apristas' murder of a number of army officers. Sánchez Cerro was assassinated by an activist in 1933, and in 1935 the same fate befell Antonio Miró Quesada, owner of the conservative newspaper *El Comercio*. In January 1947 an APRA terrorist campaign culminated in the assassination of Francisco Graña Garland, the right-wing editor of *La Prensa* newspaper. In the end, though, such violence proved to be counter-productive, for it earned the party the enduring enmity of the military and the conservative press. APRA also showed itself unwilling to collaborate with other reformist parties which shared a similar agenda, as it was clearly jealous of competitors trespassing on what it regarded as its patch. When Fernando Belaúnde Terry came to power in 1963, for instance, it adopted an obstructionist strategy in Congress to block his reformist programme.

In addition to suffering persecution, Apristas had their loyalty tested by Haya's ambiguous leadership, aimed at conciliating the party's militant and moderate wings. The militants were convinced that armed insurrection was the only means by which they would gain power but they were repeatedly frustrated by Haya's habit of withholding support at the last minute for revolutionary conspiracies which he had originally encouraged or at least connived at. In October 1948 an uprising at Callao, organized by the militants and involving sections of the navy, was suppressed because the expected support did not materialize. In reality, to win political acceptance, Haya had opted to pursue a strategy of changing the party's radical image by moderating its rhetoric and watering down its programme. He also adopted a policy of so-called *convivencia* (coexistence), entering into marriages of convenience with conservative politicians. In 1956 APRA backed the candidature of oligarch Manuel Prado, who rewarded its support by legalizing the party, and in 1962 and 1963 the policy was taken to an extreme that aroused widespread disbelief when a coalition was formed between APRA and the party of Odría, the old enemy who had outlawed and persecuted it.

Dyed-in-the-wool loyalists retained their faith in their leader, clinging to the belief that he was pursuing a pragmatic strategy that would bring the party to power without betraying its principles. Others were dismayed by the strategy and by APRA's perceived move to the right. Disenchantment led many to abandon its ranks to join more radical parties. In 1959 its extreme left-wing faction broke away to form a splinter group, APRA Rebelde, which in 1962 re-branded itself as the Movimiento de Izquierda Revolucionaria (Movement of the Revolutionary Left) and launched a guerrilla campaign in the Andean highlands.

Nor did the strategy produce the desired result, for Haya never succeeded in attaining the presidency. In 1962 he came first in the elections and, though he lacked the necessary majority to win outright, his victory seemed a foregone conclusion, but once again APRA's hopes were frustrated when the military effectively imposed their veto by publicly claiming that there had been electoral fraud. Likewise in 1968, as the end of Belaúnde's term in office approached, Haya was favourite to succeed him, but the armed forces staged a coup and set up a military government headed by General Juan Velasco Alvarado.

The military were motivated not just by their traditional antipathy towards APRA. Within the army a liberal officer corps had come to prominence, who believed that the only effective way of maintaining internal security against the threat posed by the radical left was by implementing reforms to bring about effective national development and social equality. Since they perceived APRA as having grown into a conservative party and a pillar of the established order, they deemed that the only way that such a project would be carried through was by undertaking it themselves. The military, in other words, put into practice the programme which APRA had traditionally advocated. Not only were the Apristas robbed of power yet again but they were left aggrieved that the same military who had always persecuted them had now stolen their revolution from them.

Six years after Haya's death APRA finally achieved power when his young protégé Alan García won the 1985 election by a landslide. While counting on the party's traditional support, García repackaged APRA's image to appeal to all sectors by campaigning for a reformist programme based on consensus and technical expertise. Unfortunately the expectations he created were to give way to disappointment and disillusionment. An initial period of economic growth was followed by galloping inflation—which at one stage in 1988 reached 7,000 per cent—and recession. Lacking a coherent strategy to cope with the crisis, García became increasingly erratic and as a result of his constant changes of policy the consensus he had created collapsed into political and economic chaos. García's term in office left both him and APRA severely discredited and many Apristas came to believe that he had done more to destroy the party than the hostile governments which had persecuted it for decades.

Yet the story of APRA is far from being a history of failure. Though it occupied the presidency only once, it was the major grouping in Congress on several occasions and also exercised power and influence through its control of unions and local councils. Moreover, by setting an agenda for social change and by leading the challenge to the oligarchy's hold on power, APRA significantly shaped the course of Peruvian history. Above all, it changed the way in which ordinary Peruvians thought of themselves by giving them a sense of their own worth and of their right to a better future.

The Grand Boulevards

Throughout the colonial period and until the early twentieth century the area between the old city wall and the sea was predominantly rural. There were several outlying settlements, of course. A town had grown up around the port of Callao; the villages of Magdalena (renamed Pueblo Libre at the time of Independence) and Surco had originated as Indian *reducciones*; and there were seaside villages at Miraflores, Barranco and Chorrillos. Most of the land, however, was occupied by small farms and haciendas.

The district of San Isidro, for example, takes its name from the hacienda on which it was built in the 1920s. The nobleman Antonio de Ribera acquired the land as an *encomienda* in 1560 by marrying the widow of a half-brother of Francisco Pizarro. The estate then passed through the hands of various owners before becoming the property of Spanish merchant Isidro de Abarca, the Count of San Isidro, in the second half of the eighteenth century. The colonial hacienda house still survives (Av. Paz Soldán 920) and when the district was created the developers also preserved part of the estate as a feature. El Olivar is a grove of olive trees planted in the early colonial period and nearby is an olive-press, also dating from colonial times. San Isidro, in that sense, illustrates a major aspect of the introduction of Spanish culture to Peru. The Spaniards soon adapted to American foodstuffs like corn and potatoes, and many of these were quickly taken back to Europe.

Nonetheless, they retained a preference for their customary Mediterranean diet and *encomenderos* quickly redirected agricultural production away from native crops to European plants like wheat, grapes and olives to satisfy the culinary tastes of the Spanish settlers. Within a few decades, the Spaniards had effectively transformed the ecology of the country.

Other relics of the Lima valley's rural past can also be seen in Surco and Chorrillos, where the main buildings of the Hacienda San Juan Grande and the Hacienda Villa have been conserved and restored. Both estates were owned and run by the Jesuits, who became the most powerful landowner in the coastal region, and they convey an idea of the prosperity of the religious orders in the colonial period. The Hacienda Villa, in particular, was a major commercial enterprise, since in an area where small to medium-sized properties were the norm it had a slave population of over 400 engaged in the cultivation of sugar cane, a profitable export crop.

In the colonial period and in the first half of the nineteenth century travel between the city and the outlying settlements could be a risky business. In colonial times it was common for bands of runaway slaves to go about raiding farms and robbing travellers on the roads. In the long run they were usually hunted down and brought to justice—in December 1667 twenty-six mulatto bandits were captured and executed—but the persistence of the problem indicates that the authorities were never able to assert effective control over the capital's hinterland. Later, in the early decades after independence, the instability caused by frequent coups and rebellions led to a breakdown of law and order and enabled bandits to operate under the guise of political partisans. The problem is illustrated by Ricardo Palma's "El sombrero del padre Abregú" (Father Abregú's Hat). The story describes a well-known local character, a priest who every weekend would journey from the city to the seaside village of Barranco to say Sunday mass at a hermitage there. Father Abregú cut a somewhat eccentric figure, since he rode perched on a mule and wore a high-brimmed clerical hat. But, as Palma explains, he had good reason for travelling in this fashion. He had been in the habit of riding on horseback and wearing a Panama hat until one day in 1835 he fell into the hands of bandits. Things might have gone badly for him, but after robbing him of what little he had the bandit leader took a liking to him and, though taking his horse, gave him a mule in exchange and told him to wear a clerical hat in future so that his men would recognize him and know not to molest him. Palma uses the anecdote to evoke the climate of the times, when travellers venturing beyond the city wall lived in terror of being assaulted on the roads.

Under the guise of being partisans of a political cause, the bandits committed hundreds of felonies and the roads were impassable for timid honest folk... Stories of robberies, murders and other outrages in unpopulated country were the daily topic of conversation among the capital's citizens, who did not dare go outside the walls without first making an act of contrition in lieu of the last sacraments.

The roads were fairly primitive, and in the nineteenth century foreign travellers disembarking at Callao regularly commented on the poor state of the road to the capital. The situation improved in the 1850s when two railway lines were constructed linking Lima to Callao and Miraflores-Barranco-Chorrillos, leaving from stations located respectively at what are now the Plaza San Martín and the Palace of Justice. But if we are to believe Gladys, the protagonist of Enrique A. Carrillo's short novel *Cartas de una turista* (Letters from a Tourist, 1905), the service was not particularly reliable, the half-hour journey to Chorrillos being operated by "a sluggish train that leaves when it feels like it and arrives when it can." Later, in 1906, the railway service was replaced by electric trams which continued to function until the 1950s, allowing people to live in the suburbs and commute to work in the city. One of these trams is on display in the Museo de la Electricidad in Barranco.

For Lima to grow, a modern road system was required, and one of the elements in the grand design for the city's modernization was a series of avenues radiating from the ring road and linking the centre to outlying districts. The first, opened in 1899, was the Avenida Brasil, which provided improved communication with Pueblo Libre (formerly Magdalena and sometimes known as Magdalena Vieja) and from there continued to the sea, leading to the development of Magdalena del Mar (also known as Magdalena Nueva) as a neighbourhood for the affluent middle class and, later, to the creation of the neighbouring district of San Miguel. The Avenida Venezuela, opened in 1924, was built to improve the transport of goods to and from the port of Callao. The most handsome of these boulevards, opened in 1921, is the Avenida Arequipa, a dual carriageway running to Miraflores with a tree-lined promenade in the middle. In the 1960s, as traffic levels increased, the Paseo de la República expressway—the Vía Expresa, popularly known as *el zanjón* (the big ditch) because it is a cut below the level of the adjacent streets—was opened to facilitate speedy travel between central Lima and San Isidro and Miraflores. A coast road was also built linking the seaside communities between Callao and Chorrillos.

Expanding Lima came to take the form of a triangle whose tips were the city centre, Callao and Chorrillos. Improved communications led both to the growth of existing communities and to new urban developments on the fringes of the new avenues. One such development, dating from the late 1920s, was the district of Santa Beatriz flanking the Avenida Arequipa at the level of the Estadio Nacional. Santa Beatriz was a sign of things to come. The original expansion of the city had been restricted to the area around the former city wall, partly because transport facilities were limited, partly because the elites still retained an ideal of gracious urban living. Now, from the 1920s onwards, improved public transport and the advent of the motor car made it possible to live further out. Moreover, exposure to images of North American and European lifestyles had given the middle classes the ambition to have a house of their own with garden at front and rear, and by the end of the twentieth century a progressive process of urban development had completely built over the green land contained with the triangle.

Avenida Arequipa

Avenida Arequipa, the most magnificent of Lima's grand boulevards, is the legacy of President Augusto B. Leguía, who ruled Peru throughout the 1920s. It was Leguía who implemented the project and in his honour the road was initially named Avenida Leguía. Yet now the only public recognition of him is an inconspicuous monument on block 24 in the district of Lince, for he was so hated that after his overthrow his enemies set out to efface his memory. The opprobrium in which he was held is easy to understand. He had ruled dictatorially, his regime had been riddled with corruption, he ran the country into debt. He also offended nationalists by pragmatically resolving border disputes and by increasing the influence of North American capitalism. His real crime, however, was that he opened the door to a process of social change that threatened the Peruvian establishment.

Not that he was in any way a revolutionary. A successful businessman of provincial origin, he had been a member of the Partido Civil and as its representative served as president between 1908 and 1912. Even so, by the standards of the time he was a progressive and, disenchanted by the opposition he had encountered from the party's conservative wing, he distanced himself from it and won the 1919 election by capitalizing on middle-class discontent with the closed oligarchic society controlled by the *civilistas*. When his victory was challenged in the courts he mounted a pre-emptive coup and packed Congress with his supporters. Thereafter he ruled as a strongman who did not hesitate to imprison or deport those who opposed him, and he had himself re-elected in 1925 and again in 1929 in controlled elections. There were two main sides to his declared intention of creating a Patria Nueva (New Fatherland). The first was to break the political control of the *civilista* elites, to encourage the rise of a strong middle class as a political force and, to a limited extent, to improve the situation of the working classes and the indigenous peasantry. He was successful to the extent that the *civilistas* were never able to make a come-back, while the 1920s saw a significant increase in the number of middle-class professionals, small businessmen and public employees. On the other hand, though some measures were taken to protect indigenous communities, his initiatives with regard to the lower classes tended to be purely token gestures, such as the creation of an annual Day of the Indian.

Leguía's second aim was to turn Peru into a modern country. This involved major projects outside the capital, such as the construction of 11,000 miles of new roads to open up the interior, irrigation schemes which brought 100,000 acres of the coastal desert into cultivation, and a sanitation campaign which eliminated yellow fever in the northern coastal region. Lima itself was transformed almost beyond recognition. One indication of the scale of the modernization carried out was that whereas in 1919 the Paseo Colón was virtually the only paved street, by 1930 almost 90 per cent of the city's roads were tarmacked. All this had to be paid for, of course. To do so, Leguía encouraged foreign investment, leading to the establishment of a vast North American economic empire made up of great enterprises like the Cerro de Pasco Copper Corporation and the International Petroleum Company, and he was accused of selling out the country to foreign capital. He also borrowed heavily; between 1918 and 1929 Peru's foreign debt rose from $10 million to $100 million. In the end economic crisis caused by the developing worldwide depression brought about his overthrow in 1930.

As can be gauged from the avant-garde poetry of the period, Leguía's project was in tune with the aspirations of the country's middle classes. In a poem written in 1916 Alberto Hidalgo identifies himself with Kaiser Wilhelm in his war against France, implying that they are allies in the common cause of exterminating a decadent civilization:

And Emperor and Bard—you and I—arm in arm
we'll march together as conquerors on depraved Paris.

Bearing in mind that the Creole elites of the period took France as their cultural model, the poem was effectively a declaration of war against the conservative Aristocratic Republic and everything it represented. The following year Hidalgo moved from his native Arequipa to Lima, where he published books celebrating the beauty of cars, aeroplanes, motor cycles, sport and war, manifestations of a dynamic creative spirit which was sweeping away the antiquated and forging a brave new future. Yet the work which best expresses the desire to see Peru break with the past and embrace modernity is Carlos Oquendo de Amat's *5 metros de poemas* (5 metres of poems, 1927). In "New York" the modern city is evoked as a limitless panorama of exciting possibilities, as is suggested at the end of the poem when, as dawn breaks, morning appears bearing a sign offering itself for hire:

And the morning
goes along like the girl next door
in her tresses
she has pinned a sign

> *THIS MORNING*
> *IS FOR HIRE*

The Leguía years were a creative period in the literary field, with the publication of major works like César Vallejo's *Trilce* (1922), Oquendo de Amat's *5 metros de poemas* and Martín Adán's avant-garde novel *La casa de cartón* (The Cardboard House, 1929). These were also years of intense intellectual activity, much of it centred around magazines like José Carlos Mariátegui's *Amauta* (1926-30), a journal of socialist orientation aimed at promoting both a deeper understanding of Peru and a widening of its cultural horizons. *Amauta* included contributions from prominent foreign intellectuals and articles on science, geography, politics, art and history and generally sought to keep its readers abreast with new developments in all those fields. It also published poetry and fiction, providing an outlet for young Peruvian writers, whatever their political affiliations. In particular, it promoted two literary currents: *indigenismo*, which championed the Andean peoples and their culture, and the avant-garde, which was bringing Peruvian literature into line with the international mainstream. For Mariátegui those two currents complemented each other in the struggle to break with the legacy of colonialism and to create a Peru that combined modernity with the rediscovery of its Andean roots.

While most of Peru's intellectuals welcomed Leguía's modernizing ambitions, few of them regarded them as going far enough, and a feature of the period was the publication of works articulating a more radical vision of the nation's future. The most influential of these was Mariátegui's *Siete ensayos de interpretación de la realidad peruana* (Seven Interpretative Essays on Peruvian Reality, 1928), a Marxist analysis of

Peruvian society and its history. The thrust of Mariátegui's argument was that as a result of the colonial experience Peru had failed to produce either a capitalist bourgeoisie or an industrial working class. He attributed the nation's backwardness to the persistence of semi-feudal structures and relations in the countryside and proposed that national progress could only be achieved by breaking the dominance of the land-owning oligarchy through a programme of agrarian reform which would restore land to the indigenous communities, whose collective traditions should be built on to construct a new society. As a political thinker Mariátegui was to exercise enormous influence and is still revered by the Peruvian left.

If Leguía's programme failed to satisfy the likes of Mariátegui, the country's conservatives thought it had gone much too far, as the 1920s had seen the spread of radical ideas and the emergence of organized left-wing political movements with the founding of APRA in 1924 and the Socialist Party in 1928. Their response was to seek to close the floodgates in order to maintain their hold on power, and Leguía's overthrow in 1930 was to usher in a period of repression presided over by military officers Luis M. Sánchez Cerro, Oscar R. Benavides and, later, Manuel A. Odría. Their collective mentality was aptly summed up by Sánchez Cerro in a description of himself: "When you see me lashing the indolent and lazy rabble with a piece of bread in one hand and a whip in the other, say that it is Sánchez Cerro trying to put the masses on the right track." A reminder of that era is the Colombian Embassy on block 31 of Av. Arequipa, where APRA leader Haya de la Torre spent five years as a refugee during the Odría dictatorship.

The climate of repression introduced by Sánchez Cerro left its mark on the country's literature. In the 1920s the literary scene was effervescent, and the writing of the period exuded a sense that change was in the air. In the 1930s, conversely, poetry became inward-looking and hermetic. Emilio Adolfo Westphalen, author of *Las ínsulas extrañas* (The Strange Islands, 1933) and *Abolición de la muerte* (Abolition of Death, 1935), stated that "the prevailing social regime offered me no prospect of leading a life that I considered liveable," and that poetry became for him a means of combating the discouragement caused by the socio-political state of the country. Influenced by Spanish mystic poetry and by surrealism, his verse revolves around the struggle to access an alternative space. In one poem, a tree raising itself up to the heavens and banging its head against the sky serves as a metaphor, not only of man's striving to transcend human limitations, but more particularly of Peruvians' struggle to rise above the repressive conditions in which they are forced to live:

A tree raises itself up to the very limits of the heavens that roof it
It beats with dispersed voice
The tree against the sky against the tree

Similarly, the dominant poetic trend of the 1940s was a so-called "pure poetry", which turned its back on contemporary social reality to take refuge in the timeless world of literature. Its leading exponent was Martín Adán (1908-85), whose major work, the collection of sonnets *Travesía de extramares* (Voyage through the Outer Seas, 1950), takes the poet on a lonely voyage of exploration of the uncharted realms of the imagination in quest of an ineffable absolute apprehended in the moment of poetic inspiration:

My stupefaction!... stay with me... stock-still... instant
After instant!... my agnition... because I'm awe-struck!...
My epiphany!... orgasm blinded me!...
Overflowing emptiness of my breast!...

Let it suffice me, this infinity of my emanated soul...
Catastasis beyond metaplasm!...
Let entelechy... witness of my nothingness...
Not conceive... I who unastounds me!...

My ecstasy... stay with me!... Insistent be the monstrosity
That wasn't insistent in this instant!... whether you consist
Of me or be a god who adds himself to me!...

Divine vanity... where I absent myself
From him who I am in vain... where you're far from me,
Someone I!... endure for me, My Eternity!

The 1950s were to witness an upsurge of socially committed poetry, represented primarily by a group of poets—Gustavo Valcárcel,

Alejandro Romualdo, Juan Gonzalo Rose and Manuel Scorza—who were forced into exile during the Odría dictatorship. Such verse reiterates the poets' obstinate faith in eventual victory over the forces of oppression. Romualdo's "Canto coral a Túpac Amaru" (Choral Chant to Túpac Amaru) evokes the eighteenth-century revolutionary leader as a symbol of the social struggle and employs the rhythm of a litany to express the inevitability of the coming revolution:

> *They'll blow him up*
> *with dynamite. In a body,*
> *they'll carry him, they'll drag him. By force*
> *they'll blow him up:*
> *and they won't be able to kill him!*
>
> *They'll try to blow him up and they won't be able to.*
> *They'll try to smash him and they won't be able to.*
> *They'll try to kill him and they won't be able to.*
>
> *On the third day of suffering,*
> *when they think it's all over and done,*
> *shouting "Liberty!" throughout the earth,*
> *he'll return.*
> *And they won't be able to kill him!*

Part Five
THE EXPANDING METROPOLIS

Petroperú

Overlooking the Vía Expresa (Paseo de la República 3361) is the headquarters of Petroperú, the state oil company. Like the former Ministry of Fisheries, now the Museo de la Nación (Av. Javier Prado Este 2465), it is one of a series of functional and unbeautiful concrete government buildings erected by the military regime that ran the country between 1968 and 1980. Yet, more than just another emblem of state bureaucracy, the Petroperú building encapsulates the changes which Lima and Peru have experienced in modern times. Within days of seizing power the military expropriated the holdings of the International Petroleum Company, a subsidiary of Standard Oil, which virtually controlled the country's oil industry and was perceived as a symbol of Peru's economic and political dependence on the United States. The military's intention was to signal that this was not just another coup. They styled their regime the Revolutionary Government of the Armed Forces and drew up a programme aimed at implementing the reforms which reformist parties like APRA and Fernando Belaúnde's Acción Popular had promised but had failed to fulfil. General Juan Velasco Alvarado, the new Head of State, spelt out what they were about in his message to the nation on the first anniversary of the coup:

> We're living a revolution. It's time that everyone understand it. Every genuine revolution replaces a political, social and economic system by another that is qualitatively different. Just as the French Revolution wasn't carried out to prop up the monarchy, ours wasn't carried out to defend the established order in Peru, but to change it fundamentally, in all its essential aspects.

By the 1960s pressure for social change had been mounting, as the literature of the period seems to suggest. In the essay *Lima la horrible* (Lima the Horrible, 1964) Sebastián Salazar Bondy argues that Lima is an essentially conservative city which has never been able to shake off the weight of its colonial past and denounces the anachronistic power wielded by the old elites. Antonio Cisneros, in the title-poem of *Canto ceremonial contra un oso hormiguero* (Ceremonial Song Against an Ant-eater, 1968), satirizes the corruption and exploitation of the traditional ruling oligarchy in the predatory activities of an ageing homosexual, depicted as an antediluvian monster who has somehow outlived the historical changes which should logically have made it extinct:

> *I can still see you in the Plaza San Martín [...]*
> *oh your tongue*
> *how it snakes through the whole city*
> *tower of babel that spills*
> > *onto the first unwary*
> > *& the second*
> > *& the third*

Another young middle-class poet, Javier Heraud (1942-63), became an iconic figure when he was killed in an abortive guerrilla operation. His brief body of work traces the evolution that led him to political militancy. "El nuevo viaje" (The New Journey) explains the process that led him to leave behind the alienating environment of coastal Peru, associated with capitalist exploitation, and to head for the mountains, a symbol both of guerrilla activism and of a future utopia:

> *You can't stroll*
> *along the sands*
> *if there are oppressive snails*
> *and submarine spiders.*
> *And yet,*
> *walking a little,*
> *turning to the left,*
> *you reach the mountains*
> *and the rivers.*

From the 1930s onwards the military as an institution had been changing, increasingly recruiting from the middle- and lower-middle classes officers who recognized the need for fundamental social change.

A new mentality developed which saw the major threat to national stability as being the widespread poverty and injustice which fuelled left-wing radicalism. Such officers were profoundly influenced by the guerrilla movement launched in the Andes in the early 1960s, since at the same time as they were suppressing it they saw at first hand the conditions which had engendered it. Many officers, such as Velasco himself, came from humble backgrounds and, while believing in a disciplined society, their personal experience had made them eager to do away with the old order. In the end what determined the military's intervention was their perception that none of the political parties was capable of effecting the necessary reforms and that the only way of achieving them was by initiating them themselves.

The Velasco regime instituted a sweeping programme of agrarian reform which expropriated large estates and plantations and redistributed the land to the peasants who worked it. At the same time it sought to promote industrial development by bringing key sectors of the economy under state control; by 1975 state enterprises accounted for 31 per cent of the Gross Domestic Product. Unfortunately, the reforms carried out by the military were seriously flawed and failed to achieve their goals of redistributing wealth and promoting development. Nonetheless, they radically changed Peruvian society in two significant ways.

Firstly, they broke the power of the old oligarchy once and for all. This dramatic shift is dramatized in the novels of Jaime Bayly, which are set in the 1980s and portray the decomposition of the country's social and economic elite. *Los últimos días de "La Prensa"* (The Last Days of *La Prensa*, 1996) narrates the demise of the famous conservative newspaper that had been the champion of a traditional liberal free market and one of the country's most prestigious and influential periodicals. Expropriated by the military, it was restored to its owners in the early 1980s but it had lost all sense of direction and drifted into terminal decline. The disorientation of the former dominant class is personified in the novel by an old man who broods on the loss of his hacienda as a result of the agrarian reform and nurses the dream of having it restored to him. And in *No se lo digas a nadie* (Don't Tell Anyone, 1994) a member of the Creole upper classes acknowledges that their day is drawing to a close and that the future of Peru lies with the mixed-race majority:

You have to accept an irreversible fact: we whites, who were masters of this country, are on our way out; we're encircled and we're getting fewer and fewer. The cholos *are kicking us out little by little. After all, it's only natural, that's the way it had to be. The* cholos *are the majority. They're the masters of this country.*

The Velasco era also raised the expectations and self-esteem of lower-class Peruvians and helped bring about a cultural shift with regard to the racism which had always been at the root of social relations in Peru. Official discourse adopted a new terminology intended to signal respect for social sectors who had previously been stigmatized. Thus, the term "Indian" was replaced by *campesino* (peasant) and the squatter settlements known as *barriadas* were renamed *pueblos jóvenes* (young towns). The government also set up an organization called SINAMOS (Sistema Nacional de Movilización Social)—the acronym translates as "without masters"—to mobilize controlled popular support to help achieve its objectives. Though on the whole it was something of a failure, SINAMOS did prove successful in the squatter settlements, where it nurtured effective neighbourhood self-help committees which, after the military regime's demise, evolved into autonomous grassroots organizations. The success of the military's drive for greater social inclusiveness is reflected in the new constitution which marked the return to democracy, as it extended the vote to previously disenfranchised illiterates. The changed social climate is evoked in Carlos Zavaleta's story "Una nueva era" (A New Era, 1984), where the protagonist returns to Peru after an absence of ten years and, to his amazement, sees an Indian couple in full native dress wandering like tourists around the Plaza Mayor, the centre of Spanish and Creole power since colonial times. It is a phenomenon that he interprets as evidence that the old social and racial barriers are finally breaking down:

Jaime caught sight of an apparently genuine Indian couple who, like them, were heading towards the square [...] As far as he knew, never before would they have dared venture into that square that was the sanctuary of power [...] The Indian and his wife slowly entered the square, as though at the end of a centuries-long journey. The came to the huge light on the perimeter and looked impassively at the Cathedral and Pizarro's Palace and then, slow but indestructible, they continued walking, while Jaime [...] kept watching them as though seeing noteworthy beings who had instituted a new phase in history.

Petroperú is now a relic of a bygone age, and though parts of it have been sold off it is the only major state enterprise not yet fully privatized. The philosophy that had prevailed in the Velasco period privileged state intervention to regulate the economy in order to redistribute wealth and promote development. In the 1990s, during the presidency of Alberto Fujimori, Peru adopted the neo-liberal economic model inaugurated in the previous decade by Ronald Reagan and Margaret Thatcher, the new orthodoxy being that a free market was the most effective way of creating prosperity. Inheriting a massive economic crisis, Fujimori introduced a draconian stabilization package which slashed price subsidies and social spending and raised interest rates and taxes. This was followed by a series of measures designed to restructure the economy, such as the privatization of state enterprises, the deregulation of financial and labour markets and tax and tariff reform. To achieve what was euphemistically called "flexibility of labour", laws protecting workers' rights were set aside and stability of employment became a thing of the past.

The privatization programme generated huge sums for the treasury, the most spectacular sale being that of the state-owned telephone and telecommunications companies to an international consortium headed by Telefónica of Spain for a massive $2 billion, which prompted newspapers to joke that Atahualpa's ransom had finally been repaid. The reduction of trade tariffs from 66 per cent to 15.7 per cent led to an increase in imports as the middle and upper classes acquired mobile phones, cable television and all the other trappings of late-twentieth-century capitalist society. Peru was swiftly incorporated into the new global system as foreign companies bought into its economy and as it bought into the products and ethos of the new western capitalism.

Fujimori's neo-liberal strategy proved effective in that it not only stabilized the economy but succeeded in reactivating it. The results are visible in the physical appearance of the capital. In the 1980s Lima was a sorry spectacle of crumbling decay as a result of economic crisis, terrorist attacks and the ever-increasing influx of migrants, yet by the end of the century it had given itself a make-over and was blossoming again. On both sides of the Vía Expresa impressive state-of-the-art office blocks house the headquarters of the major banks, and American-style shopping malls have sprung up everywhere.

Unfortunately, in Peru, as elsewhere, the social costs of neo-liberalism and globalization have been enormous. There has been little evidence of the trickle-down effect that was claimed for the free market and instead the gap between rich and poor has widened. In the 1990s, as work-forces were slimmed down, 77.4 per cent of Lima's economically active population was unemployed or underemployed. And as earnings diminished, cushions such as subsidies on basic foodstuffs and transport were removed. By 2000 almost half of Peruvians were living below the poverty line, and soup kitchens became a part of life in the capital's shanty towns. That precarious struggle for subsistence, too, is unfortunately visible in the streets of today's Lima, where throngs of men and women line the kerbs with piles of every conceivable item for sale, and at traffic lights cars are besieged by vendors offering everything from chewing-gum to pirated books and CDs.

San Isidro

Created in the 1920s as an intermediate community between the city centre and Miraflores, San Isidro initiated a process of outward expansion that was to culminate in the urbanization of the whole Lima valley. Its history, however, goes much further back. It was originally a pre-Columbian settlement, a relic of which survives in the form of the Huaca Huallamarka, a shrine and burial centre (Nicolás de Ribera 201). During the colonial period the land became an hacienda, whose olive grove, El Olivar, was retained as a focal point for the new district. What makes San Isidro one of Lima's most attractive areas is that alongside modern development remnants of its pre-urban past have been preserved.

San Isidro was designed as a housing development on the North-American model, with houses and chalets surrounded by gardens. Its focal point was the Olivar, around which it grew up as an elegant, upper-class residential district, with houses built in a variety of styles according to the taste of the owner: neocolonial, Tudor etc. The district also reflects the Leguía government's policy of encouraging suburban development by promoting the creation of prestigious facilities that would make outlying areas desirable places to which to move from the city centre. Among such facilities was the Lima Golf Club (Av. Camino Real, cuadra 7), which opened in 1924. Another was the Country Club (Los Eucaliptos 590), a luxury hotel in a rural setting but with access to the city. Built in a style that has been described as Californian Spanish, it had gardens, parks, a golf course and a polo field and, in addition to hosting guests like famous bullfighters, film stars and foreign dignitaries, it became a social centre for Lima's elites. The Country Club went into decline during the economic crisis of the 1980s, but has since been refurbished and reopened under new management.

In its early decades San Isidro was an enclave of Lima's elites, as Alfredo Bryce Echenique describes it in *Un mundo para Julius* (A World for Julius, 1970), a novel portraying the lifestyle of the Creole oligarchy in the 1950s. Julius' family spend several months in residence at the Country Club while waiting to move into their new mansion and are regulars at the Golf Club. While football was the sport of the masses, golf was very much the preserve of the privileged classes and, enclosed on all sides, the Club was a visible expression of social status and social exclusion. This separateness is made evident by the glimpse which the novel offers of the hidden world inside:

The golfers and their wives would enter the dining-room, looking tanned—in fact, elegantly tanned—and one could tell that they were agile and in excellent economic shape [...] Then the men left to play another round of golf [...] There was always someone from England, a few Americans and maybe a German as well. They would speak in English or Spanish, but no matter which language they used they always added delicious foreign words [...] If you were on the outside looking in over the wall at the scene I'm describing, you'd be convinced that life couldn't be happier or more beautiful.

Significantly, the new mansion to which the family move is located in Monterrico, which is described as being "more like San Isidro than San Isidro itself". By the 1950s, San Isidro was already being displaced as the up-market residential area, as the suburbs in their turn became increasingly populated and the more affluent moved out to luxurious new homes in the eastern fringe of the city, close to the Andean foothills, in districts like La Molina, San Borja, Monterrico, Camacho and Las Casuarinas. That process was accelerated in the 1960s with the opening of the Vía Expresa and the Avenida Javier Prado Este intersection, which facilitated travel between these new suburbs and the centre.

From the 1950s San Isidro duly became less exclusive, growing in size and population and taking on a more middle-class character as people increasingly moved away from the city centre to the suburbs. It also reconstituted itself as businesses, too, relocated in the district. Since then it has developed into Lima's major financial centre, and all the main institutions have their headquarters there in state-of-the-art modern corporate buildings. Its American-style shopping mall in Camino Real was the first in the city, and in the same avenue is one of the capital's most active cultural centres, that of the Catholic University

(PUCP). San Isidro, in short, is a dynamic and vibrant district that has managed to acquire the trappings of modernity while retaining its elegance.

Pueblo Libre and Surco

As Lima expanded, existing rural communities likewise grew and were absorbed into the city as districts. Santa María Magdalena and Santiago de Surco were founded in the late sixteenth century as *reducciones* overseen by the Franciscans, that is, as settlements where indigenous communities were congregated to facilitate religious indoctrination and acculturation in the Spanish way of life. Designed on the model of Spanish colonial cities, both settlements were built around a central square and a church, though Magdalena deviates from the norm in that the church is not actually located in the square, the reason apparently being that its site was determined by a grant of land from the local Indian chieftain. Neither church is the original building, both of them having been rebuilt in the eighteenth century.

Both districts retain traces of their rural past. In Magdalena two colonial hacienda houses have survived: the Casa-hacienda Orbea (corner of Av. San Martín and Av. Roberto Acevedo), which still belongs to the family, and the Casa-hacienda Cueva, which now functions as the Museo Arqueológico Rafael Larco Herrera (Av. Bolívar 1515). In Surco the main buildings of the Hacienda San Juan Grande, an estate owned and run by the Jesuits, have been conserved and restored. Surco was also a grape-growing area. Though the vine had been introduced by the Spaniards in the sixteenth century, local commercial production took off in the nineteenth century, thanks to the initiative of Italian immigrants. In the 1930s vineyards occupied some 1,100 acres, producing grapes both for the table and for the production of wine and pisco. Today only three vineyards survive, but the district continues to celebrate an annual grape harvest festival.

In the colonial period both settlements were used by viceroys as rural retreats. The building facing on to Magdalena's Plaza Bolívar was the country residence of Peru's penultimate viceroy, Joaquín de la Pezuela. Here Pezuela conducted negotiations with representatives of the patriot forces during the struggle for independence. Later San Martín used it as a retreat and Bolívar made it his headquarters, and because of its association with the independence cause the district was rechristened Pueblo Libre (Freetown), though it still continued to be referred to as Magdalena. The house contains an important collection of historical paintings and portraits of viceroys, presidents and other political figures.

Formerly the National History Museum, the house is now part of the Museo Nacional de Antropología, Arqueología e Historia. The Archaeology Museum, located on the side of the square to its right, was founded in 1945, bringing to a culmination the life's work of Julio C. Tello (1880-1947), who worked tirelessly to promote the study of archaeology in Peru and was the Museum's first Director. The founding father of Peruvian archaeology, Tello carried out major research on pre-Inca cultures, particularly Paracas and Chavín, and on the basis of his field-work published ground-breaking studies of the pre-Columbian past such as *Introducción a la historia antigua del Perú* (Introduction to the Ancient History of Peru, 1922). His many important discoveries include the famous Chavín Obelisk, which is on display in the Museum.

Pueblo Libre was more quickly absorbed into the expanding city. With the opening of the Avenida Brasil in 1899, it became more easily accessible and began to grow. The area between it and the sea was likewise developed, coming to be known as Magdalena del Mar or Magdalena Nueva to distinguish it from the original Magdalena, which was sometimes called Magdalena Vieja. Surco, on the other hand, was bypassed by the railway line to the seaside village of Chorrillos which opened in 1858 and it remained predominantly rural until the 1950s, after which it underwent a rapid process of urbanization. As a result of its relatively recent development Surco has a more modern air to it than Pueblo Libre. This is most noticeable in its Jockey Plaza (Av. Javier Prado, cuadra 42), Lima's largest and trendiest shopping mall.

Callao

Callao is not officially part of Lima, since it is a separate administrative district comprising the town itself and neighbouring communities like Bellavista, La Perla and La Punta and with a total population of 600,000. *Chalacos*, as its inhabitants are called, also have a distinct sense of local identity encapsulated in the slogan "¡Chim Pum Callao!", an idiomatic expression of support for the district. Yet, geographically and historically, Callao has always been closely linked to Lima. Indeed, one of the reasons why Pizarro chose Lima as the site for the capital was the proximity of a sheltered harbour at Callao. During the colonial period it was the principal port for Spanish commerce in the Pacific. There goods from Spain and other parts of the colonies were unloaded and transported to Lima by road, following the route of present-day Avenida Colonial. From there bullion from Peru's silver mines was shipped to Panama, where it was transported overland and then carried to Spain by convoy. Until independence foreign trade was monopolized by Spain. With the lifting of trade restrictions European merchants, notably the British, moved in to exploit the new market and by the mid-nineteenth century a number of foreign businesses had established themselves in the port. Foremost among them was the Pacific Steam Navigation Company, whose former premises still stand on the corner of Avenida King and Avenida Independencia. By the 1870s Pacific Steam had become the largest steamship company in the world. Its ships ran a regular service between Liverpool and Callao, initially via the Straits of Magellan and later via the Panama Canal.

In addition to being an international port, Callao has played a vital role in internal communications. The construction of a national roadway system only really got under way in the 1930s and 1940s, when the Central Highway and the Panamerican Highway were built. Before then the easiest form of travel to and from Lima and many parts of the country was by sea. Goods and passengers were shipped from Callao to ports like Mollendo, Salaverry, Pacasmayo and Paita and from there continued the journey overland to Arequipa, Trujillo, Cajamarca, Piura and their respective hinterlands. Merchandise and travellers going to the capital made the same journey in reverse.

Given that Callao has traditionally been Lima's gateway to the world, it is appropriate that its airport should also be located in the area. The airport is named after Jorge Chávez, a Peruvian aviator who was the first person to fly over the Alps. The avenue leading to it bears the name of Elmer Faucett, an American pilot who in 1921 made the first flight across the Andes. In 1928 he formed Aerolíneas Faucett, which for most of the twentieth century was one of Peru's major domestic airlines, providing a daily service between the capital and most provincial cities.

The wealth passing through the port made it a target for predators. In 1579 Francis Drake sailed into the bay and seized a ship laden with merchandise. The Dutch pirates Joris van Spielbergen and Jacques

L'Hermite attacked the port in 1615 and 1624 respectively. To protect against such assaults the harbour was fortified. Overlooking the bay is the Castillo del Real Felipe, a fortress whose building was begun in 1747 and completed in the 1770s. The outer perimeter is over a mile long and the rampart over fifteen feet high. The fortress' effectiveness as a stronghold was revealed during the Wars of Independence when its guns kept the patriot fleet at bay for four years until it was eventually taken by siege in 1821. Later, after independence had effectively been won, royalist forces under Brigadier José Ramón Rodil seized the fortress in 1824 and kept up resistance for two years. A later dispute with Spain was resolved when the garrison's batteries drove off an attack by a Spanish fleet in 1866. The fortress houses a museum of military history, with displays from pre-colonial days to modern times. Nearby, on Avenida Jorge Chávez, the Museo Histórico Naval del Perú has displays illustrating the history of the Peruvian navy.

Nearby La Perla is home to another military institution, the Escuela Militar Leoncio Prado, which in addition to its role in training young men for an army career functions as a secondary boarding school. The school is the setting for *La ciudad y los perros*, the novel which launched Mario Vargas Llosa to international celebrity and was adapted to the cinema screen by Francisco Lombardi in 1985. The novel centres around the death of a cadet shot during a military exercise. A friend claims that he was murdered as a punishment for informing on a misdemeanour committed by his classmates, but the authorities hush up the matter and pass it off as an unfortunate accident. The plot functions primarily as a linking device, since Vargas Llosa's main concern is to use the enclosed environment of the school to explore the class and racial divisions of Peruvian society, the prevalence of *machista* values and the corruption of the country's elites. The school authorities, not surprisingly, saw the novel as a defamation of their institution and reacted with outrage, staging a ceremonial burning of the book.

A minor character in the novel—Fontana, the effeminate teacher of French—was based on poet and painter César Moro (1903-56), who taught at the school. Moro was actively involved with the surrealist movement, first in Paris in the late 1920s and early 1930s and later in Mexico City from 1938 to 1948. Detesting his native city, which he dubbed "Lima the Horrible", he left Peru in his youth and spent most of his life in voluntary exile before returning to live out his last years as a lonely, marginal figure. His life and work were a repudiation of the environment in which he grew up. He was openly homosexual; he dropped his given name—Alfredo Quispez Asín—in favour of a pseudonym; and with the exception of *La tortuga ecuestre* (The Equestrian Turtle), dating from the late 1930s, he opted to write his verse in French. Rebelling against the western rationalist tradition, he adopts the figure of the madman as emblem of his poetics in "A vista perdida" (Lost to Sight):

> *I'll never renounce the impudent luxury the sumptuous wildness of*
> *furs like the finest fasces hanging from cords and sables*
> *The immense landscapes of saliva with small fountain-pen*
> *cannons*
> *Saliva's violent sunflower*
> *The word designating the object proposed by its opposite*
> *The tree as a minute nightlight*
> *The loss of faculties and the acquisition of insanity*
> *Aphasiac language and its intoxicating perspectives*
> *Logoclonia tics rages interminable yawning*
> *Stereotypes prolix trains of thought [...]*
> *The grandiose boreal twilight of schizophrenic thought*
> *The sublime delirious interpretation of reality*
> *I'll never renounce the primeval luxury of your giddy fallings oh*
> *diamond-like madness*

Off the coast from the port is the uninhabited island of San Lorenzo, which during the colonial period was used by pirates as a refuge and where Charles Darwin carried out fieldwork in 1835. Close by is the small rocky island of El Frontón, for many decades a notorious penal settlement and political prison. El Frontón is the main setting for Alberto Durant's *Alias "La Gringa"* (1991), a film evoking the contradictions of Peruvian society by showing common criminals and Shining Path militants sharing the same space.

Though founded in 1537, Callao is a relatively modern town, as in 1746 it was destroyed by a massive earthquake and a huge tidal wave which wiped out most of its population. So great was the wave that it is said to have reached as far as the eighteenth-century church of

Nuestra Señora del Carmen (corner of Av. Colonial and Av. Faucett), situated at La Legua, a place so called because it was one league from the port on the old road to Lima. The older part of the town—in and around the Plaza Dos de Mayo—has a number of fine buildings, many of them with a wooden balcony running along the façade. Though most have been badly neglected, they recall the affluence which Callao enjoyed in the second half of the nineteenth century as a result of the opening of the country to foreign commerce and the establishment of foreign businesses in the port. Another of the town's attractions is its seafood restaurants, since Callao is the country's largest fishing port and has a long culinary tradition. It also has its own locally produced beer, Pilsen Callao. To ask for any other brand in Callao is a definite *faux pas*.

Sarita Colonia: Folk Saint
In the port's Baquíjano Cemetery stands a cramped concrete-block shrine to a modern folk saint, Sarita Colonia. Though frowned upon by the Church, her cult has taken hold and the walls of the shrine are covered with thousands of plastic plaques thanking her for the miracles she has worked. From the few facts that are known about her life, it would seem that it was not particularly remarkable. Born in the Andean region in 1914, she moved to Callao with her family when she was a child. She apparently dreamed of becoming a nun, but her mother died when she was fifteen and she was forced to take work as a market vendor and maid to support the family. Throughout her hardships she maintained a devout piety and became known for her acts of charity. In 1940 she died of malaria at the age of twenty-six and was buried in a mass grave.

All sorts of posthumous legends have grown up around her: that she was unjustly accused of theft or that she miraculously escaped an attempted rape. Such accretions to her biography reflect the experience of her devotees, who regard her as being just like them. She has become, in fact, the saint of the capital's marginalized. She is particularly revered by prostitutes, petty criminals and transvestites, who invoke her protection before venturing out into the street. Her following includes those struggling to make a living in the informal economy, taxi and bus drivers, maids and the unemployed. Initially the cult seems to have been fairly localized but from the 1970s it was taken up by the new waves of migrants who settled in shanty towns around the capital and who saw in her someone who had shared their experience. Indeed, alongside the religious aspect of the cult, she has become a cultural icon, a symbol of identity for migrants struggling to establish a place for themselves in the city.

The cult has also given rise to a minor industry producing Sarita Colonia kitsch. The only photograph of her that exists was taken when she was a young girl of about twelve, but that image has been endlessly recycled on cards, framed pictures, candles, T-shirts, stickers, tattoos etc., and buses, taxis, lorries, shops, restaurants and all sorts of businesses display images of the folk saint. The Sarita Colonia phenomenon has also impinged on the arts. The pop group Los Mojarras' first album (1994) was entitled *Sarita Colonia*, and the sleeve features an image of Sarita tattooed on the chest of a criminal. The refrain of the title song sums up her significance for the people of Lima's shanty towns:

Sarita Colonia, patron saint of the poor,
I want no more sorrow, I want no more tears.

In literature the phenomenon is explored in Eduardo González Viaña's magic-realist novel *Sarita Colonia viene volando* (Sarita Colonia Comes Flying, 1990), and in painting Sarita figures in a picture by Carlos Enrique Polanco on display in the Museo del Banco Central de Reserva. Entitled "Los santos", it shows the interior of a church with images of Santa Rosa on the left, San Martín de Porras on the right and Sarita Colonia in the middle, symbolizing an ideal future in which she will have been incorporated into the Peruvian Church's pantheon of saints and the marginalized masses, whose icon she is, integrated into national society. That such a situation is still a long way off is indicated by the fact that the picture was excluded from an exhibition of paintings of Santa Rosa held in the cathedral in 1995.

The Church's response to the cult of Sarita Colonia is symptomatic of the hierarchy's continuing remoteness from the lives of ordinary Peruvians. The Peruvian Church had traditionally been conservative and identified with the country's upper classes. But from the late 1950s onwards, in common with the Church in other parts of Latin America, it came to adopt a more progressive stance in response to the modernizing policies of John XXIII and Paul VI, to growing pressure for social change and to a drift from Catholicism among sectors of the lower and middle classes. Key figures in the development of a new concept of the Church's mission were Juan Landázuri Ricketts, appointed archbishop of Lima in 1955, and his auxiliary Luis Bambarén, appointed in 1968. Landázuri believed that the Church should distance itself from established social structures and forces and that it should not only endorse social change but actively promote it by playing a guiding role in the country's development and encouraging a sense of social responsibility in political leaders and the population generally.

Bambarén was assigned the task of overseeing Lima's squatter settlements and encouraged priests, nuns and lay people to live in the shanty towns and to work pastorally and in community projects. The foot-soldiers of the Church's new commitment to the poor were idealistic young clerics who went to live among the inhabitants of the shanty towns and isolated rural areas and saw it as their responsibility not merely to minister to them and to administer charity but to support them in their struggles and to empower them by helping them form their own self-help organizations. Ideological rationale was provided, above all, by Father Gustavo Gutiérrez, one of the leading proponents of liberation theology, who in *Teología de Liberación* (Liberation Theology, 1971) argued that, to truly give witness to the gospel, the Church had to join the poor in their political struggle for liberation from poverty and injustice.

Such developments were viewed with unease by many members of the hierarchy, who regarded liberation theology as Marxist socialism in disguise, and in the 1980s the Catholic right regained control of the Peruvian Church following the election of conservative Pope John Paul II in 1978. New appointees tended to be conservatives, such as Augusto Vargas Alzamora, who succeeded the retiring Landázuri as archbishop of Lima in 1990, and conservative movements such as Opus Dei and Sodalitium Vitae exercised a growing influence within the Church. The hierarchy have reiterated their commitment to the Church's social mission and continue to support community projects in shanty towns and rural parishes, but they now refrain from speaking out on social and political matters, focusing instead on the defence of traditional Catholic teaching in areas such as divorce, abortion and birth control, and clergy deemed to be too radical or political have found themselves disciplined.

The present situation, in fact, seems to be one in which a progressive clergy, inspired by the ideals of liberation theology, are being kept in check by a conservative hierarchy.

The failure of the Church to reach out to large sectors of the country's masses is also reflected in the dramatic spread of evangelical Protestant groups such as the Pentecostals, the Mormons, Jehovah's Witnesses and the Seventh Day Adventists. Between 1960 and 1985 such groups achieved an astonishing growth rate of 470 per cent and by the end of the century there were reckoned to be around 1.5 million members of evangelical churches in Peru. This phenomenon was partly the result of aggressive proselytizing, backed up by funding from the United States, but is also to be explained by the fact those movements preached a message that appealed to people disaffected with Catholic traditionalism and scared by the revolutionary radicalism which they associated with liberation theology.

Perhaps the major factor, however, has been the Church's chronic shortage of priests, particularly in rural areas and in the slums and poor neighbourhoods of the cities. Peru depends heavily on foreign priests to staff its churches and even then its ratio of priests to laity stood at 1: 8,425 in 1991. As a result many areas lack pastoral attention. Not only has this given evangelical Protestants the opportunity to step into the gap, but it explains an important feature of Peruvian religiosity. In colonial times the Church successfully imposed its religion on Peru's indigenous peoples and created a predominantly Catholic country. However, since then as now there was a shortage of priests to give people a firm grounding in the faith, evangelization was fairly rudimentary. Pre-Christian beliefs and practices survived beneath the veneer of the new religion and to this day a popular religion made up of diverse elements coexists alongside orthodox Catholicism, one of its expressions being the cult of Sarita Colonia. In effect, though 90 per cent of Peruvians are classified as Catholics, many of them are so in name only.

Miraflores

Just as San Isidro replaced the old city centre as Lima's business district, so Miraflores became the main area for shopping, restaurants, cafés and entertainment. Like Pueblo Libre and Surco, it was originally established as a settlement for the indoctrination of the Indians, but the local indigenous population was small and it consisted of only a few houses. In the latter part of the eighteenth century it became one of several rural places of recreation for the city's elites and, though at that time it could not rival Chorrillos in popularity, French traveller Flora Tristan described it in the 1830s as "the most beautiful place I have seen in South America." Yet it was only in the middle of the nineteenth century that the village began to become developed, mainly because a number of affluent European immigrants chose to establish themselves in the area. Unfortunately, its development was interrupted by the War of the Pacific. Miraflores was one of the main lines of defence against the invading Chileans and when it was overrun the village was sacked and left in ruins. The post-war period saw a slow process of recovery. Whereas Chorrillos and Barranco were the fashionable holiday resorts, Miraflores was more of a quiet little village where people chose to settle and bring up their families. In 1900 its population was still only 1,283, but with the advent of motor transport, the opening of the Avenida Arequipa in 1921 and the construction of the Vía Expresa in the 1960s, it underwent a steady and increasingly rapid process of growth, particularly from the 1940s onwards, and by 2000 it had a population of around 200,000.

Not everyone welcomed this development and many looked back nostalgically to the days when Miraflores was a quiet little village. Julio Ramón Ribeyro's story "Los eucaliptos" (The Eucalyptus Trees, 1956) describes the history of the neighbourhood in which he grew up and of the urbanization which transformed it and stripped it of its character. The same author's "Tristes querellas en la vieja quinta" (Sad Squabbles in the Old Condominium, 1974) records the thoughts of an old man on the changes which he has seen in his lifetime:

The whole resort had changed as well. From being a place of recreation and sea-bathing, it had turned into a modern city criss-crossed by wide asphalt avenues. The old Republican mansions of avenues like Pardo, Benavides, Grau, Ricardo Palma, Leuro and of the seaside promenades had been relentlessly demolished to build on their sites apartment buildings of ten and fifteen storeys, with glass balconies and underground garages. Memo nostalgically recalled his strolls of yesteryear through tree-lined streets with low-rise houses, streets that were perfumed, peaceful and quiet, where a car rarely passed and where children could still play football. The resort was now nothing more than a prolongation of Lima, with all its traffic, its bustle, its commercial and bureaucratic apparatus. Those who loved calm and flowers had moved to other districts and abandoned Miraflores to a new middle class, hard-working and with no taste, prolific and showy, who knew none of the old habits of politeness and tranquility and who had created a noisy, soulless city of which they were absurdly proud.

Miraflores was traditionally an upper-class enclave. In Mario Vargas Llosa's *La ciudad y los perros*, its exclusiveness is signalled by the observation that outsiders who on Sundays come from other parts of the city to ogle the girls promenading in the local park find themselves in the same position as cinema-goers fantasizing about the inaccessible female stars on the screen: "Alberto and Emilio took two turns around the park, observing their friends, their acquaintances and the outsiders who had come from Lima and Magdalena and Chorrillos to look at the girls, who must have reminded them of movie stars."

Miraflores is no longer the elite residential zone it once was, but it remains an enclave of sorts, and though members of the lower classes work there and families from poorer districts visit it for Sunday outings, it is very much the area of the comfortable, westernized middle classes and there is also a considerable foreign presence.

Today's Miraflores is a hybrid of the traditional and the trendy. Old streets with traditional housing coexist alongside high-rise apartment buildings and modern hotels and banks, European-style cafés alongside McDonald's, KFC and Pizza Hut, cultural institutions alongside discos. It is also a district geared towards tourism, with many hotels, shops selling antiques and local crafts and a handicraft market in Avenida Petit Thouars.

Miraflores effectively has two centres. The first is the area around the Parque Central at the end of the Avenida Arequipa. Here are the town hall and the parish church, both of them twentieth-century constructions replacing earlier buildings. It is in this area that most of the shops are located, particularly in Avenida Larco, though high-street shopping is increasingly giving way to American-style malls. Here, too, are to be found cafés like the Haití and the Vivaldi. Off the Avenida Diagonal is a pedestrianized side street full of pizzerias and clubs. The

Parque Kennedy frequently stages performances of music, mime and popular theatre. On Sundays and public holidays local artists offer their paintings and crafts for sale in the Parque Central.

The other centre is the seafront running along the cliff top overlooking the Pacific Ocean. This is the scene of pleasant parks and gardens like the Parque Salazar and the Parque del Amor. At the end of Avenida Larco, beneath the Parque Salazar, is a modern leisure and shopping complex called LarcoMar. Constructed on three levels, it includes among its facilities cafés, restaurants, shops, cinemas and a disco.

Of historical interest is a pre-Colombian structure, the Huaca Pucllana (popularly known as the Huaca Juliana), situated on block 8 of General Borgoño. Miraflores is also home to a number of important cultural institutions. The Museo Amano (Retiro 160) has a magnificent collection of pre-Columbian textiles and ceramics, particularly from the Chancay period. The house where the great nineteenth-century writer Ricardo Palma lived the latter years of his life has been preserved as a museum, the Casa Museo Ricardo Palma (General Suárez 189) and is a fine example of a middle-class residence of the early twentieth century. The house of historian Raúl Porras Barrenechea (Colina 398) is a research institute of the University of San Marcos and has a programme of public lectures. The town hall has an art gallery which stages regular exhibitions. The Centro Cultural Ricardo Palma (Larco 770) has a busy programme of cultural events, as do the Alianza Francesa (Av. Arequipa 4595), the Asociación Cultural Peruano-Británica (Av. Arequipa 3495) and the Instituto Cultural Peruano Norteamericano (Av. Angamos Oeste 160).

The Costa Verde

In the late colonial period it became the custom for Lima's elites to take holidays by the sea. The custom became more generalized in the course of the nineteenth century as it was taken up by the middle classes and it was further encouraged when communication was improved, first in the 1850s with the construction of railway lines linking Lima to Callao and Chorrillos and later in 1906 when the train was superseded by the electric tram. In the twentieth century, as Lima's population grew and as new roads and the advent of motor transport made travel easier, the city's seaside resorts ceased to be the preserve of the elites, and throughout the summer thousands flock to the beaches at the weekend.

The main beach area is the bay of Miraflores, known as the Costa Verde. Stretching from La Punta to Chorrillos, it is linked by a modern coast road as well as by roads on the cliff tops above. As indicated by the name Barranco, Lima's seaside resorts are located on the top of

sandy cliffs (*barrancos*), which meant that until modern times access to the beaches was difficult, though Barranco itself had a funicular. A feature of the local ecology were the trickles of water which filtered through the cliffs into beachside caves, where first fishermen and later bathers would shower after coming out of the sea, and Chorrillos derives its name ("trickles") from that phenomenon. An effect of this filtration was that vegetation grew on the cliffs, and as a result this stretch of coast received its name the Costa Verde (Green Coast). The name still survives, though ecological changes have caused the greenery to disappear.

The fashionable resort of the nineteenth century was Chorrillos. It was originally an Indian fishing village and when its first church was established in the late seventeenth century it was dedicated to St. Peter, the patron saint of fishermen. Each year, on his feast day (29 June), the statue of the saint is paraded through the streets and then the procession is transferred to boats and does a tour of the bay. Chorrillos is still an important fishing port and is famous for its fish restaurants.

By the 1840s Chorrillos had become a flourishing holiday resort, and the local indigenous community found a new source of income by providing services to visitors. They built rustic houses which they rented out to holiday-makers and supplied and guided mules to take bathers down the cliffs to the beach. Another of their services is illustrated in one of Pancho Fierro's water-colours, where a young bare-chested Indian, acting as a *bañador* (bathing attendant), holds a lady's hand as she timidly ventures into the sea. Foreign travellers often described Chorrillos as the Peruvian equivalent of European resorts like Brighton but, like the young Englishwoman in Enrique A. Carrillo's novel *Cartas de una turista* (Letters from a Tourist, 1905), others tended to regard it as a "modest little village putting on airs of being an aristocratic spa" and invariably complained about the rustic quality of the housing. In the 1820s Englishman Gilbert Mathison lamented that "every approach to comfort or delicate convenience, much less luxury, is absolutely wanting."

By European standards the houses were certainly fairly basic, and whereas Brighton was urban, Chorrillos was rustic and holiday homes were constructed, not to reproduce urban comforts, but as functional seasonal accommodation. Known as *ranchos*, they were built on the same principle as the shacks of fishermen and peasants. They were simple structures, usually of one floor, built with adobe and *quincha*, with a veranda where the inhabitants could enjoy the open air and the view while being sheltered from the sun, and with a railing separating them from the street. With the affluence of the guano era, housing became more solid, luxurious and ornate, but the basic structure and the name were retained. The *rancho* was a typical form of housing of the Lima area, examples of which are to be found not only in seaside settlements like Chorrillos, Barranco and Miraflores, but also in former rural communities like Pueblo Libre.

Chorrillos' period of splendour came during the 1860 and 1870s, at the height of the guano boom, when the capital's best families built opulent holiday homes and an elegant seafront promenade was constructed. During the War of the Pacific, however, the town was sacked and laid waste by the Chileans and, though it subsequently recovered towards the end of the century, it was on a much more modest scale. A feature of the coastal landscape is the architecturally eclectic Club de Regatas, an elite sports club with its own private beach, founded in 1875.

In the 1950s and 1960s the bay known as La Herradura (The Horseshoe) became Lima's most popular beach, but in the 1970s its popularity declined as the sea was contaminated by sewage emissions. Today Chorrillos has lost its elitist character and is socially mixed. Its continuing attractiveness as a residential area is attested by the modern apartment buildings which have sprung up along the front, but—perhaps appropriately, given its Indian origins—provincial migrants have also settled in its peripheral neighbourhoods.

In the early decades of the twentieth century Barranco displaced Chorrillos as Lima's most fashionable resort. Originally an Indian fishing settlement, it had already by the end of the seventeenth century become a recreation spot for Spaniards and Creoles, who acquired rural properties and built simple holiday homes. A link with colonial times is provided by the Ermita de la Santísima Cruz. In the middle of the eighteenth century Indian fishermen reported that the outline of Christ on the Cross had mysteriously appeared on the cliff face. A small chapel was built as a centre of pilgrimage and over the years it was enlarged and rebuilt, culminating in the church standing today. The Ermita was the heart of the locality and a village slowly grew up around it, but it was badly damaged by an earthquake in 1940 and has been closed ever since.

In the nineteenth century Barranco became a holiday centre for rich Limeñan families, as well as for British and German residents, and as in Chorrillos they built *ranchos* as summer residences, a good example being the house of the Nugent family in Avenida Grau. In 1870 the gulley leading down to the beach was turned into an attractive promenade, the Bajada de los Baños, and a few years later a wooden bridge, the Puente de los Suspiros (Bridge of Sighs) was erected over it. At the end of the bridge, in the little square in front of the Ermita, stands a bust of singer and songwriter Chabuca Granda, who celebrated

the bridge in one of her compositions. Though it, too, was sacked by the Chileans, Barranco suffered less than Chorrillos since it was not in the front line and it was more successful in recovering. Many prominent families opted to establish permanent homes there, and its population increased from 866 in 1876 to 5,911 in 1908. Constructed in a variety and combination of styles that constitutes part of Barranco's charm, these residences reflect the affluence enjoyed by the Creole bourgeoisie of the early twentieth century and their desire that their homes should be a visual statement of their status and good taste. The Paseo Sáenz Peña, in particular, contains a number of such houses and conveys a feel of the Barranco of that period. Among the more opulent examples are the mansions of the Rossel Ríos family in Avenida Grau and the Osma family in the Avenida Pedro de Osma (now a museum of colonial art). In modern times the continuing popularity of Barranco has led to the construction of apartment blocks along the seafront and on the cliffs beyond the Bajada de los Baños, with large windows and balconies to take advantage of the sunshine and the view. On the whole, such buildings have been designed to fit in with the adjacent older structures and Barranco remains one of Lima's most beautiful areas.

Two of Peru's major poets were natives of Barranco: José María Eguren (1874-1942) and Rafael de la Fuente Benavides (1908-85), who wrote under the pen-name Martín Adán. Eguren's house still stands in the Plazuela de San Francisco. Adán's youthful avant-garde novel, *La casa de cartón* (The Cardboard House, 1928), describes the experience of an adolescent growing up in Barranco in the 1920s. Since the 1980s Barranco has been transformed into Lima's bohemian quarter, and much of the older housing has been refurbished and turned into public establishments such as art galleries, cafés, bars and clubs. It has become a place where young writers and artists congregate and take part in cultural activities like experimental theatre and literary recitals. It has also become famous for its nightlife, and the area around the attractive modern Plaza Municipal is particularly lively.

Another resort which attracted holiday-makers from the nineteenth century onwards was La Punta, close to Callao. Unlike Miraflores, Barranco and Chorrillos, it is located at sea-level and its front gives easy access to the beach, though that advantage is offset somewhat by the fact that the beach is comprised of pebbles. Perhaps because it had an important Italian colony, La Punta has the air of a European seaside resort and provided all the expected facilities: pier, promenade, bandstand, entertainments. Particularly popular in the 1930s and 1940s, it was later somewhat sidelined as the city expanded southwards, but it remains pleasant little seaside community.

Though people still bathe and practise water sports there, the sea off the Costa Verde has become polluted in recent decades. It is still a very attractive place for a stroll, a particularly pleasant walk being the cliff top road from Miraflores to Barranco, but for bathing Limeñans now more commonly go further afield to newer beach resorts that over the years were developed along the coast. To the north the most important resort is Ancón, which like Chorrillos and Barranco has been an established holiday town since the mid-nineteenth century. But most modern development has taken place to the south, where there is a continuous string of beach resorts, the most popular being El Silencio. The largest is San Bartolo, which has grown into a flourishing town.

Limeñan Cuisine

Lima is widely acknowledged to be the gastronomic capital of South America. One reason for the excellence of its cuisine is that, because of its location, it is able to count on fresh, high-quality produce all the year round and, thanks to Peru's ecological and climatic diversity, it has access to a wide variety of produce. Another is that it has evolved out of a long process of cultural exchange involving native peoples, Spaniards, Africans and immigrants from Europe (particularly Italian and French) and Asia (Chinese and Japanese) and that it has been enriched by the culinary traditions of the country's various regions.

In addition to restaurants providing international cuisine, Lima has numerous Italian, Chinese and Japanese restaurants, reflecting the impact of immigration from those countries. Limeñans are especially fond of *chifas* (Chinese restaurants), where traditional Chinese cooking has been adapted to local tastes, and there are hundreds of them dotted around the city. Local cuisine—usually referred to as *comida criolla* (Creole food)—can be enjoyed in excellent small family restaurants as well as in more sophisticated establishments like A Puerta Cerrada (Bolognesi 752, Barranco), El Señorío de Sulco (Malecón Cisneros 1470, Miraflores) and José Antonio (Bernardo Monteagudo 200, San Isidro). But for someone spending only a few days in the city the best way to gain a sense of the range and quality of Limeñan cuisine is to visit one of a number of restaurants—like the Vista al Mar in Miraflores' Larcomar complex—which lay on a lavish buffet for Sunday lunch.

Limeñan cuisine is varied, but certain basic elements feature regularly. White rice is the most common accompaniment and dishes like *Arroz con pato* (rice with duck) or *Arroz con camarones* (rice with prawns) are usually to be found on restaurant menus. Another standard accompaniment is *salsa criolla* (Creole sauce), a mixture of chopped onions, hot peppers and parsley, seasoned with salt, oil and lemon juice. For seasoning the most common ingredient is *ají* (Peruvian hot pepper), of which there are five varieties. It is used in most dishes and sauces and has given its name to hot spicy dishes like *Ají de gallina* (spicy chicken casserole). One of its varieties, *rocoto*, is served stuffed with minced meat and other ingredients in the popular traditional dish, *rocoto relleno*. Another source of seasoning is the Peruvian lemon, which came to Peru from North Africa via Spain. It is smaller than the usual variety and has a particularly acid juice which gives a distinctive flavour to many of Lima's best known dishes.

Given that Peru has rich fishing grounds off its Pacific coast, it is hardly surprising that seafood should figure prominently in local cooking. It comes in many forms: as a *chupe* (a seafood chowder), as a *parihuela* (a seafood stew akin to bouillabaisse), as a *sudado* (cooked in fish stock), *a lo macho* (fish covered with shellfish in sauce), as a *picante de mariscos* (spicy shellfish) etc. Particularly popular is *ceviche* (sometimes written *cebiche*), which has virtually become the national dish. Its origins go back to pre-Hispanic times when the inhabitants of the coast ate their fish raw and seasoned with hot peppers or marinated in a sour grenadine-like local fruit. Later lemons, garlic and onions, introduced by the Spaniards, became key ingredients. The classic *ceviche* is made with freshly caught white fish such as *corvina* (sea bass), which is cut into small pieces, mixed with onion and seasoned with salt, garlic and hot pepper. It is then left to marinate for a few minutes in lemon juice and served immediately. There are, however, many variants of *ceviche*, since it can be made with any seafood or combination of seafoods. The dish is traditionally accompanied by two Peruvian staples: *choclo* (corn on the cob) and *camote* (sweet potato).

Potatoes, too, have a central place in Limeñan cuisine. It was Peru that gave the potato to the world and it has over 4,000 varieties. Of these the best are the yellow potato and the sweet potato, which have a unique flavour and texture. Potatoes are served in every conceivable form and constitute the basis of two of Lima's best loved dishes. As its name indicates, *papa a la huancaína* (potatoes in the style of Huancayo) is an example of how in cooking as well as in other areas of culture the capital has absorbed regional traditions. It is a simple but extremely tasty dish consisting of boiled yellow potatoes covered in a creamy sauce of cheese and hot peppers, served on a bed of lettuce and accompanied by slices of boiled egg and black olives. *Causa*, whose name derives from the Quechua *kausay* (necessary sustenance/staff of life), is a refreshing dish for hot summer days. A layered loaf of yellow potato purée with fillings of seafood and mayonnaise between the layers, it is chilled in the refrigerator before serving.

Other traditional dishes are local favourites. Served with a hot pepper sauce, the classic *anticucho* (kebab) is made with cow heart, but variants use chicken breast, chicken liver and fish. Tamales are a mixture of seasoned corn paste and pieces of pork wrapped in a banana leaf and boiled. They are served with Creole sauce. An adaptation of Chinese cooking, *lomo saltado* consists of strips of beef sautéed with pre-fried potato chips, chopped onion and tomato, strips of hot pepper, soya sauce and vinegar and served on a bed of white rice.

Lima is also famous for the variety of its pastries and desserts, a tradition dating back to colonial times, when convents specialized in the making of confectionery. The proximity of the coastal sugar plantations encouraged a sweet tooth and molasses is a basic ingredient of traditional dishes. Other key ingredients are fruit, dried fruit and spices. Among the most typical desserts are *mazamorra morada* (purple corn custard), a concoction of purple corn, sweet potato flour, fruit, dried fruits and sugar served sprinkled with cinnamon; *suspiro de limeña* (a Lima lady's sigh), a mixture of sweet cream and whipped egg yolks topped with sweet wine meringue; and *bien me sabe* (tastes nice), small sponge cakes containing honey, fruit and walnuts.

The classic Limeñan aperitif is pisco sour, made with pisco (a grape-based liquor) blended with lemon juice, corn syrup, egg white and ice and served with a few drops of bitters on the top. Beer is often drunk with meals, the two local brands being Cristal and Pilsen Callao,

though regional beers from Cuzco and Arequipa are also popular. Wine-drinkers will find two acceptable national wines: Tacama and Ocucaje. A favourite non-alcoholic drink is *chicha morada*, made from purple corn and fruit. But the drink most commonly consumed in restaurants is Inca Kola, a local carbonated soft drink that outsells Coca-Cola and has virtually become a symbol of national identity.

Squatter Settlements

Since the 1940s the development of Lima and, indeed, of the country as a whole has been distorted by an increasingly massive influx of migrants from the provinces. While Lima and other coastal cities began to experience industrialization, the countryside continued to languish in underdevelopment, and pressure on meagre resources was exacerbated by demographic growth brought about by access to modern medicines. At the same time, the horizons of rural people were broadened by the expansion of the mass media with the advent first of radio and then television, while newspapers were more widely read as a result of increasing levels of literacy, and the city came to be viewed by many as the path to a better life. The agrarian reform of the Velasco era also had the effect of loosening people's ties to the land, and the flight from the countryside was further fuelled by a succession of crises, such as the cataclysmic devastation wrought in large areas of the country by floods and drought in 1983 and the bloody civil war waged between the army and the Maoist guerrilla movement Sendero Luminoso in the 1980s and early 1990s. As peasants abandoned the land and flocked to the cities, Peru was transformed in the space of a few decades from a rural country into a predominantly urban society. The main focus of migration was, of course, the capital and by the 1980s two-thirds of Lima's population were migrants or children of migrants.

Unfortunately, the city lacked the infrastructure to absorb such an influx. Because of the modest nature of Peru's incipient industrialization, the demand for labour was small in comparison to the numbers looking for jobs and many found themselves struggling to subsist. Housing, too, was in short supply. The first waves of migrants tended to settle in the districts of the old city centre, which quickly became saturated. Subsequent migrant groups responded by establishing squatter settlements on the city's periphery and later on its barren desert hinterland. By the 1990s half of Lima's inhabitants lived in such settlements, concentrated in so-called "cones", triangular zones stretching outwards from the city to the north, south and east. Some have developed into veritable satellite towns. The largest is thought to be San Juan de Lurigancho, with some 760,000 inhabitants, while Comas, San Martín de Porras and Villa El Salvador, have populations of around a half-million.

Not surprisingly, much of the literature dealing with the migration process tends to focus on the frustration of the migrants' dreams of a better life. In Enrique Congrains Martín's "El niño de Junto al Cielo" (The Boy from Next to Heaven, 1954), that process is described allegorically through the adventures of Esteban, a ten-year-old boy recently arrived in Lima from the provinces who sets out to explore the city for the first time. His illusions are symbolized by the secret name he has given to the shanty town where his family has settled on the Cerro del Agustino, one of the hills overlooking Lima. Since he conceives of it as being literally "Next to Heaven", he has privately christened it so, thereby evoking the image of the capital nursed by the migrants, who are drawn there by the belief that it is an earthly paradise where all their dreams will be realized. Initially, Esteban is encouraged to feel optimistic about the future the city holds in store for him when, shortly after he sets out, he finds a ten-*soles* banknote lying on the ground. The banknote, of course, stands for the lure that attracts the migrants to the capital, the dream of streets paved with gold, the promise of an affluence that will liberate them from poverty and enable them to shape their own lives. Subsequently, however, Esteban is cheated out of his money and his faith in the benevolence of the city when he falls victim to a confidence trick worked on him by Pedro, a street-wise urchin with whom he makes friends and whom he artlessly tells about his lucky find. Pedro persuades him to invest his money in a joint business venture—buying and selling magazines—only to abscond with both the capital and the profits, leaving him stranded and penniless. In a wider sense that deception comes to symbolize the defrauded expectations of the whole migrant community, lured to Lima by the promise of a better life only to end up disappointed and disillusioned by the harsh reality of the capital. The expedition which takes Esteban from his hilltop shanty town to the streets of central Lima can be read as a metaphorical journey, not only in that it brings him down to earth from the heights of his unworldly innocence, but in that by so doing it replicates the bitter road travelled by so many of the country's migrant masses.

Julio Ramón Ribeyro's "Los gallinazos sin plumas" (The Featherless Buzzards, 1954) evokes the poverty and squalor of the shanty towns through the story of two young brothers, Enrique and Efraín, who each morning go out foraging for food for their grandfather's pig. The boys are part of a whole army of human scavengers who eke out a meagre livelihood rummaging among the city's refuse, in the dustbins of residential districts and public buildings and even on the municipal rubbish dumps. The dehumanizing poverty in which the new urban population lives is signalled by the fact that on the rubbish dump the boys, the featherless buzzards of the title, are reduced to the primitive level of the scavenger birds alongside which they root for scraps of food:

> *From then on, Efraín and Enrique made their trek to the rubbish dump on Wednesdays and Sundays. Soon they became part of the strange fauna of those places and the buzzards, accustomed to their presence, worked at their side, cawing, flapping their wings, poking with their yellow beaks, as if helping them to uncover the trail of the precious filth.*

A similarly bleak portrayal of the migrant experience is provided by one of Peruvian cinema's best films, *Gregorio* (1985), a collective production by the Grupo Chaski. The film is essentially a docu-drama, with a fictional narrative serving as a thread linking the documentary together. Gregorio and his mother travel to Lima from their home in the Andes to join up with his father, who has migrated ahead of them. Shortly after they have established themselves in a new shanty town, the father falls ill and dies, his constitution weakened by overwork. Initially, Gregorio and his mother pull together to keep the household going, she by working as a washerwoman and seamstress, he by supplementing her earnings as a shoe-shine boy in the city centre. Yet he is emotionally distraught when his mother initiates a relationship with another man and he becomes involved with a gang of homeless street children, under whose influence he drifts into thieving and smoking marihuana. In an attempt to reconcile himself with his mother he offers her the proceeds of a robbery, but succeeds only in alienating her and the gang (for whom he was holding the money), and the closing shots show him travelling alone in a bus into the city centre, an ending that leaves open the question of how he will survive in the streets of the capital. Filmed almost entirely in the streets, *Gregorio* captures the feverish rhythm of a crowded and overpopulated city and, starkly but without sensationalism, evokes the hard daily life of its inhabitants, epitomized by the children of the shanty towns, who are forced to assume a premature adulthood with which they are not emotionally equipped to cope. The film seems to imply that for migrants from the countryside the move to Lima merely means swapping one form of hardship for another and at the emotional cost of losing their identity.

A different perspective is offered by writers from the ranks of the squatter community, who present the creation of shanty towns as the first phase in a process whereby the marginalized provincial majority were opening a space for themselves in national society. The working-class poet Leoncio Bueno's "Wayno de Comas" (Huayno of Comas) depicts the invasion of lands to establish the shanty town of Comas in 1958 as the opening of a front in the war to create an egalitarian and multiracial society:

> *I speak here, in this place, behind*
> *the barbed wire of the social struggle.*
> *I speak here, where before there was nothing,*
> *each day I hear the growth of my cries,*
> *of my voice, subversive in this land taken*
> *by the momentum of so many. [...]*
> *One day the masses said: Do we exist or not?*
> *We took these hills, a great work is being raised*
> *harnessed to the thrust of the space age.*
> *Tomorrow gringo historians, sociologists, psychologists,*
> *   anthropologists will come.*
> *They'll say: "How intwesting… Wis Koumas a lunag landscape?"*
> *Exactly. The masses came,*
> *they had no water to drink*
> *but they sowed trees.*

The foundation of Comas is represented as an epic feat destined to cause disbelief among scholars of the future and comparable to the achievement of the American astronauts who landed on the moon. It is so in a literal sense, in that the settlers have created a flourishing community out of a barren wasteland reminiscent of a lunar landscape. It is even more so in a symbolic sense, in that that they have planted the seeds of a new society in which the outsider will at long last have a place.

Likewise, Cronwell Jara's *Patíbulo para un caballo* (Scaffold for a Horse, 1989), set in 1948, recounts the successful resistance of the inhabitants of the fictional shanty town of Montacerdos to the authorities' attempts to evict them from the land where they have squatted. The cordon the police set up around the community can be read a symbol of exclusion, of the class barriers erected by the dominant minority to preserve its privilege. But the metaphor is also two-sided, as the barricades erected by the settlers to repulse the police are an emblem of popular resistance, an assertion of the migrants' determination to fight back against an unjust social order and to achieve a better future for themselves and their families. In the end, the connotations of the novel's central symbol turn out to be the reverse of what they originally appeared to be. Though the narrative revolves around the settlers' struggle to defend themselves against police attempts to dislodge them, it is ultimately the established order which is under siege. As migrants from all the various regions of the country, the inhabitants of Montacerdos represent Peru's underclasses who are beginning to mobilize. Accordingly, it is the old system that is on the defensive, struggling to contain a mass movement which threatens to overwhelm the traditional social structure and to transform the racial and cultural character of the nation. With the eventual lifting of the siege, the right of the underclasses to a place in national society is officially recognized. The novel does not exaggerate the extent of the settlers' victory. Montecerdos remains a shanty town and its inhabitants continue to struggle to survive in conditions of squalor and deprivation. Yet the victory is nonetheless significant, since it marks the start of a slow but relentless process of social change. The government's response to the resistance put up by the settlers reflects a pragmatic recognition by the ruling establishment that the migrant sector now constitutes a political force which has to be wooed and placated. And the penetration of the city by the settlers of Montacerdos, albeit as humble street vendors, labourers and artisans, points ahead to a progressive opening up of Peruvian society and to a dynamic of upward social mobility. That process is exemplified by the narrator Maruja, who from childhood in the shanty town progresses to become a university student.

So-called shanty towns were, in fact, the means by which the migrants created their own living space. Most settlements came into being through mass invasions of unoccupied land. Such invasions were planned and organized like a military campaign. An engineer or engineering student was contracted to draw up a plan of the future community, assigning plots to individuals and reserving areas for public buildings (schools, health centres, community council) and places of recreation (parks, sports fields). The invasion usually took place at night or in the early hours of the morning and usually on a public holiday to reduce the possibility of a quick reaction by the authorities. The site was marked out and the ground cleared and in a matter of hours makeshift houses consisting of panels of woven reeds were in place.

A general assembly would elect a committee to run the settlement's affairs, to negotiate with the authorities to regularize its position and to bring in public services like water, sewerage, electricity and roads. In the main, that work was carried out by the settlers themselves, with little support from the state. Indeed, in the early stages of the migration process the authorities tended to opt for a policy of evicting squatters. Yet as the plight of the migrants blossomed into a major social issue, the Church and other groups and organizations began to take up their cause and to provide assistance; and as they came to be a political constituency more numerous than the capital's traditional population, politicians of all persuasions began to woo them and when in power colluded in land invasions and provided services to the new settlements. In the 1970s, in particular, the military government promoted a self-help programme directed by the state. Symptomatic of this gradual official recognition of squatter settlements was the evolving terminology used to describe them, since they were initially known as "barriadas" (shanty towns) but were subsequently upgraded to "pueblos jóvenes" (young towns).

In time, settlements which started out as a collection of precarious structures without services gradually develop into proper townships with solidly constructed houses and modern amenities. Such is the case of older communities like San Martín de Porras and Comas, which started as migrant settlements in the 1940s and 1950s, and of Villa El Salvador, which is unique in that it was founded with government support in the 1970s as a planned model community. These settlements have paved streets, municipal gardens, schools and electricity, water and sewerage systems, and San Martín de Porras and Villa El Salvador even boast modern shopping malls and multiplex cinemas. At the same time, the constant influx of migrants has led to the continual creation of new settlements and it is estimated that nearly a third of Lima's population live in precarious shanty towns lacking basic services. Thirty per cent of the city's inhabitants have no running water; 46 per cent lack drainage; 28 per cent lack electricity; 38 per cent have no public lighting. Lima's squatter settlements thus continue to be an emblem of the socio-economic inequality of Peruvian society and an indictment of the failure of the Peruvian state to provide for the welfare of its citizens.

The Other Path

Faced with the lack of job opportunities, migrants were obliged to devise alternative ways of earning a living, and on the margin of the official economy emerged a vast informal economy whose activities were unregulated and untaxed. Its most visible manifestation was street trading, which in 1986 was carried out by an estimated 91,455 people, located mainly in the popular districts and almost 60 per cent of whose activity was devoted to the sale of foodstuffs. The informal sector also came to dominate the capital's transport system by providing bus services between the squatter settlements and the rest of the city; in the mid-1980s it accounted for 93 per cent of Lima's transport fleet. The informal economy also included a large number of small businesses and workshops, accounting for 45.7 per cent of Peru's economically active population and 38.9 per cent of its GDP by the end of the 1980s. In *The Other Path: The Invisible Revolution in the Third World* (1989) neo-liberal economist Hernando de Soto romanticizes these informal workers by depicting them as grassroots examples of the capitalist entrepreneurial spirit:

> *They have demonstrated their initiative by migrating, breaking with the past without any prospect of a secure future, they have learned how to identify and satisfy others' needs and their confidence in their abilities is greater than their fear of competition. When they start something, they know that there is always a risk of failure. Every day they face dilemmas: what and how are they going to produce? What are they going to make it with? At what prices will they buy and sell? Will they manage to find long-term customers? Behind every product offered or manufactured, behind all the apparent disorder or relative illegality, are their sophisticated calculations and difficult decisions.*
>
> *This ability to take risks and calculate is important because it means that a broad entrepreneurial base is already being created. In Peru, informality has turned a large number of people into entrepreneurs, into people who know how to seize opportunities by managing available resources, including their own labour, relatively efficiently. [...]*
>
> *This new business class is a very valuable resource: it is the human capital essential for economic takeoff. It has meant survival for those who had nothing and has served as a safety valve for societal tensions. It has given mobility and productive flexibility to the wave of migrants, and is, in fact, doing what the state could never have done: bring large numbers of outsiders into the country's money economy.*

There is a considerable element of truth in De Soto's depiction of Lima's new migrant population. They are certainly far from being passive victims of socio-economic disadvantage, since by their own initiative, hard work and determination they have constructed homes for their families, found means of subsisting and, in some cases, even prospered. They also represent a potential that the state has so far failed to harness.

Yet it is a travesty to portray them as budding capitalists who need only to be freed from the shackles of state regulation in order to blossom. In using them to promote his own neo-liberal agenda, De

Soto is guilty both of overstating the case and of being selective with the facts. On the one hand, though the informal sector has thrown up examples of self-made capitalists, it is made up mainly of desperate street vendors and artisans who earn barely enough to get by, while those employed in unregulated backstreet workshops manufacturing goods for sale on the streets have no legal rights or protection. And as the experience of the 1990s demonstrated, the economic model which he proposes disastrously aggravated the plight of the lower sectors.

On the other hand, though the move to the city has forced migrants to learn to compete in order to survive, one of the strengths of their settlements are neighbourhood associations born of the Andean community tradition and collective cooperation in initiatives such as the pooling of resources in communal kitchens has been a leading strategy in combating poverty. The story of the migrants' struggle to triumph over adversity and build a better future for themselves and their families is truly uplifting, not simply because of the initiative which they have displayed, but because they have demonstrated the effectiveness of community values in a society where they are sadly lacking.

Huaynos and Chicha

In the early days of the shanty towns the authorities adopted a policy of evicting settlers in a futile attempt to discourage migration from the countryside. They did so in response to the fears and prejudices of Lima's middle classes, who were concerned that an influx of migrants from the sierra would swamp their city, changing its character and lowering its tone. Those fears are evoked in Antonio Cisneros' "Crónica de Lima" (Chronicle of Lima, 1968), where the shanty towns ringing the capital are likened to the encampment of a barbarian horde:

> On the sandy hills
> barbarians from the south and east have built
> a camp that's bigger than the whole city, and they have other gods.

In the event, the flow of migrants could not be contained and has often been described as an invasion. In the eyes of some, it was nothing less than a process of re-conquest whereby Peru's subaltern peoples were reclaiming the country taken from their ancestors by the conquistadors.

Thus, José María Arguedas, in the prose poem "A nuestro padre creador Tupac Amaru" (To our Father Creator Tupac Amaru, 1972), depicts the rural migrants as a conquering host slowly but surely turning the former centre of Spanish and Creole power into an Andean city by altering its ethnic composition and imposing their traditions and customs:

> *We have come to the immense village of the masters and we are over-turning it...We are thousands of thousands, here, now. We are united; we have gathered village by village, name by name, and we are closing in on this immense city which hated us, which despised us as horse shit. We will turn it into a town of men who intone the hymns of the four regions of our world.*

To a considerable extent, the capital has become Andeanized, as the migrants brought their own culture with them and it came to pervade the city's public spaces. Every Sunday huge and enthusiastic crowds of migrants flocked to establishments known as *coliseos folklóricos* which, from the late 1940s onwards, staged performances of Andean music and dance featuring artists from the different regions of the sierra. So popular were the *coliseos* that by the mid-1950s there were around fifteen of them, the most important being the Coliseo Nacional, a circus tent in La Victoria, and the Coliseo Cerrado del Puente del Ejército, a sports ground in the city centre. But as the flow of migration steadily increased and as the migrants became better organized, the *coliseos* were displaced as the main centres of Andean cultural expression by provincial clubs, enabling migrants from the same area or region to maintain links with one another and with their place of origin. These clubs held regular Sunday gatherings, celebrated their local festivals with traditional dances and songs and organized functions to raise money to support their home community. They often also had a football team competing in a district league, and matches were usually followed by music and dancing.

Recognizing a new market opportunity, the mass media were soon catering to the demand for Andean music among the migrant community. The first discs were cut in the late 1940s, and by the 1970s recordings of Andean music were being produced by all the major companies and by a number of small companies specializing in that market. Andean music sold more records than any other form of music, and one company reportedly had sales of 100,000 units a month. From the mid-1950s, too, certain radio stations began to introduce programmes of Andean music into their schedules and by the 1980s there were four stations targeted at the migrant population and providing them with a regular diet of music from the sierra. Star performers like El Picaflor de los Andes (Alberto Gil Mallma), El Jilguero del Huascarán (Ernesto Sánchez Fajardo) and La Pastorita Huaracina (María Alvarado Trujillo) became national celebrities; such was their popularity that when the first-named died in 1975 over 100,000 people turned out for his funeral to pay their last respects. And by the 1970s the Andean *huayno*—like the *vals criollo*, a combination of music, song and dance—ranked first in terms of popularity among the urban public.

Andean culture has always been characterized by its great regional diversity and to some extent that diversity was replicated in the urban environment. If the provincial clubs came to flourish at the expense of the *coliseos folklóricos*, it was because they put on cultural events that kept homesick migrants in touch with their local roots, and some of the smaller record companies were able to thrive by specializing in the music of particular regions. Yet as records and radio became Andean music's main vehicle of diffusion, it inevitably underwent a process of standardization, since the aim of the mass media was to reach as wide an audience as possible. It is that which explains why the *huayno* came to predominate over other forms of Andean music as the cultural expression *par excellence* of the migrant masses. Since the colonial period the *huayno* had been most common genre throughout the Andean area, with numerous local and regional variants and different forms of instrumental accompaniment. The fact that it was pan-Andean in character, yet allowed for local variations, meant that it was a genre with which all migrants from the sierra could identify.

In the 1970s a new musical phenomenon emerged among the migrant community's younger generation: *chicha* or *cumbia andina*. *Chicha* took its name from the fermented maize beer that was traditional in the Andes and brewed by Andean migrants in the shanty towns. As its alternative name suggests, it was a kind of syncretism of the *huayno* and the tropical rhythms of the Colombian *cumbia*, which became extremely popular throughout Latin America in the 1960s, the successful combination of the two genres being made possible by the fact that they had similar rhythmic structures. At the same time, *chicha* was distinctively modern in that it adopted the sophisticated electronic equipment and presentational style typical of western pop and rock. Making use of electric guitars, drums, synthesizers and sometimes the electric organ and with powerful amplifiers projecting their music to the furthest corners, bands played to mass audiences in public squares, football stadiums and dance halls known as *chichódromos* located in popular districts like El Cercado, Breña and Pueblo Libre. Leading groups like Los Shapis, Alegría, Chacalón and La Nueva Crema built up a massive following, and so popular did *chicha* become among the youth of the lower classes that it sold more records in Peru than international superstars Julio Iglesias and Michael Jackson put together. Los Shapis' hit "El Aguajal" alone sold over a million copies in three years.

The evolution from *huayno* to *chicha* mirrors the history of the capital's migrant community. The *huayno* had its origins in the countryside and for homesick migrants, uprooted from a traditional rural way of life and transplanted to an alien urban environment, it provided both an emotional link with the world they had left behind and a means whereby they resisted acculturation and retained a sense of

their own distinct identity. Whether singing the vicissitudes of love or the beauty of the Andean landscape or evoking traditional festivals, the music and the lyrics of the *huayno* conjured up for exiled *serranos* images of the beloved land from which they were now separated. Ernesto Sánchez Fajardo's "Carrito de regreso" (The Car Home), for example, expresses the migrant's yearning for his home village:

Hurry, hurry, little car, along the highway.
Cross, cross the plateaux and the mountains.
Take me back to my blessed land,
for my heart is dying for those places.
When I reach my land I'll live content
by the side of my cholita *whom I love so much.*
I want no more of people slighting me
and looking at me with malevolence.

Chicha, on the other hand, though it grew out of the *huayno*, was very much an urban phenomenon, the cultural expression of the children of migrants who had been born and brought up in the city and for whom the city was their home environment. And while the *huayno*, though itself tending towards standardization, retained regional variations, *chicha* was characterized by a more uniform style, as there began to emerge among the young of the migrant community a more generalized sense of identity based on Andean descent rather than local regional roots. Its appropriation of western technology and western presentational techniques does not imply a slavish adoption of western ways, but rather reflects second-generation migrants' familiarity with modernity and their sense of themselves as having joined the modern world.

It should be stressed that *chicha* did not displace the *huayno* but that they coexisted. Though the two genres reflect the experience of different generations, the provincial clubs that kept Andean traditions alive were also one of the main venues for *chicha* and it was not uncommon for a session of traditional music for parents to be followed by a session of *chicha* for the young folk. Nor on the whole does it seem that the younger generation rejected the culture of their parents but rather that they respected it as their heritage. Indeed, the fact that *chicha* had its origins in the *huayno* would seem to indicate that, though they eagerly embraced modernity, the younger generation saw their identity as rooted in the Andean tradition and the young people who thronged to the *chichódromos* did so not as mere spectators but to join in as part of a collectivity re-enacting the combination of music, song and dance characteristic of the festivities of their elders.

Chicha also distinguished itself both from western popular music and from the *huayno*, which looked back to the rural past, in that some of its most successful lyrics centred on the experience of the new urban masses. Los Shapis' hit "Así es mi trabajo" (It's my job) became the anthem of the *ambulantes*, the migrants who, lacking employment opportunities, turned to small-scale street trading to make a living:

> *In my house/I have my wares*
> *to go tomorrow/to sell in the street.*
> *I'm not ashamed of it,/it's my job.*
> *I steal from no one,/I cheat no one.*
> *Please leave me alone/don't take my wares from me.*
> *To work in the city/is what I want, not to rob.*

Chicha continues to be the popular music of the youth of Lima's migrant community. Now more commonly known as *tecnocumbia*—a name regarded as more prestigious—it has evolved in major ways. Firstly, though *chicha* originated in Lima, its popularity soon spread to other parts of the country and many of its leading stars are now singers and bands who first made their name in the provinces and then went on to take the capital by storm. Indeed, the most popular and successful performer of the late 1990s was a native of the Amazon region, Rossy War. Secondly, socially informed music of the early phase has given way to a kind of "*chicha* lite" that is more melodious and sweetly romantic. Thirdly, it has shed much of its Andean flavour and, reflecting the globalization of the 1990s, has become more cosmopolitan and eclectic in the best postmodern manner. Rossy War, for example, favours outfits that simultaneously play on her Amazon origins and project her as the Peruvian equivalent of international pop stars like Madonna and her (inaccurate) anglicization of her name—Rosa Guerra—is symptomatic of a bid to be a player on the international scene. To talk of the Andeanization of Lima is, therefore, to misrepresent the process that has been taking place in the capital. In fact, the evolution of *chicha* reflects the way in which Lima has become a melting-pot where regional traditions are converging with western modernity to produce a new and distinctive popular culture. Yet it would be difficult to claim that it is symptomatic of the emergence of a shared sense of national identity. *Chicha's* public are Lima's *cholos*, the inhabitants of the city's *pueblos jóvenes* and working-class districts, and in middle- and upper-class residential areas it is rarely heard, except when domestic servants listen to it on the radio. There are indications that the watered-down version of the 1990s is becoming more widely accepted, particularly in the wake of the inroads it has made abroad in countries like Argentina, but even so, the musical preferences of middle-class youth are more likely to be *salsa* and western pop. Lima remains a city culturally divided.

Literature since 1940

Conventionally the verse of the poets who emerged in the 1940s and 1950s or who produced their main work during that period is classified as "pure poetry" or "social poetry". Among those associated with the former were Martín Adán, Jorge Eduardo Eielson and Javier Sologuren, who turned their backs on their environment to take refuge in the timeless world of literature, creating in poems of rigorous formal perfection an alternative space where life is lived at a higher level. The most accomplished of the latter category were Alejandro Romualdo and Juan Gonzalo Rose. Both trends can be seen as a response to the repressive climate of an era when the oligarchy allied itself with the military to maintain its hold on power and contain pressure for social change. But the classification itself is somewhat simplistic, since so-called "pure poetry" was far from being merely escapist and produced major poems on the human condition, while the social poets also wrote about personal experience. Nor can all poets of the period be so neatly categorized. The work of Blanca Varela expresses her experience as a woman and her love-hate relationship with Lima, but centres above all on the human condition, its dominant notes being a rebellious dissatisfaction and a lucid awareness of life's ultimate absurdity. Carlos Germán Belli developed a highly original mock-classical manner which indirectly voices social criticism by giving expression to the frustrations of the country's middle classes and, in his later work, serves as a vehicle for metaphysical meditations. Belli's early work conveys particularly effectively the atmosphere of the period of oligarchic domination, evoking the image of an anachronistic society bypassed by modernity. Replicating the discourse of Spanish pastoral poetry of the sixteenth and seventeenth centuries, he makes frequent inter-textual allusions to the mythical Arcadia that was the setting for that poetry, but such allusions function as an ironic contrast, for the valley inhabited by the Peruvian shepherd-poet is a cold, arid, inhospitable land where he lives in

bondage as the serf of cruel feudal lords and where he must toil
ceaselessly to survive at the most basic level. Recurrent motifs such as
fetters and the foot pressing down on his neck convey his humiliating
condition of servitude:

> *Deaf, maimed, dumb, one-eyed, lame,*
> *I live with the chassis of my neck*
> *beneath the plump foot of the horrid master, [...]*
> *and we live in pits, without leisure to mitigate*
> *the iron or wood of the great fetter.*

The 1960s constituted a major watershed in modern Peruvian
poetry. The spread of modern systems of communication brought
about a universal broadening of horizons and an internationalization of
culture, and the period was marked by a liberalization of the
socio-political climate and a trend towards greater permissiveness in all
aspects of life. Reflecting the spirit of the age, a new generation of poets
adopted a poetic manner marked by freer, more open forms and by a
colloquial conversational tone that was often jokey and irreverent.
Foremost among them was Antonio Cisneros, whose verse is
characterized by a devastating irony, which he wields to debunk the
mythologies of the ruling establishment and voice his antipathy towards
its staid bourgeois lifestyle. The poets of the 1970s were to continue and
develop the poetic manner of their predecessors, going even further in
their cultivation of a colloquial language and tone and incorporating
into their verse references to the paraphernalia of modern city life, in
order to capture the spirit of the new society that was emerging as a
result of industrialization, mass migration to the cities and the
revolutionary policies of the Velasco regime. Outstanding among them
is Abelardo Sánchez León, whose work expresses the alienation of an
individual estranged from the traditional, exclusive bourgeois world in
which he grew up and unsure of his place in the changing society
around him. Yet the main feature of the period was the emergence of
writers of humble extraction, such as Enrique Verástegui and José
Watanabe, who broke the middle classes' traditional monopoly of
literature and were the literary expression of a provincial lower class
claiming a place and a voice in national society. This democratization of
poetry was to continue in the 1980s with the appearance of a whole

generation of women poets such as Carmen Ollé, Giovanna Pollarolo, Mariela Dreyfus, Patricia Alba and Sonia Luz Carrillo.

In the narrative field the 1950s saw the advent of a generation of writers—Enrique Congrains Martín, Carlos Eduardo Zavaleta, Eleodoro Vargas Vicuña, Julio Ramón Ribeyro—who sought to modernize Peruvian writing by assimilating the technical developments of mainstream western fiction. Though they also dealt with regional life, their work was mainly urban, reflecting the impact of the industrialization of the coast and the shift of population from the rural areas to the cities, particularly Lima. Congrains Martín, in the stories of *Lima, hora cero* (Lima, Zero Hour, 1954) and in the novel *No una sino muchas muertes* (Not One but Many Deaths, 1957), portrays the hardships and frustrated ambitions of the new urban masses, while much of Ribeyro's fiction focuses on those from the middle classes who find themselves socially displaced because of their inability to compete in the new society. The outstanding figure of the generation was Ribeyro, who in addition to three novels produced a huge corpus of short fiction dealing with universal as well as national themes and is recognized as one of Latin America's major short-story writers.

The technical innovations of the 1950s generation formed part of a continent-wide trend that was to culminate in the 1960s with the so-called "boom" in Spanish-American fiction. In Peru the two main representatives of the new narrative were José María Arguedas and Mario Vargas Llosa. Already an established novelist, Arguedas was inspired by the example of his young compatriots to renovate his narrative style and produced his best work in the latter stages of his career. In addition to the works already mentioned, he left an important uncompleted novel *El zorro de arriba y el zorro de abajo* (The Fox of Above and the Fox of Below, 1971), which explores the new society which was emerging as a result of industrialization and mass migration. Vargas Llosa was to become one of the superstars of Latin American fiction. In the course of his career he has produced a vast corpus of writing, but his best novels are reckoned to be his first three, in which he deploys a complex style involving multiple narrators and a fragmented narrative that constantly switches time and place. *La ciudad y los perros* describes the enclosed environment of a military college as a microcosm of national society. *La Casa Verde* (The Green House, 1966) focuses on the interior of the country, conveying an image of Peru as a nation divided by geography, culture, race and class. *Conversación en La Catedral* explores political corruption and its corrosive effect on Peruvian society. Among the second wave of so-called "new novelists" who came to the fore in the 1970s, Alfredo Bryce Echenique won international acclaim with *Un mundo para Julius*, in which he depicts the privileged world of the Creole oligarchy.

In recent decades Peruvian fiction has continued to be marked by the sophistication of its narrative technique. But probably the most significant development has been the success of writers from lower-class backgrounds whose work seeks to give a history to the traditionally excluded elements of national society. Gregorio Martínez, in the stories of *Tierra de caléndula* (Marigold Land, 1975) and the novels *Canto de sirena* (Siren Song, 1977) and *Crónica de músicos y diablos* (Chronicle of Musicians and Devils, 1991), re-creates the experience of the Afro-Peruvian peasantry of the southern coastal region. Cronwell Jara's novel *Patíbulo para un caballo* (Scaffold for a Horse, 1989) is a foundational myth recounting the story of migrants' conquest of a space in the city. Miguel Gutiérrez's *La violencia del tiempo* (The Violence of Time, 1992) is a saga recounting the history of a humble *mestizo* family over several generations. Paralleling changes which have been taking place in the country at large, fiction has thus begun to reflect the multiracial character of Peruvian society and to promote a multicultural model of nationhood.

The Future

The term *chicha*, which was coined to describe the customs of the migrant community, has come to be used in some quarters to define the new Lima, the inference being that with the uncontrolled growth of the city the whole of society has become "informalized" as old standards have broken down. It is on this so-called *chicha* culture that novelist Alfredo Bryce Echenique focuses in an essay written shortly after his return to Lima in the 1990s. He describes the dismay he experienced at finding how the city had changed during his thirty-odd years' absence:

> *Compared to the city I left three long decades ago, today's Lima is much less jolly, less lively, less human, and less inhabitable. It may well be that eyes accustomed to it don't perceive the magnitude of the transformations, but mine, those of a man who one fine day decided he*

*didn't give a damn and took off, have yet to shake off the painful shock
and total anguish of what they see.*

People tell you that nowadays Lima is chicha—*tasteless, cheap,
pretentious—and they go their merry way.* Chicha: *the president,
the traffic, the music, the climate, Peruvian television, hyperpatrio-
tism, Peru's soccer team ("They played like Peruvians and lost," an
expert explained to me after yet another defeat [...]). Everything is*
chicha, *our souls are* chicha, *being eccentric is* chicha, *corruption is*
chicha, *moral degradation is* chicha, *and of course the sociologists who
invented the word* chicha *are* chicha.

So it's a chicha *vicious circle, which is why you find this man who
returned grinding his teeth. He lacks* chicha *reflexes,* chicha *defence
mechanisms,* chicha *offence mechanisms, aggression mechanisms and
even more the dehumanized means to see without seeing [...]. And
he lacks the* chicha *capacity to survive the savage decibels of* chicha
volume and the annoying noises that are all noises and chicha *into
the bargain.*

*To overlook all that, people have to ride bareback on the wild
mustang of vulgarity and violence, ignoring the ugliness in the ugli-
est and most expensive neighbourhood (there is no most-beautiful
neighbourhood any more), the hunger and misery, unemployment
and homelessness, ignoring our infamous social contract whereby
everyone speaks in hushed tones (which is preferable, considering how
badly they speak, especially on* chicha *television, which is all television), ignoring the stoplights where all the vendors who ever existed
lurk. [...]*

*But I'm no expert in these matters. I'm just a voice crying out in
a* chicha *desert.*

If Bryce is unhappy about what has become of Lima, architect Juan
Günther Doering, a town-planning expert, is even gloomier about its
future:

*If Lima's demographic and urban growth continues, [...] there is no
doubt that the city's only future is one of chaos, anarchy and a wors-
ening of the poverty that already afflicts a large part of its population.
The city will go on expanding in a disordered fashion, based on the
construction of wretched hovels, till it covers all the cultivated space*

that still exists in the Chillón, Rímac and Lurín valleys, as well as the arid ravines of the hills that delimit those valleys. Given the ever more difficult features of those terrains, this expansion will be carried out with a very low density of construction, thereby making it even more expensive to provide public services and, therefore, making their installation impossible in these new settlements. [...] By 2010 the city will have overspilled the inhabitable areas of Lima province that lie between the Pacific Ocean and the Andean cordillera, and will have begun to make inroads into the neighbouring valleys of the Chancay and Chilca rivers, both of which are more than 70 kilometres' distance from the city centre.

In effect, the enormous influx of migrants from the provinces has distorted Lima's development and it is now a city faced with a tremendous crisis. It has run out of space to accommodate more migrants, it lacks the resources to provide basic services for its growing population, and its industrial growth is unable to match the demand for jobs. Lima, in this sense, is now paying the penalty for the privileged position it enjoyed down the centuries. From its foundation the city has been Peru. It was here that political power was concentrated. It flourished as Peru's point of contact with the outside world, growing rich by exporting the country's resources and using the proceeds to turn itself into a city that could emulate European capitals. Later, when the country began to become industrialized, eighty per cent of industrial development was in the Lima-Callao area. In the meantime, the provinces in general and rural areas in particular stagnated in poverty and underdevelopment. The centralization of educational institutions and white-collar occupations in the capital meant that aspiring middle-class provincials were obliged to migrate to better themselves. Later, rural poverty and the myth of opportunities provided by the big city led to a concerted movement of population from the countryside. Today Lima is indeed Peru in that, as a popular saying goes, all of Peru is in Lima.

At the same time, Lima is singularly dependent on the rest of Peru for its food, its water, its electric energy and its revenue from minerals, oil and gas, and the precariousness of the city's existence and its dependence on the rest of the country were brought home to Limeñans by the sabotage campaign waged by Shining Path in the 1980s and early

1990s. Water, in particular, is a serious problem, for supplies are limited and rationing is often necessary, particularly when rainfall is low in the Andean highlands.

Theoretically at least, the most obvious solution to Lima's problems would be to reverse the course of history by pursuing a policy of decentralization and regional development, thereby discouraging the flow of migrants to the capital. Such a policy has often featured in official rhetoric but efforts to put it into effect have been desultory, partly because of lack of political will, partly because the unfortunate fact is that the state lacks the resources to make whole-scale regional development feasible. Moreover, in a very real sense Lima's primacy over the rest of the country is self-perpetuating, since its economic and demographic growth has the effect of reinforcing both its political importance and its claim to a greater share of national resources.

If migration to the capital looks likely to continue, it is also hard to see how Lima can control the rising birth rate that is the other major factor in its disproportionate growth, since the root cause of the population explosion is not that women are producing large numbers of offspring but that improvements in basic health care have meant that people who in the past would have died at an early age are now growing up to produce children who in their turn produce more children. Nor is it easy to envisage Peru achieving the kind of dramatic economic take-off that would enable Lima to create jobs for its growing population and to acquire the revenue to provide essential services, since 25 per cent of the country's export earnings go to servicing its foreign debt and its economy remains largely dependent on the export of minerals, oil and gas, with most of its manufactures coming from abroad. It is difficult, therefore, to be optimistic about Lima's future.

Yet, in one respect at least, Lima is a much better place that when I first got to know it in the mid-1960s. As a result of migration the capital now more truly reflects Peru's multiracial and multicultural diversity and it is a more open society where, despite appalling poverty, ordinary people have opportunities to gain an education and to better themselves. There is still a long way to go, of course. The different classes continue to inhabit different worlds within the same shared urban space and in some quarters the Andean migrants are grudgingly accepted as an unavoidable fact of life rather treated as social equals. Nonetheless, it is to be expected that over time significant sectors of the migrant population will improve their social and economic status and slowly but inevitably there is emerging a consensus that Peru's only future is as a rainbow nation.

Finally, it is above all the extraordinary resilience of Lima's ordinary people that inspires faith in its future. When one sees not just the ingenuity, determination and long hours of hard work with which they prevail over the precariousness of their daily lives, but also their dogged pursuit of qualifications that will enable them to get on in life, it hard to believe that they and their city will fail to endure and thrive.

FURTHER READING

Adán, Martín, *The Cardboard House*. St. Paul, MN: Graywolf Press, 1990.

Angrand, Léonce, *Imagen del Perú en el siglo XIX*. Lima: Milla Batres, 1972.

Anton, Ferdinand, *Ancient Peruvian Textiles*. London: Thames and Hudson, 1987.

Bayly, Jaime, *No se lo digas a nadie*. Barcelona: Seix Barral, 1994.

————, *Los últimos días de "La Prensa"*. Barcelona: Seix Barral, 1996.

Bedoya, Ricardo, *Un cine reencontrado: diccionario ilustrado de las películas peruanas*. Lima: Universidad de Lima, 1997.

Belli, Carlos Germán, *El pie sobre el cuello*. Montevideo: Alfa, 1967.

Bernales Ballesteros, Jorge, *Lima, la ciudad y sus monumentos*. Sevilla: Escuela de Estudios Hispano-Americanos, 1972.

Bonfiglio, Giovanni, *Los italianos en la sociedad peruana: una visión histórica*. Lima: Asociación Italianos del Perú, 1993.

Bowser, Frederick P., *The African Slave in Colonial Peru 1524-1650*. Stanford, CA: Stanford University Press, 1974.

Bryce Echenique, Alfredo, *A World for Julius*. Austin: University of Texas Press, 1992.

Calderón, Gladys, *La casa limeña. Espacios habitados*. Lima: Siklos, 2000.

Cisneros, Antonio, *The Spider Hangs Too Far from the Ground*. London: Cape Goliard Press, 1970.

Cisneros Sánchez, Manuel, *Pancho Fierro y la Lima del 800*. Lima: Seix y Barral, 1975.

Cobo, Bernabé, *Fundación de Lima*. In *Obras*, 279-460. Biblioteca de Autores Españoles 91. Madrid: Atlas, 1956.

Congrains Martín, Enrique, *Lima, hora cero*. Lima: Círculo de Novelistas Peruanos, 1954.

Contreras, Carlos and Marcos Cueto, *Historia del Perú contemporáneo*. Lima: Red para el Desarrollo de las Ciencias Sociales en el Perú, 1999.

Cortázar, Pedro Felipe, *Lima*. Vol. 5 of Documental del Perú. Lima: Inca, 1984.

Custer, Tony, *The Art of Peruvian Cuisine*. Lima: Ganesha, 2000.

Del Busto Duthurburu, José Antonio, *Breve historia de los negros del Perú*. Lima: Fondo Editorial del Congreso del Perú, 2001.

Del Valle Caviedes, Juan, *Obra completa*. Caracas: Biblioteca Ayacucho, 1984.

Descola, Jean, *Daily Life in Colonial Peru 1710-1820*. London: George Allen and Unwin, 1968.

De Soto, Hernando, *The Other Path: The Invisible Revolution in the Third World*. New York: Harper and Row, 1989.

Fuentes, Manuel Atanasio, *Lima: apuntes históricos, descriptivos, estadísticos y de costumbres*. Lima: Fondo del Libro / Banco Industrial del Perú, 1985).

García Bryce, "La arquitectura en el Virreinato y la República". In *Historia del Perú*, IX, 9-166. Lima: Mejía Baca, 1980.

Günther Doering, Juan and Guillermo Lohmann Villena, *Lima*. Madrid: MAPFRE, 1992.

Herrera Cornejo, H. Andrés, *La Lima de Eugenio Courret, 1862-1934*. Lima: Novecientos Seis, 2001.

Higgins, James, *A History of Peruvian Literature*. Liverpool: Francis Cairns, 1987.

Holligan de Díaz-Límaco, *Peru in Focus: A Guide to the People, Politics and Culture*. London: Latin America Bureau and New York: Interlink Books, 2000.

Jara, Cronwell, *Patíbulo para un caballo*. Lima: Mosca Azul, 1989.

Juan, Jorge and Antonio de Ulloa, *A Voyage to South America*. New York: Alfred A. Knopf, 1964.

Klarén, Peter Flindell, *Peru: Society and Nationhood in the Andes*. New York and Oxford: Oxford University Press, 2000.

La Riva-Agüero, José de, "Lima española". In *Obras Completas*, VI, 363-97. Lima: Pontificia Universidad Católica del Perú, 1968..

Lavalle, José Antonio, and José Alejandro González García, eds., *Arte textil del Perú*. Lima: Industria Textil Piura, 1989.

Lloréns Amico, José Antonio, *Música popular en Lima: criollos y andinos*. Lima: Instituto de Estudios Peruanos, 1983.

Lockhart, James, *Spanish Peru 1532-1560. A Colonial Society*. Madison, WI: University of Wisconsin Press, 1968.

Martínez, Gregorio, *Crónica de músicos y diablos*. Hanover, NH: Ediciones del Norte, 1991.

Matos Mar, José, *El desborde popular*. Lima: Instituto de Estudios Peruanos, 1986.

Méndez Guerrero, Manuel et al., *Lima*. Madrid: Instituto de Cooperación Iberoamericana, 1986.

Middendorf, Ernst W., *Perú: observaciones y estudios del país y sus habitantes durante una permanencia de 25 años*. 3 vols. Lima: Universidad Nacional Mayor de San Marcos, 1973-1974.

Miller, Laura et al., *Lima obrera 1900-1930. Tomo II*. Lima: Ediciones El Virrey, 1987.

Miller, Robert Ryal, ed., *Chronicle of Colonial Lima: The Diary of Josephe and Francisco Mugaburu, 1640-1697*. Norman: University of Oklahoma Press, 1975.

Morimoto, Amelia, *Los japoneses y sus descendientes en el Perú*. Lima: Fondo Editorial del Congreso del Perú, 1999.

Morris, James, *Cities*. London: Faber and Faber, 1963.

Palma, Ricardo, *Tradiciones peruanas completas*. Madrid: Aguilar, 1964.

———, *Peruvian Traditions*. New York: Oxford University Press, 2004.

Pintura contemporánea (Primera parte 1820-1920). Lima: Banco de Crédito del Perú, 1975.

Pintura contemporánea (Segunda parte 1920-1960). Lima: Banco de Crédito del Perú, 1976.

Pintura en el Virreinato del Peru. Lima: Banco de Crédito del Perú, 1989.

Porras Barrenechea, Raúl, *Pequeña antología de Lima. El río, la puente y la alameda*. Lima: Instituto Raúl Porras Barrenechea, 1965.

Radiguet, Max, *Lima y la sociedad peruana*. Lima: Biblioteca Nacional del Perú, 1971.

Ribeyro, Julio Ramón, *Cuentos completos*. Madrid: Alfaguara, 1994.

———, *Marginal Voices: Selected Stories*. Austin: University of Texas Press, 1993.

Ricketts, Mónica, ed., *Lima. Paseos por la ciudad y su historia*. Lima: Adobe, 1999.

Rugendas, Johann Moritz, *El Perú romántico del siglo XIX*. Lima: Milla Batres, 1975.

Salazar Bondy, Sebastián, *Lima la horrible*. Mexico City: Era, 1964.

Salinas y Córdova, Buenaventura de, *Memorial de las historias del Nuevo Mundo Pirú*. Lima: Universidad Nacional Mayor de San Marcos, 1957.

Siu Kam Wen, *El tramo final*. Lima: Lluvia, 1985.

Stein, Steve, *Lima obrera 1900-1930. Tomo I*. Lima: Ediciones El Virrey, 1986.

Tord, Luis Enrique, "Historia de las artes plásticas en el Perú". In *Historia del Perú*, IX, 167-345. Lima: Mejía Baca, 1980.

—— and Pedro Gjurinovic, *El Palacio de Torre Tagle y las casonas de Lima / The Torre Tagle Palace and the Old Mansions of Lima*. Lima: Asociación de Funcionarios del Servicio Diplomático del Perú, 2001.

Trazegnies Granda, Fernando de, *En el país de las colinas de arena*. Lima: Ponteficia Universidad Católica del Perú, 1995.

Tristan, Flora, *Peregrinations of a Pariah 1833-34*. Boston: Virago/Beacon Travelers, 1986.

Varela, Blanca, *Canto villano: Poesía reunida, 1949-1983*. Mexico City: Fondo de Cultura Económica, 1986.

Vargas Llosa, Mario, *The Time of the Hero*. London: Picador, 1986.

——, *Conversation in The Cathedral*. London: Faber and Faber, 1993.

——, *Aunt Julia and the Scriptwriter*. London: Picador, 1984.

Velarde, Héctor, *Arquitectura peruana*. Lima: Studium, 1978.

——, *El barroco: arte de conquista*. Lima: Universidad de Lima, 1980.

Zavaleta, Carlos E., *Cuentos completos*, 2 vols. Lima: Ricardo Angulo Basombrío, 1997.

Index of Literary & Historical Names

INDEX OF PLACES